Dear Sister,

This book is given with much Love. May it bring you a closer walk with God and peace only he can give

Love

Barbara

1-1-23

Radiant Religion

Daily Meditations on Happiness in Christian Living

Radiant Religion

Daily Meditations on Happiness in Christian Living

Ellen G. White

Pacific Press®
Publishing Association
Nampa, Idaho | www.pacificpress.com

Cover design: Daniel Añez

Cover design resources: GettyImages.com | Jasmina00, GettyImages.com | EXTREME-PHOTOGRAPHER, GettyImages.com | Delbars

Published by Pacific Press® Publishing Association

Printed in the United States of America

Purchase additional copies of this book by calling toll-free 1-800-765-6955 or by visiting http://www.adventistbookcenter.com.

ISBN 978-0-8163-6859-4

May 2022

Contents

Foreword

R*adiant Religion* was the first daily devotional book drawn from Ellen G. White's writings. It was compiled by the Missionary Volunteer (Youth) Department of the General Conference in 1946, and eventually allowed to go out of print because all of the readings were selected from other available published sources written by Ellen G. White.[1]

Immersed in a global society saddened by the terrible impact of World War II, the compilers searched for content related to happiness in Ellen White writings. For the most part, the daily readings are shorter than those found in subsequent devotionals, and each one is closely tied to that day's memory verse. They also include secondary Bible verses that were inserted into the readings of the original compilation by the editors of the Inter-American Division Publishing Association in their edition.

In times when organized religion is seen in a negative light by many, this collection of thoughts from the inspired pen of Ellen G. White argues that real joy can be found in a relationship with God that is illuminated by the Bible and sustained by the basic principle that God Himself desires us to be happy.

"All heaven is interested in the happiness of man. Our heavenly Father does not close the avenues of joy to any of His creatures".[2]

—The Editors

---

1. This description is provided by the White Estate. See egwwritings.org/en/book/14039/info

2. Ellen G. White, *Steps to Christ (Washington, DC: Review and Herald*®, 1956), 43.

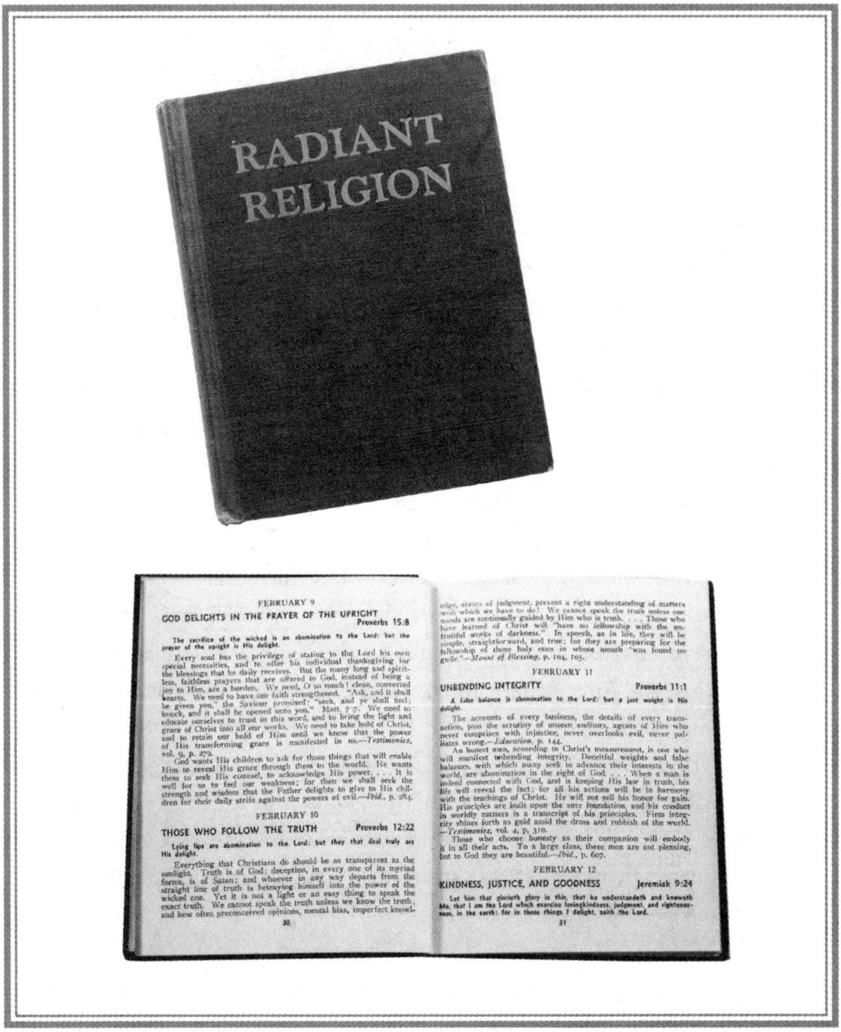

Cover and sample of the inside pages of the 1946 edition of *Radiant Religion* by Ellen G. White.

JANUARY 1
Rejoice and Be Glad

God Invites Us to Rejoice Always

Rejoice always.

—1 Thessalonians 5:16, NKJV

All heaven is interested in the happiness of man. Our heavenly Father does not close the avenues of joy to any of His creatures.—*Steps to Christ*, 46.

He has made provision that all may be holy and happy if they choose. Sufficient light has been given to this generation, that we may learn what our duties and privileges are, and enjoy the precious and solemn truths in their simplicity and power.—*Testimonies for the Church*, vol. 2, 693.

The world's Redeemer accepts men as they are, with all their wants, imperfections, and weaknesses; and He will not only cleanse from sin and grant redemption through His blood, but will satisfy the heart-longing of all who consent to wear His yoke, to bear His burden. It is His purpose to impart peace and rest to all who come to Him for the bread of life. He requires us to perform only those duties that will lead our steps to heights of bliss to which the disobedient can never attain. The true, joyous life of the soul is to have Christ formed within, the hope of glory.—*Steps to Christ*, 46.

Fellowship With Him

Sing to Him, sing psalms to Him;
Talk of all His wondrous works!
Glory in His holy name;
Let the hearts of those rejoice who seek the LORD*!*
Seek the LORD *and His strength;*
Seek His face evermore!

—Psalm 105:2–4, NKJV

MAN, CREATED FOR FELLOWSHIP WITH GOD, can only in such fellowship find his real life and development. Created to find in God his highest joy, he can find in nothing else that which can quiet the cravings of the heart, can satisfy the hunger and thirst of the soul. He who with sincere and teachable spirit studies God's word, seeking to comprehend its truths, will be brought in touch with its Author; and, except by his own choice, there is no limit to the possibilities of his development.—*Education*, 124.

No man can really enjoy life without religion. Love to God purifies and ennobles every taste and desire, intensifies every affection, and brightens every worthy pleasure. It enables men to appreciate and enjoy all that is true, and good, and beautiful.—*Messages to Young People*, 264.

To have the consciousness that the eye of the Lord is upon us, and that His ear is open to our prayers, is a satisfaction indeed. To know that we have a never-failing Friend to whom we can confide all the secrets of the soul, is a happiness which words can never express.—*Counsels on Health*, 628.

Trusting and Loving Him

Let all who take refuge in you be glad;
let them ever sing for joy.
Spread your protection over them,
that those who love your name may rejoice in you.
Surely, Lord, you bless the righteous;
you surround them with your favor as with a shield.
—Psalm 5:11, 12, NIV

WE MAY REJOICE IN HOPE. Our Advocate is in the heavenly sanctuary, pleading in our behalf. Through His merits we have pardon and peace. He died that He might wash away our sins, clothe us with His righteousness, and fit us for the society of heaven, where we may dwell in light forever. Dear brother, dear sister, when Satan would fill your mind with despondency, gloom, and doubt, resist his suggestions. Tell him of the blood of Jesus, that cleanses from all sin. You cannot save yourself from the tempter's power, but he trembles and flees when the merits of that precious blood are urged. Then will you not gratefully accept the blessings Jesus bestows? Will you not take the cup of salvation that He presents, and call on the name of the Lord?—*Testimonies for the Church*, vol. 5, 316.

All your happiness, peace, joy, and success in this life are dependent upon genuine, trusting faith in God. . . . Believe in Jesus as one who pardons your sins, one who wants you to be happy in the mansions He has gone to prepare for you. He wants you to live in His presence; to have eternal life and a crown of glory.—*Messages to Young People*, 410.

Because the Lord Reigns

Let the heavens rejoice, and let the earth be glad;
And let them say among the nations, "The LORD reigns."
—1 Chronicles 16:31, NKJV

THE WORLD that Satan has claimed and has ruled over with cruel tyranny, the Son of God has, by one vast achievement, encircled in His love and connected again with the throne of Jehovah. Cherubim and seraphim, and the unnumbered hosts of all the unfallen worlds, sang anthems of praise to God and the Lamb when this triumph was assured. They rejoiced that the way of salvation had been opened to the fallen race and that the earth would be redeemed from the curse of sin. How much more should those rejoice who are the objects of such amazing love!—*Thoughts From the Mount of Blessing*, 104.

With eager desire all heaven had waited for the end of His tarrying in a world marred by the curse of sin. The time had now come for the heavenly universe to receive their King. . . .

With joy unutterable, rulers and principalities and powers acknowledge the supremacy of the Prince of life. . . .

Songs of triumph mingle with the music from angel harps, till heaven seems to overflow with joy and praise. Love has conquered. The lost is found. Heaven rings with voices in lofty strains proclaiming, "Blessing, and honor, and glory, and power, be unto Him that sitteth upon the throne, and unto the Lamb forever and ever." Revelation 5:13. . . .

From that scene of heavenly joy, there comes back to us on earth the echo of Christ's own wonderful words, "I ascend to My Father, and your Father; and to My God and your God." John 20:17. The family of heaven and the family of earth are one. For us our Lord ascended, and for us He lives.—*The Desire of Ages*, 832–835.

Let the Righteous Be Glad

Let the righteous be glad;
Let them rejoice before God;
Yes, let them rejoice exceedingly.

—Psalm 68:3, NKJV

WHATEVER IS DONE to the glory of God is to be done with cheerfulness, not with sadness and gloom. There is nothing gloomy in the religion of Jesus. If Christians give the impression by a mournful attitude that they have been disappointed in their Lord, they misrepresent His character and put arguments into the mouth of His enemies. Though in words they may claim God as their Father, yet in gloom and sorrow they present to the world the aspect of orphans.

Christ desires us to make His service appear attractive, as it really is. Let the self-denials and the secret heart trials be revealed to the compassionate Saviour. Let the burdens be left at the foot of the cross, and go on your way rejoicing in His love who first loved you.—*Thoughts From the Mount of Blessing*, 88.

By your appointment they stand today,
for all things are your servants.
If your law had not been my delight,
I would have perished in my misery.
I will never forget your precepts,
for by them you have given me life.

—Psalm 119:91-93, NRSV

He Who Fears God

Blessed is the one who fears the LORD *always,*
but whoever hardens his heart will fall into calamity.

—Proverbs 28:14, ESV

WITHOUT THE FEAR OF GOD no one can be truly happy.—*Testimonies for the Church*, vol. 4, 434.

"God is greatly to be feared in the assembly of the saints, and to be had in reverence of all them that are about Him" (Psalm 89:7).

Those who realize the greatness and majesty of God, will take His name on their lips with holy awe. He dwelleth in light unapproachable; no man can see Him and live.—*Early Writings*, 122.

"Wherefore . . . , let us have grace, whereby we may serve God acceptably with reverence and godly fear" (Hebrews 12:28).

True reverence for God is inspired by a sense of His infinite greatness and a realization of His presence. With this sense of the Unseen, every heart should be deeply impressed. . . . "Holy and reverend is His name," [Psalm 111:9.] the psalmist declares. Angels, when they speak that name, veil their faces. With what reverence, then, should we, who are fallen and sinful, take it upon our lips!—*Gospel Workers*, 178.

O LORD *God of hosts,*
who is as mighty as you, O LORD*?*
Your faithfulness surrounds you. . . .
The heavens are yours, the earth also is yours;
the world and all that is in it—you have founded them.

—Psalm 89:8, 11, NRSV

He Who Trusts God

Those who listen to instruction will prosper;
those who trust the Lord will be joyful.

—Proverbs 16:20, NLT

If we will but listen, God's created works will teach us precious lessons of obedience and trust. From the stars that in their trackless courses through space follow from age to age their appointed path, down to the minutest atom, the things of nature obey the Creator's will. And God cares for everything and sustains everything that He has created. He who upholds the unnumbered worlds throughout immensity, at the same time cares for the wants of the little brown sparrow that sings its humble song without fear. When men go forth to their daily toil, as when they engage in prayer; when they lie down at night, and when they rise in the morning; when the rich man feasts in his palace, or when the poor man gathers his children about the scanty board, each is tenderly watched by the heavenly Father. No tears are shed that God does not notice. There is no smile that He does not mark.

If we would but fully believe this, all undue anxieties would be dismissed. Our lives would not be so filled with disappointment as now; for everything, whether great or small, would be left in the hands of God, who is not perplexed by the multiplicity of cares, or overwhelmed by their weight. We should then enjoy a rest of soul to which many have long been strangers.—*Steps to Christ*, 85, 86.

The Meek

"Blessed are the meek,
For they shall inherit the earth."

—Matthew 5:5, NKJV

MEEKNESS IS A PRECIOUS GRACE, willing to suffer silently, willing to endure trials. Meekness is patient and labors to be happy under all circumstances. Meekness is always thankful and makes its own songs of happiness, making melody in the heart to God. Meekness will suffer disappointment and wrong, and will not retaliate. Meekness is not to be silent and sulky. A morose temper is the opposite of meekness; for this only wounds and gives pain to others, and takes no pleasure to itself.—*Testimonies for the Church*, vol. 3, 335.

A meek and quiet spirit will not be ever looking out for happiness for itself, but will seek for self-forgetfulness and find sweet content and true satisfaction in making others happy.—*Testimonies for the Church*, vol. 3, 536.

The world's Redeemer had a greater than angelic nature, yet united with His divine majesty were meekness and humility that attracted all to Himself. . . .

The meekness of Christ, manifested in the home, will make the inmates happy; it provokes no quarrel, gives back no angry answer, but soothes the irritated temper and diffuses a gentleness that is felt by all within its charmed circle. Wherever cherished, it makes the families of earth a part of the one great family above.—*Thoughts From the Mount of Blessing*, 14, 16.

The Merciful

Whoever despises his neighbor is a sinner,
but blessed is he who is generous to the poor.

—Proverbs 14:21, ESV

"YE HAVE THE POOR WITH YOU ALWAYS," Christ said, "and whensoever ye will ye may do them good." . . . Mark 14:7.

In placing among them the helpless and the poor, to be dependent upon their care, Christ tests His professed followers. By our love and service for His needy children we prove the genuineness of our love for Him. To neglect them is to declare ourselves false disciples, strangers to Christ and His love.—*The Ministry of Healing*, 205.

Jesus sought to correct the world's false standard of judging the value of men. He took His position with the poor, that He might lift from poverty the stigma that the world had attached to it. He has stripped from it forever the reproach of scorn, by blessing the poor, the inheritors of God's kingdom.

. . . He dwelt among the lowly. He set at naught the artificial distinctions of society. The aristocracy of birth, wealth, talent, learning, rank, He ignored. . . .

. . . He ate with publicans and sinners, and mingled with the common people, not to become low and earthly with them, but in order by precept and example to present to them right principles, and to uplift them from their earthliness and debasement.—*The Ministry of Healing*, 197.

As you open your door to Christ's needy and suffering ones, you are welcoming unseen angels. You invite the companionship of heavenly beings. They bring a sacred atmosphere of joy and peace. They come with praises upon their lips, and an answering strain is heard in heaven. Every deed of mercy makes music there. The Father from His throne numbers the unselfish workers among His most precious treasures.—*The Desire of Ages*, 639.

At Peace With God and Man

Deceit is in the heart of those who devise evil,
But counselors of peace have joy.
—Proverbs 12:20, NKJV

He who is at peace with God and his fellow men cannot be made miserable. Envy will not be in his heart; evil surmisings will find no room there; hatred cannot exist. The heart that is in harmony with God is a partaker of the peace of heaven and will diffuse its blessed influence on all around. The spirit of peace will rest like dew upon hearts weary and troubled with worldly strife.—*Thoughts From the Mount of Blessing*, 27.

"Blessed are the peacemakers." The peace of Christ is born of truth. It is harmony with God. The world is at enmity with the law of God; sinners are at enmity with their Maker; and as a result they are at enmity with one another. But the psalmist declares, "Great peace have they which love Thy law: and nothing shall offend them." Psalm 119:165. Men cannot manufacture peace. Human plans for the purification and uplifting of individuals or of society will fail of producing peace, because they do not reach the heart. The only power that can create or perpetuate true peace is the grace of Christ. When this is implanted in the heart, it will cast out the evil passions that cause strife and dissension. "Instead of the thorn shall come up the fir tree, and instead of the brier shall come up the myrtle tree;" and life's desert "shall rejoice, and blossom as the rose." Isaiah 55:13; 35:1.—*The Desire of Ages*, 302.

He Whose Helper Is God

Happy is he who has the God of Jacob for his help,
Whose hope is in the LORD his God.

—Psalm 146:5, NKJV

WHEN, AFTER HIS SIN IN DECEIVING ESAU, Jacob fled from his father's home, he was weighed down with a sense of guilt. Lonely and outcast as he was, separated from all that had made life dear, the one thought that above all others pressed upon his soul, was the fear that his sin had cut him off from God, that he was forsaken of Heaven. In sadness he lay down to rest on the bare earth, around him only the lonely hills, and above, the heavens bright with stars. As he slept, a strange light broke upon his vision; and lo, from the plain on which he lay, vast shadowy stairs seemed to lead upward to the very gates of heaven, and upon them angels of God were passing up and down; while from the glory above, the divine voice was heard in a message of comfort and hope. Thus was made known to Jacob that which met the need and longing of his soul—a Saviour. With joy and gratitude he saw revealed a way by which he, a sinner, could be restored to communion with God.—*Steps to Christ*, 19.

Jacob's history is an assurance that God will not cast off those who have been betrayed into sin, but who have returned unto Him with true repentance.—*Patriarchs and Prophets*, 202.

Happy are those whose transgression is forgiven,
whose sin is covered.
Happy are those to whom the LORD imputes no iniquity,
and in whose spirit there is no deceit.

—Psalm 32:1, 2, NRSV

Delight in Christ's Name

In Your name they rejoice all day long,
And in Your righteousness they are exalted.

—Psalm 89:16, NKJV

THE NAME OF THE LORD" is "merciful and gracious, long-suffering, and abundant in goodness and truth, . . . forgiving iniquity and transgression and sin." Exodus 34:5–7. Of the church of Christ it is written, "This is the name wherewith she shall be called, The Lord our Righteousness." Jeremiah 33:16. This name is put upon every follower of Christ. It is the heritage of the child of God.—*Thoughts From the Mount of Blessing*, 106.

The disciples were to carry their work forward in Christ's name. Their every word and act was to fasten attention on His name, as possessing that vital power by which sinners may be saved. Their faith was to center in Him who is the source of mercy and power. In His name they were to present their petitions to the Father, and they would receive answer. They were to baptize in the name of the Father, the Son, and the Holy Spirit. Christ's name was to be their watchword, their badge of distinction, their bond of union, the authority for their course of action, and the source of their success.—*The Acts of the Apostles*, 28.

Blessed are the people who know the joyful sound!
They walk, O LORD, in the light of Your countenance.
In Your name they rejoice all day long,
And in Your righteousness they are exalted.

—Psalm 89:15, 16, NKJV

Your Salvation

We will rejoice in your salvation,
And in the name of our God we will set up our banners!
May the LORD *fulfill all your petitions.*

—Psalm 20:5, NKJV

ALL HEAVEN IS INTERESTED in our salvation. The angels of God, thousands upon thousands, and ten thousand times ten thousand, are commissioned to minister to those who shall be heirs of salvation. They guard us against evil and press back the powers of darkness that are seeking our destruction. Have we not reason to be thankful every moment, thankful even when there are apparent difficulties in our pathway? —*Testimonies for the Church*, vol. 6, 63.

God desires that the receivers of His grace shall be witnesses to its power. Those whose course has been most offensive to Him He freely accepts; when they repent, He imparts to them His divine Spirit, places them in the highest positions of trust, and sends them forth into the camp of the disloyal to proclaim His boundless mercy. He would have His servants bear testimony to the fact that through His grace men may possess Christlikeness of character, and may rejoice in the assurance of His great love. —*The Desire of Ages*, 826.

May he grant your heart's desires
and make all your plans succeed.
May we shout for joy when we hear of your victory
and raise a victory banner in the name of our God.
May the LORD *answer all your prayers.*

—Psalm 20:4, 5, NLT

The Law of God

For I delight in the law of God,
in my inner being.

—Romans 7:22, ESV

THE PSALMIST DECLARES of the good man: "His delight is in the law of the Lord, and in His law doth he meditate day and night." He refers to his own experience, and exclaims: "O how love I Thy law! it is my meditation all the day." "Mine eyes prevent the night watches, that I might meditate in Thy word."—*Testimonies for the Church*, vol. 4, 526.

The will of God is expressed in the precepts of His holy law, and the principles of this law are the principles of heaven. The angels of heaven attain unto no higher knowledge than to know the will of God, and to do His will is the highest service that can engage their powers.

But in heaven, service is not rendered in the spirit of legality. When Satan rebelled against the law of Jehovah, the thought that there was a law came to the angels almost as an awakening to something unthought of. In their ministry the angels are not as servants, but as sons. There is perfect unity between them and their Creator. Obedience is to them no drudgery. Love for God makes their service a joy. So in every soul wherein Christ, the hope of glory, dwells, His words are re-echoed, "I delight to do Thy will, O My God: yea, Thy law is within My heart." Psalm 40:8.—*Thoughts From the Mount of Blessing*, 109.

But his delight is in the law of the LORD,
And in His law he meditates day and night.

—Psalm 1:2, NKJV

Celebrate the Truth

Love is patient. . . . It does not rejoice at wrongdoing,
but rejoices with the truth.
—1 Corinthians 13:4, 6, ESV

LOVE "REJOICETH NOT IN INIQUITY, but rejoiceth in the truth." He whose heart is imbued with love is filled with sorrow at the errors and weaknesses of others; but when truth triumphs, when the cloud that darkened the fair fame of another is removed, or when sins are confessed and wrongs corrected, he rejoices. —*Testimonies for the Church*, vol. 5, 169.

The word of God—the truth—is the channel through which the Lord manifests His Spirit and power. Obedience to the word produces fruit of the required quality—"unfeigned love of the brethren." This love is heaven-born and leads to high motives and unselfish actions.—*The Acts of the Apostles*, 519.

Since you have purified your souls in obeying the truth
through the Spirit in sincere love of the brethren,
love one another fervently with a pure heart.
—1 Peter 1:22, NKJV

Love isn't easily upset.
Love doesn't tally wrongs or celebrate injustice;
but truth—yes, truth—is love's delight!
—1 Corinthians 13:5, 6, VOICE

Every Good Thing

"Afterward you may go and celebrate
because of all the good things the LORD *your God*
has given to you and your household.
Remember to include the Levites and the foreigners
living among you in the celebration."

—Deuteronomy 26:11, NLT

GOD GAVE DIRECTION to the Israelites to assemble before Him at set periods, in the place which He should choose, and observe special days wherein no unnecessary work was to be done, but the time was to be devoted to a consideration of the blessings which He had bestowed upon them. At these special seasons they were to bring gifts, freewill offerings, and thank offerings unto the Lord, according as He had blessed them. The manservant and maidservant, the stranger, the fatherless and widow, were directed to rejoice that God had by His own wonderful power brought them from servile bondage to the enjoyment of freedom.—*Testimonies for the Church*, vol. 2, 573.

Shall we not keep holy festivals unto God? Shall we not show that we have some enthusiasm in His service? With the grand, ennobling theme of salvation before us, shall we be as cold as statues of marble? If men can become so excited over a match game of cricket, or a horse race, or over foolish things that bring no good to anyone, shall we be unmoved when the plan of salvation is unfolded before us? Let the school and the church henceforth have festivals of rejoicing unto the Lord.—*Counsels to Parents, Teachers, and Students*, 371.

The Source of Every Blessing

"They took strong cities and a rich land,
And possessed houses full of all goods,
Cisterns already dug, vineyards, olive groves,
And fruit trees in abundance.
So they ate and were filled and grew fat,
And delighted themselves in Your great goodness."
—Nehemiah 9:25, NKJV

GOD IS THE SOURCE OF EVERY BLESSING to His creatures, and . . . to Him man's gratitude is due for the good gifts of His providence.

"He giveth to all life, and breath, and all things." Acts 17:25. . . . And it is God who gives men power to get wealth. Deuteronomy 8:18. As an acknowledgment that all things came from Him, the Lord directed that a portion of His bounty should be returned to Him in gifts and offerings to sustain His worship.—*Patriarchs and Prophets*, 525.

The first that ripened of every product of the land was consecrated to Him. . . .

Thus the people were constantly reminded that God was the true proprietor of their fields, their flocks, and their herds; that He sent them sunshine and rain for their seedtime and harvest, and that everything they possessed was of His creation, and He had made them stewards of His goods.—*Patriachs and Prophets*, 526.

In the seventh month came the Feast of Tabernacles, or of ingathering. This feast acknowledged God's bounty in the products of the orchard, the olive grove, and the vineyard. It was the crowning festal gathering of the year. The land had yielded its increase, the harvests had been gathered into the granaries, the fruits, the oil, and the wine had been stored, the first fruits had been reserved, and now the people came with their tributes of thanksgiving to God, who had thus richly blessed them.

This feast was to be pre-eminently an occasion of rejoicing. . . . The labors of the harvest being ended, and the toils of the new year not yet begun, the people were free from care, and could give themselves up to the sacred, joyous influences of the hour. —*Patriarchs and Prophets*, 540.

Supreme Love

"If you return to the Almighty, you will be restored:
If you remove wickedness far from your tent
and assign your nuggets to the dust,
your gold of Ophir to the rocks in the ravines,
then the Almighty will be your gold, the choicest silver for you.
Surely then you will find delight in the Almighty
and will lift up your face to God."

—Job 22:23–26, NIV

THOU SHALT LOVE THE LORD THY GOD with all thy heart, and with all thy soul, and with all thy mind. This is the first and great commandment" (Matthew 22:37, 38).

The first four commandments allow no separation of the affections from God. Nor is anything allowed to divide, or share, our supreme delight in Him. Whatever divides the affections, and takes away from the soul supreme love to God, assumes the form of an idol. Our carnal hearts would cling to our idols and seek to carry them along; but we cannot advance until we put them away, for they separate us from God.—*Testimonies for the Church*, vol. 1, 289.

If we would but think of God as often as we have evidence of His care for us we should keep Him ever in our thoughts and should delight to talk of Him and to praise Him. We talk of temporal things because we have an interest in them. We talk of our friends because we love them; our joys and our sorrows are bound up with them. Yet we have infinitely greater reason to love God than to love our earthly friends; it should be the most natural thing in the world to make Him first in all our thoughts, to talk of His goodness and tell of His power.—*Steps to Christ*, 102.

The Joy of Knowing That God Is Our Helper

Because you are my help,
I sing in the shadow of your wings.

—Psalm 63:7, NIV

THE CHRISTIAN ALWAYS HAS a strong helper in the Lord. The way of the Lord's helping we may not know; but this we do know: He will never fail those who put their trust in Him. Could Christians realize how many times the Lord has ordered their way, that the purposes of the enemy concerning them might not be accomplished, they would not stumble along complainingly. Their faith would be stayed on God, and no trial would have power to move them. They would acknowledge Him as their wisdom and efficiency, and He would bring to pass that which He desires to work out through them.—*Prophets and Kings*, 576.

We are to be one with Christ as He is one with the Father, and the Father will love us as He loves His Son. We may have the same help that Christ had, we may have strength for every emergency; for God will be our front guard and our rearward. He will shut us in on every side.—*Testimonies to Ministers and Gospel Workers*, 386.

In his own strength man is strengthless; but in the might of God he may be strong to overcome evil and to help others to overcome. Satan can never gain advantage of him who makes God his defense.—*Prophets and Kings*, 175.

Then let us not cast away our confidence, but have firm assurance, firmer than ever before. "Hitherto hath the Lord helped us," and He will help us to the end. 1 Samuel 7:12.—*Steps to Christ*, 125.

He who dwells in the secret place of he Most High
Shall abide under the shadow of the Almighty.
I will say of the LORD, *"He is my refuge and my fortress;*
My God, in Him I will trust."

—Psalm 91:1, 2, NKJV

The Lord Is Our Strength

The LORD is my strength and my shield;
My heart trusted in Him, and I am helped;
Therefore my heart greatly rejoices,
And with my song I will praise Him.

—Psalm 28:7, NKJV

THE CARE OF GOD is over the weakest of His children. No act of cruelty or oppression toward them is unmarked by Heaven. Over all who love and fear Him, His hand extends as a shield.—*Patriarchs and Prophets*, 300.

Because of the increasing power of Satan's temptations, the times in which we live are full of peril for the children of God, and we need to learn constantly of the Great Teacher, that we may take every step in surety and righteousness.—*Counsels to Parents, Teachers, and Students*, 322.

Those who walk humbly before God, distrustful of their own wisdom, will realize their danger and will know God's keeping care.—*Counsels to Parents, Teachers, and Students*, 323.

The great God, whose glory shines from the heavens, and whose divine hand upholds millions of worlds, is our Father. We have only to love Him, trust in Him, as little children in faith and confidence, and He will accept us as His sons and daughters, and we shall be heirs to all the inexpressible glory of the eternal world. All the meek will He guide in judgment, the meek will He teach His way. If we will walk in obedience to His will, learn cheerfully and diligently the lessons of His providence, by and by He will say: Child, come home to the heavenly mansions I have prepared for you.—*Testimonies for the Church*, vol. 4, 653.

He Has Done Great Things for Us

The LORD has done great things for us,
and we are filled with joy.

—Psalm 126:3, NIV

"WHEREFORE COME OUT FROM AMONG THEM, and be ye separate, saith the Lord, . . . and I will receive you, and will be a Father unto you, and ye shall be My sons and daughters, saith the Lord Almighty."

. . . Oh, what a relationship is this! higher and holier than any earthly tie. . . . God adopts you into His family; you become members of the royal household, sons and daughters of the King who rules in the heaven of heavens. Can you desire a more exalted position than is here promised? Is not this enough? Said the angel: "What could God do for the children of men more than He has already done? If such love, such exalted promises are not appreciated, could He devise anything higher, anything richer and more lofty? All that God could do has been done for the salvation of man."—*Testimonies for the Church*, vol. 1, 510.

The Lord desires us to appreciate the great plan of redemption, to realize our high privilege as the children of God, and to walk before Him in obedience, with grateful thanksgiving. . . . He longs to see gratitude welling up in our hearts because our names are written in the Lamb's book of life, because we may cast all our care upon Him who cares for us. He bids us rejoice because we are the heritage of the Lord, because the righteousness of Christ is the white robe of His saints, because we have the blessed hope of the soon coming of our Saviour.—*Christ's Object Lessons*, 299.

He Is Merciful

Satisfy us early with Your mercy,
That we may rejoice and be glad all our days!

—Psalm 90:14, NKJV

HE UNDERSTANDS OUR WEAKNESSES and our temptations; and when we come to Him with broken hearts and contrite spirits, He accepts our repentance, and promises that, as we take hold of His strength to make peace with Him, we shall make peace with Him. Oh, what gratitude, what joy, should we feel that God is merciful!—*Testimonies for the Church*, vol. 3, 239.

It should not be difficult to remember that the Lord desires you to lay your troubles and perplexities at His feet, and leave them there. Go to Him, saying: "Lord, my burdens are too heavy for me to carry. Wilt Thou bear them for me?" And He will answer: "I will take them. 'With everlasting kindness will I have mercy on thee.' I will take your sins, and will give you peace. Banish no longer your self-respect; for I have bought you with the price of My own blood. You are Mine. Your weakened will I will strengthen. Your remorse for sin I will remove."

"I, even I, am He," the Lord declares, "that blotteth out thy transgressions for Mine own sake, and will not remember thy sins. Put Me in remembrance: let us plead together: declare thou, that thou mayest be justified." "I have not spoken in secret, in a dark place of the earth: I said not unto the seed of Jacob, Seek ye Me in vain: I the Lord speak righteousness, I declare things that are right." "Look unto Me, and be ye saved, all the ends of the earth: for I am God, and there is none else." Respond to the calls of God's mercy, and say: "I will trust in the Lord and be comforted. I will praise the Lord; for His anger is turned away. I will rejoice in God, who gives the victory."—*Testimonies to Ministers and Gospel Workers*, 519, 520.

He Clothes Me in His Righteousness

I will greatly rejoice in the LORD,
My soul shall be joyful in my God;
For He has clothed me with the garments of salvation,
He has covered me with the robe of righteousness,
As a bridegroom decks himself with ornaments,
And as a bride adorns herself with her jewels.

—Isaiah 61:10, NKJV

BY THE WEDDING GARMENT . . . is represented the pure, spotless character which Christ's true followers will possess. To the church it is given "that she should be arrayed in fine linen, clean and white," "not having spot, or wrinkle, or any such thing." Revelation 19:8; Ephesians 5:27. The fine linen, says the Scripture, "is the righteousness of saints." Revelation 19:8. It is the righteousness of Christ, His own unblemished character, that through faith is imparted to all who receive Him as their personal Saviour. . . .

This robe, woven in the loom of heaven, has in it not one thread of human devising. . . . When we submit ourselves to Christ, the heart is united with His heart, the will is merged in His will, the mind becomes one with His mind, the thoughts are brought into captivity to Him; we live His life. This is what it means to be clothed with the garment of His righteousness.—*Christ's Object Lessons*, 310, 311.

"The kingdom of heaven is like a king
who prepared a wedding banquet for his son. . . .
But when the king came in to see the guests,
he noticed a man there who was not wearing wedding clothes. . . .
Then the king told the attendants, 'Tie him hand and foot, and throw him outside,
into the darkness.' . . . For many are invited, but few are chosen."

—Matthew 22:2, 11, 13, 14, NIV

I Don't Fear His Divine Judgment

Love has been perfected among us in this:
that we may have boldness in the day of judgment;
because as He is, so are we in this world.

–1 John 4:17, NKJV

WHEN "THE LORD COMETH with ten thousand of His saints, to execute judgment upon all," He will also "convince all that are ungodly among them of all their ungodly deeds." Jude 14, 15. Every sinner will be brought to see and acknowledge the justice of his condemnation.—*Patriarchs and Prophets*, 393.

Then it will be seen that Satan's rebellion against God has resulted in ruin to himself and to all that chose to become his subjects. He has represented that great good would result from transgression; but it will be seen that "the wages of sin is death.". . . . Satan, the root of every sin, and all evil workers, who are his branches, shall be utterly cut off. An end will be made of sin, with all the woe and ruin that have resulted from it. Says the psalmist, "Thou hast destroyed the wicked, thou hast put out their name forever and ever. O thou enemy, destructions are come to a perpetual end." Psalm 9:5, 6.

But amid the tempest of divine judgment the children of God will have no cause for fear. "The Lord will be the hope of His people, and the strength of the children of Israel." Joel 3:16. The day that brings terror and destruction to the transgressors of God's law will bring to the obedient "joy unspeakable and full of glory." "Gather My saints together unto Me," saith the Lord, "those that have made a covenant with Me by sacrifice. And the heavens shall declare His righteousness: for God is Judge Himself."—*Patriarchs and Prophets*, 341.

"The Father judges no one but has given all judgment to the Son,
so that all may honor the Son just as they honor the Father.
Anyone who does not honor the Son does not honor the Father who sent Him."

–John 5:22, 23, NRSV

My Name Is Written in Heaven

"But don't rejoice because evil spirits obey you;
rejoice because your names are registered in heaven."
—Luke 10:20, NLT

REJOICE NOT in the possession of power, lest you lose sight of your dependence upon God. Be careful lest self-sufficiency come in, and you work in your own strength, rather than in the spirit and strength of your Master. Self is ever ready to take the credit if any measure of success attends the work. Self is flattered and exalted, and the impression is not made upon other minds that God is all and in all. . . . Rejoice that through Christ you have become connected with God, members of the heavenly family. While you look higher than yourself, you will have a continual sense of the weakness of humanity. The less you cherish self, the more distinct and full will be your comprehension of the excellence of your Saviour. The more closely you connect yourself with the source of light and power, the greater light will be shed upon you, and the greater power will be yours to work for God. Rejoice that you are one with God, one with Christ, and with the whole family of heaven.—*The Desire of Ages*, 493.

"Not everyone who says to Me, 'Lord, Lord,' shall enter the kingdom of heaven,
but he who does the will of My Father in heaven.
Many will say to Me in that day, 'Lord, Lord, have we not prophesied in Your name,
cast out demons in Your name, and done many wonders in Your name?'
And then I will declare to them, 'I never knew you;
depart from Me, you who practice lawlessness!' "
—Matthew 7:21–23, NKJV

JANUARY 26
Rejoice and Be Glad

Rejoice in Youth

Rejoice, O young man, in your youth,
And let your heart cheer you in the days of your youth;
Walk in the ways of your heart,
And in the sight of your eyes;
But know that for all these
God will bring you into judgment.

—Ecclesiastes 11:9, NKJV

SAYS THE WISE MAN, "Remember now thy Creator in the days of thy youth." But do not for a moment suppose that religion will make you sad and gloomy and will block up the way to success. The religion of Christ does not obliterate or even weaken a single faculty. It in no way incapacitates you for the enjoyment of any real happiness; it is not designed to lessen your interest in life, or to make you indifferent to the claims of friends and society. It does not mantle the life in sackcloth; it is not expressed in deep-drawn sighs and groans. No, no; those who in everything make God first and last and best, are the happiest people in the world. Smiles and sunshine are not banished from their countenance.—*Messages to Young People*, 38.

The Lord would have all His sons and daughters happy, peaceful, and obedient. Jesus says, "My peace I give unto you: not as the world giveth, give I unto you. Let not your heart be troubled, neither let it be afraid." "These things have I spoken unto you, that My joy might remain in you, and that your joy might be full." John 14:27; 15:11.—*Steps to Christ*, 124.

The joy of Christ in the soul is worth everything.—*Testimonies to Ministers and Gospel Workers*, 516.

The Eternal's law is perfect,
turning lives around.
His words are reliable and true,
instilling wisdom to open minds.

—Psalm 19:7, VOICE

How can a young person remain pure?
Only by living according to Your Word.

—Psalm 119:9, VOICE

Faithful in Prosperity

When times are good, be happy;
but when times are bad, consider this:
God has made the one
as well as the other.
Therefore, no one can discover
anything about their future.

—Ecclesiastes 7:14, NIV

God has given in His word a picture of a prosperous man—one whose life was in the truest sense a success, a man whom both heaven and earth delighted to honor. Of his experiences Job himself says:

"In the ripeness of my days,
When the secret of God was upon my tent;
When the Almighty was yet with me,
And my children were about me; . . .
The young men saw me and hid themselves,
And the aged rose up and stood; . . .
"For when the ear heard me, then it blessed me;
And when the eye saw me, it gave witness unto me;

Because I delivered the poor that cried,
The fatherless also, and him [margin], that had none to help him.
"The blessing of him that was ready to perish came upon me;
And I caused the widow's heart to sing for joy.
I put on righteousness, and it clothed me:
My justice was as a robe and a diadem."

"The blessing of the Lord, it maketh rich, and He addeth no sorrow with it." Proverbs 10:22.—*Education*, 142.

The Bible condemns no man for being rich, if he has acquired his riches honestly. Not money, but the love of money, is the root of all evil. It is God who gives men power to get wealth; and in the hands of him who acts as God's steward, using his means unselfishly, wealth is a blessing, both to its possessor and to the world.—*The Ministry of Healing*, 212.

An Expression of Faith

My inmost being will rejoice
when your lips speak what is right.

—Proverbs 23:16, NIV

GOD HAS GIVEN US the gift of speech that we may recite to others His dealing with us, that His love and compassion may touch other hearts, and that praise may arise from other souls also to Him who has called them out of darkness into His marvelous light. —*Counsels to Parents, Teachers, and Students*, 243.

The gift of speech has been greatly abused and widely perverted from its intended purpose; but let those who claim to be children of the heavenly King awake to their responsibility, and make the most of this talent.—*Counsels to Parents, Teachers, and Students*, 245.

It is a law of nature that our thoughts and feelings are encouraged and strengthened as we give them utterance. While words express thoughts, it is also true that thoughts follow words. If we would give more expression to our faith, rejoice more in the blessings that we know we have,—the great mercy and love of God,—we should have more faith and greater joy. No tongue can express, no finite mind can conceive, the blessing that results from appreciating the goodness and love of God. Even on earth we may have joy as a wellspring, never failing, because fed by the streams that flow from the throne of God.—*The Ministry of Healing*, 251.

I tell you this: on the day of judgment,
people will be called to account
for every careless word they have ever said.

—Matthew 12:36, VOICE

Celebrating His Blessings

"Also on the fifteenth day of the seventh month,
when you have gathered in the fruit of the land,
you shall keep the feast of the LORD *for seven days;*
on the first day there shall be a sabbath-rest,
and on the eighth day a sabbath-rest.
And you shall take for yourselves on the first day
the fruit of beautiful trees, branches of palm trees,
the boughs of leafy trees, and willows of the brook;
and you shall rejoice before the LORD *your God for seven days."*
—Leviticus 23:39, 40, NKJV

WELL WOULD IT BE for the people of God at the present time to have a Feast of Tabernacles—a joyous commemoration of the blessings of God to them. As the children of Israel celebrated the deliverance that God had wrought for their fathers, and His miraculous preservation of them during their journeyings from Egypt, so should we gratefully call to mind the various ways He has devised for bringing us out from the world, and from the darkness of error, into the precious light of His grace and truth. . . .

The Feast of Tabernacles was not only commemorative but typical. It not only pointed back to the wilderness sojourn, but, as the feast of harvest, it celebrated the ingathering of the fruits of the earth, and pointed forward to the great day of final ingathering, when the Lord of the harvest shall send forth His reapers to gather the tares together in bundles for the fire, and to gather the wheat into His garner. . . .

. . . When the ransomed of the Lord shall have been safely gathered into the heavenly Canaan, forever delivered from the bondage of the curse, under which "the whole creation groaneth and travaileth in pain together until now" (Romans 8:22), they will rejoice with joy unspeakable and full of glory.—*Patriarchs and Prophets*, 540–542.

JANUARY 30
Rejoice and Be Glad

Let Us Celebrate the Victory

And now my head shall be lifted up above my enemies all around me;
Therefore I will offer sacrifices of joy in His tabernacle;
I will sing, yes, I will sing praises to the LORD.

—Psalm 27:6, NKJV

WHOSO OFFERETH PRAISE," says the Creator, "glorifieth Me." Psalm 50:23. All the inhabitants of heaven unite in praising God. Let us learn the song of the angels now, that we may sing it when we join their shining ranks. Let us say with the psalmist, "While I live will I praise the Lord: I will sing praises unto my God while I have any being." "Let the people praise Thee, O God; let all the people praise Thee." Psalm 146:2; 67:5.—*Patriarchs and Prophets*, 289.

We must carry to every religious gathering a quickened spiritual consciousness that God and His angels are there, co-operating with all true worshipers. . . .

The place of worship may be very humble, but it is no less acknowledged by God. To those who worship God in spirit and in truth and in the beauty of holiness it will be as the gate of heaven.—*Testimonies for the Church*, vol. 6, 362, 363.

The temple of God is opened in heaven, and the threshold is flushed with the glory which is for every church that will love God and keep His commandments. We need to study, to meditate, and to pray. Then we shall have spiritual eyesight to discern the inner courts of the celestial temple. We shall catch the themes of song and thanksgiving of the heavenly choir round about the throne. When Zion shall arise and shine, her light will be most penetrating, and precious songs of praise and thanksgiving will be heard in the assemblies of the saints.—*Testimonies for the Church*, vol. 6, 368.

Happy are those who live in your house,
ever singing your praise. . . .
For a day in your courts is better
than a thousand elsewhere.
I would rather be a doorkeeper in the house of my God
than live in the tents of wickedness.

—Psalm 84:4, 10, NRSV

The Great Joy of Being a Christian

May you always be joyful in your union with the Lord.
I say it again: rejoice!

—Philippians 4:4, GNT

"REJOICE IN THE LORD ALWAYS: and again I say, Rejoice" (Philippians 4:4).

Forgetting our own difficulties and troubles, let us praise God for an opportunity to live for the glory of His name. Let the fresh blessings of each new day awaken praise in our hearts for these tokens of His loving care. When you open your eyes in the morning, thank God that He has kept you through the night. Thank Him for His peace in your heart. Morning, noon, and night, let gratitude as a sweet perfume ascend to heaven. —*The Ministry of Healing*, 253.

Again I say: Rejoice in the Lord. Rest in Him. You need his power, and this power you may have. Go forward firmly, valiantly, courageously. You may err in judgment, but do not lose your hold on Jesus. He is wisdom, He is light, He is power. He is to you as a great Rock in a weary land. Rest under His shadow. You need wisdom, and Jesus will give it to you. Do not be unbelieving. The more you are jostled, misapprehended, misstated, misrepresented, the more evidence you have that you are doing a work for the Master, and the more closely you must cling to your Saviour. In all your difficulties be calm and undisturbed, patient and forbearing, not rendering evil for evil, but good for evil. Look to the top of the ladder. God is above it. His glory shines on every soul ascending heavenward. Jesus is this ladder. Climb up by Him, cling to Him, and erelong you will step off the ladder into His everlasting kingdom.—*Testimonies for the Church*, vol. 8, 130.

FEBRUARY 1

Heavenly Happiness

Heaven Rejoices Over Repentant Sinners

"I say to you that likewise there will be more joy
in heaven over one sinner who repents
than over ninety-nine just persons who need no repentance."
—Luke 15:7, NKJV

HEAVEN IS FULL OF JOY. It resounds with the praises of Him who made so wonderful a sacrifice for the redemption of the human race. Should not the church on earth be full of praise? Should not Christians publish throughout the world the joy of serving Christ? Those who in heaven join with the angelic choir in their anthem of praise must learn on earth the song of heaven, the keynote of which is thanksgiving.—*Testimonies for the Church*, vol. 7, 244.

Everything in heaven is noble and elevated. All seek the interest and happiness of others. No one devotes himself to looking out and caring for self. It is the chief joy of all holy beings to witness the joy and happiness of those around them.—*Testimonies for the Church*, vol. 2, 238.

There is no jar, no discord, there. All is health, happiness, and joy.—*Testimonies for the Church*, vol. 2, 81.

"What man of you, having a hundred sheep, if he loses one of them,
does not leave the ninety-nine in the wilderness, and go after the one which is lost
until he finds it? And when he has found it, he lays it on his shoulders, rejoicing.
And when he comes home, he calls together his friends and neighbors,
saying to them, 'Rejoice with me, for I have found my sheep which was lost!' "
—Luke 15:4–6, NKJV

Satisfied With His Works

May the glory of the LORD endure forever;
May the LORD rejoice in His works.

—Psalm 104:31, NKJV

HEAVEN AND EARTH were filled with rejoicing. "The morning stars sang together, and all the sons of God shouted for joy." Job 38:7.—*Testimonies for the Church*, vol. 6, 349.

The creation was now complete. "The heavens and the earth were finished, and all the host of them." . . . Eden bloomed on earth. . . . No taint of sin or shadow of death marred the fair creation. . . .

The great Jehovah had laid the foundations of the earth; He had dressed the whole world in the garb of beauty and had filled it with things useful to man; He had created all the wonders of the land and of the sea.—*Patriarchs and Prophets*, 47.

Peace brooded over the world; for earth was in harmony with heaven. "God saw everything that He had made, and, behold, it was very good;" and He rested in the joy of His completed work.—*The Desire of Ages*, 281.

"You are worthy, O Lord,
To receive glory and honor and power;
For You created all things,
And by Your will they exist and were created."

—Revelation 4:11, NKJV

God saw all that he had made, and it was very good.

—Genesis 1:31, NIV

FEBRUARY 3
Heavenly Happiness

Christ, the Delight of the Father

"I was there when he set the limits of the seas,
so they would not spread beyond their boundaries.
And when he marked off the earth's foundations,
I was the architect at his side.
I was his constant delight,
rejoicing always in his presence."

—Proverbs 8:29, 30, NLT

THE SOVEREIGN OF THE UNIVERSE was not alone in His work of beneficence. He had an associate—a co-worker who could appreciate His purposes, and could share His joy in giving happiness to created beings. "In the beginning was the Word, and the Word was with God, and the Word was God. The same was in the beginning with God." John 1:1, 2. Christ, the Word, the only begotten of God, was one with the eternal Father—one in nature, in character, in purpose—the only being that could enter into all the counsels and purposes of God. "His name shall be called Wonderful, Counselor, The mighty God, The everlasting Father, The Prince of Peace." Isaiah 9:6. . . . And the Son of God declares concerning Himself: "The Lord possessed Me in the beginning of His way, before His works of old. I was set up from everlasting. . . . When He appointed the foundations of the earth: then I was by Him, as one brought up with Him: and I was daily His delight, rejoicing always before Him." Proverbs 8:22–30.—*Patriarchs and Prophets*, 34.

He is the image of the invisible God, the firstborn of all creation.
For by him all things were created, in heaven and on earth,
visible and invisible, whether thrones or dominions or rulers or authorities—
all things were created through him and for him.
And he is before all things, and in him all things hold together.

—Colossians 1:15–17, ESV

God Is Pleased When We Seek the Savior

Be pleased, O LORD, to deliver me;
O LORD, make haste to help me!

—Psalm 40:13, NKJV

THE SAVIOUR LONGS to manifest His grace and stamp His character on the whole world. It is His purchased possession, and He desires to make men free, and pure, and holy. Though Satan works to hinder this purpose, yet through the blood shed for the world there are triumphs to be achieved that will bring glory to God and the Lamb. Christ will not be satisfied till the victory is complete, and "He shall see of the travail of His soul, and shall be satisfied." Isaiah 53:11.—*The Desire of Ages*, 827.

Desponding soul, take courage, even though you have done wickedly. Do not think that *perhaps* God will pardon your transgressions and permit you to come into His presence. God has made the first advance. While you were in rebellion against Him, He went forth to seek you. With the tender heart of the shepherd He left the ninety and nine and went out into the wilderness to find that which was lost. The soul, bruised and wounded and ready to perish, He encircles in His arms of love and joyfully bears it to the fold of safety.—*Christ's Object Lessons*, 188.

For evils have encompassed me
beyond number;
my iniquities have overtaken me,
and I cannot see;
they are more than the hairs of my head;
my heart fails me.
Be pleased, O LORD, to deliver me!
O LORD, make haste to help me!

—Psalm 40:12, 13, ESV

FEBRUARY 5
Heavenly Happiness

God Rejoices to Bestow Blessings

"They shall be my people, and I will be their God. . . .
Yes, I will rejoice over them to do them good,
and I will assuredly plant them in this land,
with all My heart and with all My soul."
—Jeremiah 32:38, 41, NKJV

CHRIST'S LOVE for His children is as tender as it is strong. And it is stronger than death; for He died to purchase our salvation, and to make us one with Him, mystically and eternally one. So strong is His love that it controls all His powers, and employs the vast resources of heaven in doing His people good. It is without variableness or shadow of turning—the same yesterday, today, and forever. Although sin has existed for ages, trying to counteract this love and obstruct its flowing earthward, it still flows in rich currents to those for whom Christ died.

God loves the sinless angels, who do His service and are obedient to all His commands; but He does not give them grace; they have never needed it, for they have never sinned. Grace is an attribute shown to undeserving human beings. We did not seek after it; it was sent in search of us. God rejoices to bestow grace upon all who hunger and thirst for it, not because we are worthy, but because we are unworthy. —*Testimonies to Ministers and Gospel Workers*, 519.

For by grace you have been saved through faith, and that not of yourselves;
it is the gift of God, not of works, lest anyone should boast.
For we are His workmanship, created in Christ Jesus for good works,
which God prepared beforehand that we should walk in them.
—Ephesians 2:8–10, NKJV

We Are His Representatives

"Yet the Lord *set his heart in love on your ancestors alone*
and chose you, their descendants after them,
out of all the peoples, as it is today."
—Deuteronomy 10:15, NRSV

God desired to make of His people Israel a praise and a glory. Every spiritual advantage was given them. God withheld from them nothing favorable to the formation of character that would make them representatives of Himself.

Their obedience to the laws of God would make them marvels of prosperity before the nations of the world. He who could give them wisdom and skill in all cunning work would continue to be their teacher and would ennoble and elevate them through obedience to His laws. If obedient, they would be preserved from the diseases that afflicted other nations and would be blessed with vigor of intellect. The glory of God, His majesty and power, were to be revealed in all their prosperity. They were to be a kingdom of priests and princes. God furnished them with every facility for becoming the greatest nation on the earth.—*Testimonies for the Church*, vol. 6, 221, 222.

Through Israel it was His design to impart rich blessings to all peoples. Through them the way was to be prepared for the diffusion of His light to the whole world. —*Testimonies for the Church*, 221.

"His glory is His children's good; his joy, His tender Fatherhood."—*Thoughts From the Mount of Blessing*, 77.

"But you shall be for me a priestly kingdom and a holy nation.
These are the words that you shall speak to the Israelites."
—Exodus 19:6, NRSV

God Rejoices in His Chosen People

No longer will they call you Deserted,
or name your land Desolate.
But you will be called Hephzibah,
and your land Beulah;
for the LORD *will take delight in you,*
and your land will be married.

—Isaiah 62:4, NIV

IF WE ARE FAITHFUL and obedient, God will delight in us, and bless us as His own chosen peculiar people.—*Testimonies for the Church*, vol. 2, 693.

The Lord has joined His people to Himself by a solemn covenant, He promising to be their God, and they pledging themselves to be His and His alone. He declares: "I will betroth thee unto Me forever; yea, I will betroth thee unto Me in righteousness, and in judgment, and in loving-kindness, and in mercies." Hosea 2:19. And, again: "I am married unto you." Jeremiah 3:14. And Paul employs the same figure in the New Testament when he says: "I have espoused you to one husband, that I may present you as a chaste virgin to Christ." 2 Corinthians 11:2.—*The Great Controversy*, 381.

For as a young man marries a young woman,
so shall your builder marry you,
and as the bridegroom rejoices over the bride,
so shall your God rejoice over you.

—Isaiah 62:5, NRSV

Husbands, love your wives,
just as Christ loved the church and gave himself up for her.

—Ephesians 5:25, NRSV

In His Church

"For the L*ORD your God is living among you.*
He is a mighty savior.
He will take delight in you with gladness.
With his love, he will calm all your fears.
He will rejoice over you with joyful songs."
—Zephaniah 3:17, NLT

THE ELECT OF GOD are dear to His heart. They are those whom He has called out of darkness into His marvelous light, to show forth His praise, to shine as lights amid the darkness of the world. The unjust judge had no special interest in the widow who importuned him for deliverance; yet in order to rid himself of her pitiful appeals, he heard her plea, and delivered her from her adversary. But God loves His children with infinite love. To Him the dearest object on earth is His church. —*Christ's Object Lessons*, 165.

During ages of spiritual darkness the church of God has been as a city set on a hill. From age to age, through successive generations, the pure doctrines of heaven have been unfolding within its borders. Enfeebled and defective as it may appear, the church is the one object upon which God bestows in a special sense His supreme regard. It is the theater of His grace, in which He delights to reveal His power to transform hearts.—*The Acts of the Apostles*, 12.

"You are the light of the world. A city set on a hill cannot be hidden.
Nor do people light a lamp and put it under a basket, but on a stand,
and it gives light to all in the house. In the same way, let your light shine before others,
so that they may see your good works and give glory to your Father who is in heaven."
—Matthew 5:14–16, ESV

I hope to come to you soon, but I am writing these things to you so that,
if I delay, you may know how one ought to behave in the household of God,
which is the church of the living God, a pillar and buttress of the truth.
—1 Timothy 3:14, 15, ESV

FEBRUARY 9
Heavenly Happiness

God Delights in the Prayer of the Upright

The sacrifice of the wicked is an abomination to the LORD,
But the prayer of the upright is His delight.
—Proverbs 15:8, NKJV

EVERY SOUL has the privilege of stating to the Lord his own special necessities and to offer his individual thanksgiving for the blessings that he daily receives. But the many long and spiritless, faithless prayers that are offered to God, instead of being a joy to Him, are a burden. We need, oh, so much! clean, converted hearts. We need to have our faith strengthened. "Ask, and it shall be given you," the Saviour promised; "seek, and ye shall find; knock, and it shall be opened unto you." Matthew 7:7. We need to educate ourselves to trust in this word and to bring the light and grace of Christ into all our works. We need to take hold of Christ and to retain our hold of Him until we know that the power of His transforming grace is manifested in us.—*Testimonies for the Church*, vol. 9, 278.

God wants His children to ask for those things that will enable Him to reveal His grace through them to the world. He wants them to seek His counsel, to acknowledge His power. Christ lays loving claims on all for whom He has given His life; they are to obey His will if they would share the joys that He has prepared for all who reflect His character here. It is well for us to feel our weakness, for then we shall seek the strength and wisdom that the Father delights to give to His children for their daily strife against the powers of evil.—*Testimonies for the Church*, vol. 9, 284.

But he said to me, "My grace is sufficient for you,
for my power is made perfect in weakness."
Therefore I will boast all the more gladly about my weaknesses,
so that Christ's power may rest on me.
That is why, for Christ's sake, I delight in weaknesses,
in insults, in hardships, in persecutions, in difficulties.
For when I am weak, then I am strong.
—2 Corinthians 12:9, 10, NIV

God Delights in Those Who Follow the Truth

The LORD detests lying lips,
but he delights in people who are trustworthy.

—Proverbs 12:22, NIV

EVERYTHING THAT CHRISTIANS DO should be as transparent as the sunlight. Truth is of God; deception, in every one of its myriad forms, is of Satan; and whoever in any way departs from the straight line of truth is betraying himself into the power of the wicked one. Yet it is not a light or an easy thing to speak the exact truth. We cannot speak the truth unless we know the truth; and how often preconceived opinions, mental bias, imperfect knowledge, errors of judgment, prevent a right understanding of matters with which we have to do! We cannot speak the truth unless our minds are continually guided by Him who is truth. . . .

Those who have learned of Christ will "have no fellowship with the unfruitful works of darkness." Ephesians 5:11. In speech, as in life, they will be simple, straightforward, and true; for they are preparing for the fellowship of those holy ones in whose mouth "was found no guile." Revelation 14:5.—*Thoughts From the Mount of Blessing*, 68, 69.

The wrath of God is being revealed from heaven against
all the godlessness and wickedness of people,
who suppress the truth by their wickedness.

—Romans 1:18, NIV

FEBRUARY 11

Heavenly Happiness

Unbending Integrity

The LORD *detest dishonest scales,*
but accurate weights find favor with him.

—Proverbs 11:1, NIV

THE ACCOUNTS OF EVERY BUSINESS, the details of every transaction, pass the scrutiny of unseen auditors, agents of Him who never compromises with injustice, never overlooks evil, never palliates wrong.—*Education*, 144.

An honest man, according to Christ's measurement, is one who will manifest unbending integrity. Deceitful weights and false balances, with which many seek to advance their interests in the world, are abomination in the sight of God. Yet many who profess to keep the commandments of God are dealing with false weights and false balances. When a man is indeed connected with God, and is keeping His law in truth, his life will reveal the fact; for all his actions will be in harmony with the teachings of Christ. He will not sell his honor for gain. His principles are built upon the sure foundation, and his conduct in worldly matters is a transcript of his principles. Firm integrity shines forth as gold amid the dross and rubbish of the world.—*Testimonies for the Church*, vol. 4, 310.

Those who choose honesty as their companion will embody it in all their acts. To a large class, these men are not pleasing, but to God they are beautiful.—*Testimonies for the Church*, vol. 4, 607.

"Use honest scales and honest weights,
an honest ephah and an honest hin.
I am the LORD *your God, who brought you out of Egypt."*

—Leviticus 19:36, NIV

Kindness, Justice, and Goodness

" 'Let the one who boasts boast about this:
that they have the understanding to know me,
that I am the LORD, who exercises kindness,
justice and righteousness on earth,
for in these I delight,' declares the LORD."

—Jeremiah 9:24, NIV

NO FINITE MIND can fully comprehend the character or the works of the Infinite One. We cannot by searching find out God. To minds the strongest and most highly cultured, as well as to the weakest and most ignorant, that holy Being must remain clothed in mystery.—*Education*, 169.

The apostle Paul exclaims, "O the depth of the riches both of the wisdom and knowledge of God! how unsearchable are His judgments, and His ways past finding out!" Romans 11:33. But though "clouds and darkness are round about Him," "righteousness and judgment are the foundation of His throne." Psalm 97:2, R.V. We can so far comprehend His dealings with us, and the motives by which He is actuated, that we may discern boundless love and mercy united to infinite power. We can understand as much of His purposes as it is for our good to know; and beyond this we must still trust the hand that is omnipotent, the heart that is full of love.—*Steps to Christ*, 106.

"Let not the wise man boast in his wisdom, let not the mighty man boast in his might,
let not the rich man boast in his riches. but let him who boasts boast in this,
that he understands and knows me, that I am the LORD who practices
steadfast love, justice, and righteousness in the earth."

—Jeremiah 9:23, 24, ESV

God Delights in Mercy

Who is a God like You,
Pardoning iniquity
And passing over the transgression of the remnant of His heritage?
He does not retain His anger forever,
Because He delights in mercy.

—Micah 7:18, NKJV

GOD "DELIGHTETH IN MERCY." "As I live, saith the Lord God, I have no pleasure in the death of the wicked." Micah 7:18; Ezekiel 33:11. To Him the work of destruction and the denunciation of judgment is a "strange work." Isaiah 28:21. But it is in mercy and love that He lifts the veil from the future, and reveals to men the results of a course of sin.—*The Desire of Ages*, 582.

The word of God reveals His character. He Himself has declared His infinite love and pity. When Moses prayed, "Show me Thy glory," the Lord answered, "I will make all My goodness pass before thee." Exodus 33:18, 19. This is His glory. The Lord passed before Moses, and proclaimed, "The Lord, The Lord God, merciful and gracious, long-suffering, and abundant in goodness and truth, keeping mercy for thousands, forgiving iniquity and transgression and sin." Exodus 34:6, 7. He is "slow to anger, and of great kindness," "because He delighteth in mercy." Jonah 4:2; Micah 7:18.—*Steps to Christ*, 10.

He prayed to the LORD, "Isn't this what I said, LORD, when I was still at home?
That is what I tried to forestall by fleeing to Tarshish.
I knew that you are a gracious and compassionate God,
slow to anger and abounding in love,
a God who relents from sending calamity."

—Jonah 4:2, NIV

More Mercy

*Jesus said, "It is not the healthy who need a doctor, but the sick.
But go and learn what this means: 'I desire mercy, not sacrifice.'
For I have not come to call the righteous, but sinners."*
—Matthew 9:12, 13, NIV

BURNT OFFERINGS AND SACRIFICES were not acceptable to God in ancient times unless the spirit was right with which the gift was offered. Samuel said: "Hath the Lord as great delight in burnt offerings and sacrifices, as in obeying the voice of the Lord? Behold, to obey is better than sacrifice, and to hearken than the fat of rams." All the money on earth cannot buy the blessing of God nor ensure you a single victory.

Many would make any and every sacrifice but the very one they *should* make, which is to yield themselves, to submit their wills to the will of God.—*Testimonies for the Church*, vol. 4, 84.

"To obey is better than sacrifice." And without obedience and unselfish love, the richest offerings are too meager to be presented to the Possessor of all things. —*Testimonies for the Church*, vol. 3, 57.

God has commanded nothing that is unessential, and there is no other way of manifesting reverence so pleasing to Him as by obedience to that which He has spoken.—*Counsels to Parents, Teachers, and Students*, 111.

*"For I desire mercy, not sacrifice,
and acknowledgment of God rather than burnt offerings."*
—Hosea 6:6, NIV

FEBRUARY 15
Heavenly Happiness

God Delights in Our Freedom

He led me to a place of safety;
he rescued me because he delights in me.

—Psalm 18:19, NLT

CHRIST DELIGHTS to take apparently hopeless material, those whom Satan has debased and through whom he has worked, and make them the subjects of His grace. He rejoices to deliver them from suffering, and from the wrath that is to fall upon the disobedient.—*Gospel Workers*, 516.

The world is a workshop in which, through the cooperation of human and divine agencies, Jesus is making experiments by His grace and divine mercy upon human hearts. Angels are amazed as they behold the transformation of character brought about in those who yield themselves to God.—*Testimonies to Ministers and Gospel Workers*, 49.

The leaven of truth works a change in the whole man, making the coarse refined, the rough gentle, the selfish generous. By it the impure are cleansed, washed in the blood of the Lamb. Through its life-giving power it brings all there is of mind and soul and strength into harmony with the divine life. Man with his human nature becomes a partaker of divinity. Christ is honored in excellence and perfection of character. As these changes are effected, angels break forth in rapturous song, and God and Christ rejoice over souls fashioned after the divine similitude.—*Christ's Object Lessons*, 102.

And they sang a new song with these words:
"You are worthy to take the scroll and break its seals and open it.
For you were slaughtered, and your blood has ransomed people for God
from every tribe and language and people and nation."

—Revelation 5:9, NLT

God Knows the End From the Beginning

"Declaring the end from the beginning,
And from ancient times things that are not yet done,
Saying, 'My counsel shall stand,
And I will do all My pleasure.' "

—Isaiah 46:10, NKJV

HE THAT RULETH in the heavens is the one who sees the end from the beginning—the one before whom the mysteries of the past and the future are alike outspread, and who, beyond the woe and darkness and ruin that sin has wrought, beholds the accomplishment of His own purposes of love and blessing.—*Patriarchs and Prophets*, 43.

The Bible shows us God in His high and holy place, not in a state of inactivity, not in silence and solitude, but surrounded by ten thousand times ten thousand and thousands of thousands of holy beings, all waiting to do His will. Through these messengers He is in active communication with every part of His dominion. By His Spirit He is everywhere present. Through the agency of His Spirit and His angels He ministers to the children of men.

Above the distractions of the earth He sits enthroned; all things are open to His divine survey; and from His great and calm eternity He orders that which His providence sees best.—*The Ministry of Healing*, 417.

Daniel replied, "There are no wise men, enchanters,
magicians, or fortune-tellers who can reveal the king's secret.
But there is a God in heaven who reveals secrets,
and he has shown King Nebuchadnezzar what will happen in the future."

—Daniel 2:27, 28, NLT

He Gave His Son for Our Redemption

It pleased the LORD to bruise him; he hath put him to grief:
when thou shalt make his soul an offering for sin,
he shall see his seed, he shall prolong his days,
and the pleasure of the LORD shall prosper in his hand.
—Isaiah 53:10, KJV

THE PLAN FOR OUR REDEMPTION was not an afterthought, a plan formulated after the fall of Adam. It was a revelation of "the mystery which hath been kept in silence through times eternal." Romans 16:25, R.V. It was an unfolding of the principles that from eternal ages have been the foundation of God's throne. From the beginning, God and Christ knew of the apostasy of Satan, and of the fall of man through the deceptive power of the apostate. God did not ordain that sin should exist, but He foresaw its existence, and made provision to meet the terrible emergency. So great was His love for the world, that He covenanted to give His only-begotten Son, "that whosoever believeth in Him should not perish, but have everlasting life." John 3:16.—*The Desires of Ages*, 22.

He who is infinite in wisdom could devise no plan for our salvation except the sacrifice of His Son. The compensation for this sacrifice is the joy of peopling the earth with ransomed beings, holy, happy, and immortal. The result of the Saviour's conflict with the powers of darkness is joy to the redeemed, redounding to the glory of God throughout eternity. And such is the value of the soul that the Father is satisfied with the price paid; and Christ Himself, beholding the fruits of his great sacrifice, is satisfied.—*The Great Controversy*, 652.

Knowing that you were ransomed . . . with the precious blood of Christ,
like that of a lamb without blemish or spot.
He was foreknown before the foundation of the world
but was made manifest in the last times for the sake of you
—1 Peter 1:18–20, ESV

God Is Pleased With His Beloved Son

And when Jesus was baptized,
immediately he went up from the water,
and behold, the heavens were opened to him,
and he saw the Spirit of God descending like a dove
and coming to rest on him; and behold, a voice from heaven said,
"This is my beloved Son, with whom I am well pleased."
—Matthew 3:16, 17, ESV

THE WORD THAT WAS SPOKEN to Jesus at the Jordan, "This is My beloved Son, in whom I am well pleased," embraces humanity. God spoke to Jesus as our representative. With all our sins and weaknesses, we are not cast aside as worthless. "He hath made us accepted in the Beloved." Ephesians 1:6. The glory that rested upon Christ is a pledge of the love of God for us. It tells us of the power of prayer,—how the human voice may reach the ear of God, and our petitions find acceptance in the courts of heaven. By sin, earth was cut off from heaven, and alienated from its communion; but Jesus has connected it again with the sphere of glory. His love has encircled man, and reached the highest heaven. The light which fell from the open portals upon the head of our Saviour will fall upon us as we pray for help to resist temptation. The voice which spoke to Jesus says to every believing soul, This is My beloved child, in whom I am well pleased.—*The Desire of Ages*, 113.

Likewise the Spirit helps us in our weakness.
For we do not know what to pray for as we ought,
but the Spirit himself intercedes for us with groanings too deep for words.
—Romans 8:26, ESV

FEBRUARY 19

Heavenly Happiness

God Delights in Those Who Fear Him

The LORD takes pleasure in those who fear him,
in those who hope in his steadfast love.

—Psalm 147:11, ESV

ALL HEAVEN REJOICES when weak, faulty human beings give themselves to Jesus, to live His life.—*Messages to Young People*, 108.

Christ has pledged Himself to be our substitute and surety, and He neglects no one. He who could not see human beings exposed to eternal ruin without pouring out His soul unto death in their behalf, will look with pity and compassion upon every soul who realizes that he cannot save himself.

He will look upon no trembling suppliant without raising him up. He who through His own atonement provided for man an infinite fund of moral power, will not fail to employ this power in our behalf. We may take our sins and sorrows to His feet; for He loves us. His every look and word invites our confidence.—*Christ's Object Lessons*, 157.

However wretched may be the specimens of humanity that men spurn and turn aside from, they are not too low, too wretched, for the notice and love of God. Christ longs to have care-worn, weary, oppressed human beings come to Him. He longs to give them the light and joy and peace that are to be found nowhere else.—*Christ's Object Lessons*, 225.

"Come to me, all who labor and are heavy laden, and I will give you rest."

—Matthew 11:28, ESV

"Peace I leave with you; my peace I give to you. Not as the world gives do I give to you.
Let not your hearts be troubled, neither let them be afraid."

—John 14:27, ESV

Those Who Do His Will See His Love

For the L*ORD* *takes pleasure in his people;*
he adorns the humble with salvation.
Let the godly exult in glory;
let them sing for joy on their beds.

—Psalm 149:4, 5, ESV

THE CLOSEST RELATIONSHIP exists between God and His people. Not only are we objects of His sparing mercy, His pardoning love; we are more than this. The Lord rejoices over His people. He delights in them. He is their surety. He will beautify all who are serving Him with a whole heart with the spirit of holiness. He clothes them with righteousness. He loves those who do His will, who express His image.—*Testimonies to Ministers and Gospel Workers*, 414.

He is acquainted with everyone connected with His service. He knows those whose hearts He can fill with the holy oil, that they may impart it to others. Those who faithfully carry forward the work of Christ in our world, representing in word and works the character of God, fulfilling the Lord's purpose for them, are in His sight very precious. Christ takes pleasure in them as a man takes pleasure in a well-kept garden and the fragrance of the flowers he has planted.—*Testimonies for the Church*, vol. 6, 418.

To the one who does not work but trusts God who justifies the ungodly,
their faith is credited as righteousness. David says the same thing
when he speaks of the blessedness of the one to whom
God credits righteousness apart from works:
"Blessed are those
whose transgressions are forgiven,
whose sins are covered.
Blessed is the one
whose sin the Lord will never count against them."

—Romans 4:5–8, NIV

God Delights in Those Who Do His Will

It is God who works in you both to will
and to do for His good pleasure.
—Philippians 2:13, NKJV

YIELD UP YOUR WILL to the will of Jesus Christ; and as you do this, God will immediately take possession and work in you to will and to do of His good pleasure. Your whole nature will then be brought under the control of the Spirit of Christ, and even your thoughts will be subject to Him. . . .

You need to drink daily at the fountain of truth, that you may understand the secret of pleasure and joy in the Lord. But you must remember that your will is the spring of all your actions. This will, that forms so important a factor in the character of man, was at the Fall given into the control of Satan; and he has ever since been working in man to will and to do of his own pleasure, but to the utter ruin and misery of man. But the infinite sacrifice of God in giving Jesus, His beloved Son, to become a sacrifice for sin, enables Him to say, without violating one principle of His government: "Yield yourself up to Me; give Me that will; take it from the control of Satan, and I will take possession of it; then I can work in you to will and to do of My good pleasure." When He gives you the mind of Christ, your will becomes as His will, and your character is transformed to be like Christ's character.—*Testimonies for the Church*, vol. 5, 513, 515.

The person without the Spirit does not accept the things
that come from the Spirit of God but considers them foolishness. . . .
But we have the mind of Christ.
—1 Corinthians 2:14, 16, NIV

God's Pleasure in Zion

The sacrifices of God are a broken spirit;
a broken and a contrite heart, O God, you will not despise.
Do good to Zion in your good pleasure;
build up the walls of Jerusalem.

—Psalm 51:17, 18, ESV

THE LORD HAS PROVIDED His church with capabilities and blessings, that they may present to the world an image of His own sufficiency, and that His church may be complete in Him, a continual representation of another, even the eternal world, of laws that are higher than earthly laws. His church is to be a temple built after the divine similitude, and the angelic architect has brought his golden measuring rod from heaven, that every stone may be hewed and squared by the divine measurement and polished to shine as an emblem of heaven, radiating in all directions the bright, clear beams of the Sun of Righteousness.—*Testimonies to Ministers and Gospel Workers*, 17.

It is by the Spirit of truth, working through the word of God, that Christ subdues His chosen people to Himself.

In describing to His disciples the office work of the Holy Spirit, Jesus sought to inspire them with the joy and hope that inspired His own heart. He rejoiced because of the abundant help He had provided for His church.—*The Desire of Ages*, 671.

He rejoiced in the consciousness that He could and would do more for His followers than He had promised; that from Him would flow forth love and compassion, cleansing the soul temple, and making men like Him in character; that His truth, armed with the power of the Spirit, would go forth conquering and to conquer.—*The Acts of the Apostles*, 23.

FEBRUARY 23
Heavenly Happiness

The Savior Delights in Bringing Us Rest and Peace

"You have loved righteousness and hated wickedness;
therefore God, your God, has set you above your companions
by anointing you with the oil of joy."

—Hebrews 1:9, NIV

THERE ARE MANY who have an erroneous idea of the life and character of Christ. They think that He was devoid of warmth and sunniness, that He was stern, severe, and joyless. In many cases the whole religious experience is colored by these gloomy views.

It is often said that Jesus wept, but that He was never known to smile. Our Saviour was indeed a Man of Sorrows, and acquainted with grief, for He opened His heart to all the woes of men. But though His life was self-denying and shadowed with pain and care, His spirit was not crushed. His countenance did not wear an expression of grief and repining, but ever one of peaceful serenity. His heart was a wellspring of life, and wherever He went He carried rest and peace, joy and gladness.—*Steps to Christ*, 120.

"In the same way there will be more rejoicing in heaven
over one sinner who repents than over ninety-nine righteous persons
who do not need to repent."

—Luke 15:7, NIV

After he has suffered,
he will see the light of life and be satisfied;
by his knowledge my righteous servant will justify many,
and he will bear their iniquities.

—Isaiah 53:11, NIV

Delighting in God's Will and Law

Then I said, "Behold, I come;
In the scroll of the book it is written of me.
I delight to do Your will, O my God,
And Your law is within my heart.
I have proclaimed the good news of righteousness
In the great assembly;
Indeed, I do not restrain my lips."

—Psalm 40:7-9, NKJV

THE SELF-DENYING REDEEMER, throughout His pilgrimage of love on earth, was a living representation of the character of the law of God.—*Thoughts From the Mount of Blessing*, 49.

From His earliest years He was possessed of one purpose; He lived to bless others. —*The Desire of Ages*, 70.

He manifested a patience that nothing could disturb, and a truthfulness that would never sacrifice integrity. In principle firm as a rock, His life revealed the grace of unselfish courtesy.—*The Desire of Ages*, 68.

There were some who sought His society, feeling at peace in His presence; but many avoided Him, because they were rebuked by His stainless life. Young companions urged Him to do as they did. He was bright and cheerful; they enjoyed His presence, and welcomed His ready suggestions; but they were impatient at His scruples, and pronounced Him narrow and strait-laced. Jesus answered, It is written, "Wherewithal shall a young man cleanse his way? by taking heed thereto according to Thy word." . . . Psalm 119:9). . . .

When questioned why He did not join in the frolics of the youth of Nazareth, He said, It is written, "I have rejoiced in the way of Thy testimonies, as much as in all riches. I will meditate in Thy precepts, and have respect unto Thy ways. I will delight myself in Thy statutes; I will not forget Thy word." Psalm 119:14–16.—*The Desire of Ages*, 89.

Delighting in Communing With the Father

David said about him:
"I saw the Lord always before me.
Because he is at my right hand,
I will not be shaken.
Therefore my heart is glad and my tongue rejoices;
my body also will rest in hope."

—Acts 2:25, 26, NIV

CHRIST FOUND COMFORT and joy in communion with His Father. Here He could unburden His heart of the sorrows that were crushing Him. . . . As the human was upon Him, He felt His need of strength from His Father. He had select places of prayer. He loved to hold communion with His Father in the solitude of the mountain. In this exercise His holy, human soul was strengthened for the duties and trials.—*Testimonies for the Church*, vol. 2, 201.

He studied the word of God, and His hours of greatest happiness were found when He could turn aside from the scene of His labors to go into the fields, to meditate in the quiet valleys, to hold communion with God on the mountainside or amid the trees of the forest. The early morning often found Him in some secluded place, meditating, searching the Scriptures, or in prayer. With the voice of singing He welcomed the morning light. With songs of thanksgiving He cheered His hours of labor and brought heaven's gladness to the toilworn and disheartened.—*The Ministry of Healing*, 52.

One of those days, Jesus went out to a mountainside to pray,
and spent the night praying to God.

—Luke 6:12, NIV

His Loving Interest in the Human Family

*"Rejoicing in his inhabited world
and delighting in the children of man."*

–Proverbs 8:31, ESV

AT ALL TIMES and in all places Jesus manifested a loving interest in the human family, and shed about Him the light of a cheerful piety.–*Messages to Young People*, 405.

He reached the hearts of the people by going among them as one who desired their good. He sought them in the public streets, in private houses, on the boats, in the synagogue, by the shores of the lake, and at the marriage feast. He met them at their daily vocations, and manifested an interest in their secular affairs. He carried His instruction into the household, bringing families in their own homes under the influence of His divine presence. His strong personal sympathy helped to win hearts.–*The Desire of Ages*, 151.

Jesus reproved self-indulgence in all its forms, yet He was social in His nature. He accepted the hospitality of all classes, visiting the homes of the rich and the poor, the learned and the ignorant, and seeking to elevate their thoughts from questions of commonplace life to those things that are spiritual and eternal. He gave no license to dissipation, and no shadow of worldly levity marred His conduct; yet He found pleasure in scenes of innocent happiness, and by His presence sanctioned the social gathering.–*The Desire of Ages*, 150.

*On the third day a wedding took place at Cana in Galilee.
Jesus' mother was there, and Jesus and his disciples
had also been invited to the wedding.
When the wine was gone, Jesus' mother said to him,
"They have no more wine."*

–John 2:1-3, NIV

He Revealed Himself to Humble Men

At that time Jesus, full of joy through the Holy Spirit, said,
"I praise you, Father, Lord of heaven and earth,
because you have hidden these things from the wise and learned,
and revealed them to little children.
Yes, Father, for this is what you were pleased to do."

—Luke 10:21, NIV

THE HONORED MEN of the world, the so-called great and wise men, with all their boasted wisdom, could not comprehend the character of Christ. They judged Him from outward appearance, from the humiliation that came upon Him as a human being. But to fishermen and publicans it had been given to see the Invisible. Even the disciples failed of understanding all that Jesus desired to reveal to them; but from time to time, as they surrendered themselves to the Holy Spirit's power, their minds were illuminated. They realized that the mighty God, clad in the garb of humanity, was among them. Jesus rejoiced that though this knowledge was not possessed by the wise and prudent, it had been revealed to these humble men. Often as He had presented the Old Testament Scriptures, and showed their application to Himself and His work of atonement, they had been awakened by His Spirit, and lifted into a heavenly atmosphere. Of the spiritual truths spoken by the prophets they had a clearer understanding than had the original writers themselves. Hereafter they would read the Old Testament Scriptures, not as the doctrines of the scribes and Pharisees, not as the utterances of wise men who were dead, but as a new revelation from God. They beheld Him "whom the world cannot receive, because it seeth Him not, neither knoweth Him: but ye know Him; for He dwelleth with you, and shall be in you." John 14:17.—*The Desire of Ages*, 494.

He Delighted in Serving Others

"I have told you this so that my joy may be in you and that your joy may be complete."

—John 15:11, NIV

OUR SAVIOUR'S JOY was in the uplifting and redemption of fallen men. For this He counted not His life dear unto Himself, but endured the cross, despising the shame.—*Steps to Christ*, 77.

Ever before Him He saw the result of His mission. His earthly life, so full of toil and self-sacrifice, was cheered by the prospect that He would not have all this travail for nought. By giving His life for the life of men, He would win back the world to its loyalty to God.—*The Desire of Ages*, 410.

The accomplishment of the mission which He had left heaven to perform strengthened the Saviour for His labor, and lifted Him above the necessities of humanity. To minister to a soul hungering and thirsting for the truth was more grateful to Him than eating or drinking. It was a comfort, a refreshment, to Him. Benevolence was the life of His soul.—*The Desire of Ages*, 190.

The spirit of Christ's self-sacrificing love is the spirit that pervades heaven and is the very essence of its bliss. This is the spirit that Christ's followers will possess, the work that they will do.—*Steps to Christ*, 77.

"If one of you wants to be first, you must be the slave of all. For even the Son of Man did not come to be served; he came to serve and to give his life to redeem many people."

—Mark 10:44, 45, GNT

MARCH 1
Joy to the World

Happiness Is a Gift From God

For God gives wisdom and knowledge
and joy to a man who is good in his sight;
but to the sinner He gives the work of gathering and collecting,
that he may give to him who is good before God. This also is vanity and grasping for the wind.
—Ecclesiastes 2:26, NKJV

GOD IS THE SOURCE of life and light and joy to the universe. Like rays of light from the sun, like the streams of water bursting from a living spring, blessings flow out from Him to all His creatures.—*Steps to Christ*, 77.

Look at the wonderful and beautiful things of nature. Think of their marvelous adaptation to the needs and happiness, not only of man, but of all living creatures. The sunshine and the rain, that gladden and refresh the earth, the hills and seas and plains, all speak to us of the Creator's love. . . .

"God is love" is written upon every opening bud, upon every spire of springing grass. The lovely birds making the air vocal with their happy songs, the delicately tinted flowers in their perfection perfuming the air, the lofty trees of the forest with their rich foliage of living green—all testify to the tender, fatherly care of our God and to His desire to make His children happy.—*Steps to Christ*, 9, 10.

You shower him with blessings that last forever;
he finds joy in knowing Your presence and loving You.
—Psalm 21:6, VOICE

For with You is the fountain of life;
In Your light we see light.
—Psalm 36:9, NKJV

Rejoicing in the Gifts of Life

Command those who are rich in this present age not to be haughty,
nor to trust in uncertain riches but in the living God,
who gives us richly all things to enjoy.
—1 Timothy 6:17, NKJV

TO THE INFINITE LOVE of the Redeemer every human being is indebted for the gifts of life. Food and raiment and shelter, body and mind and soul—all are the purchase of His blood.—*Education*, 139.

All power is given into His hands, that He may dispense rich gifts unto men. —*Testimonies to Ministers and Gospel Workers*, 91.

Every day they are surrounded with the tokens of God's love; every day they are enjoying the bounties of His providence.—*Steps to Christ*, 121.

The plan of redemption begins and ends with a gift. . . . "God so loved the world, that He *gave* His only-begotten Son." . . . And as the crowning blessing of redemption, "*the gift of God* is eternal life through Jesus Christ our Lord."—*Testimonies for the Church*, vol. 5, 730.

He has given us the Light and Majesty of heaven, and with Him He has bestowed all the heavenly treasure. Much as He has promised us for the life to come, He bestows princely gifts in this life. As subjects of His grace, He desires us to enjoy everything that will ennoble, expand, and elevate our characters.—*The Ministry of Healing*, 405.

"Look at the birds. . . . They neither sow nor reap nor gather into barns;
yet your heavenly Father feeds them. Are you not of more value than they? . . .
. . . Consider the lilies of the field, how they grow: they neither toil nor spin;
and yet I say to you that even Solomon in all his glory was not arrayed like one of these."
—Matthew 6:26, 28, 29, NKJV

Trusting in the Lord

Rescue me and deliver me
from the hand of foreigners,
whose mouths speaks lies. . . .
Blessed are the people to whom such blessings fall!
Blessed are the people whose God is the L*ORD!*
—Psalm 144:11, 15, ESV

WE SHOULD NEVER give to the world the false impression that Christians are a gloomy, unhappy people. If our eyes are fixed on Jesus, we shall see a compassionate Redeemer, and shall catch light from His countenance. Wherever His Spirit reigns, there peace abides. And there will be joy also, for there is a calm, holy trust in God. —*The Desire of Ages*, 152.

It was God's purpose that by the revelation of His character through Israel men should be drawn unto Him. . . . All who, like Rahab the Canaanite, and Ruth the Moabitess, turned from idolatry to the worship of the true God, were to unite themselves with His chosen people. As the numbers of Israel increased they were to enlarge their borders, until their kingdom should embrace the world.

God desired to bring all peoples under His merciful rule. He desired that the earth should be filled with joy and peace. He created man for happiness, and He longs to fill human hearts with the peace of heaven. He desires that the families below shall be a symbol of the great family above.—*Christ's Object Lessons*, 290.

"Happy are you, O Israel! Who is like you,
a people saved by the L*ORD,*
the shield of your help,
and the sword of your triumph!
Your enemies shall come fawning to you,
and you shall tread upon their backs."
—Deuteronomy 33:29, ESV

Immanuel, "God With Us"

"Sing and rejoice, O daughter of Zion, for behold,
I come and I will dwell in your midst, declares the Lord."
—Zechariah 2:10, ESV

God commanded Moses for Israel, "Let them make Me a sanctuary; that I may dwell among them" (Exodus 25:8), and He abode in the sanctuary, in the midst of His people. Through all their weary wandering in the desert, the symbol of His presence was with them. So Christ set up His tabernacle in the midst of our human encampment. He pitched His tent by the side of the tents of men, that He might dwell among us, and make us familiar with His divine character and life. "The Word became flesh, and tabernacled among us (and we beheld His glory, glory as of the Only Begotten from the Father), full of grace and truth." John 1:14, R.V., margin.

Since Jesus came to dwell with us, we know that God is acquainted with our trials, and sympathizes with our griefs. Every son and daughter of Adam may understand that our Creator is the friend of sinners. For in every doctrine of grace, every promise of joy, every deed of love, every divine attraction presented in the Saviour's life on earth, we see "God with us."—*The Desire of Ages*, 23, 24.

Then I, John, saw the holy city, New Jerusalem, coming down out of heaven from God,
prepared as a bride adorned for her husband. And I heard a loud voice from heaven saying,
"Behold, the tabernacle of God is with men, and He will dwell with them,
and they shall be His people. God Himself will be with them and be their God.
And God will wipe away every tear from their eyes; there shall be no more death,
nor sorrow, nor crying. There shall be no more pain,
for the former things have passed away."
—Revelation 21:2–4, NKJV

MARCH 5

Joy to the World

Truly Happy

Light shines on the godly,
and joy on those whose hearts are right.
May all who are godly rejoice in the LORD
and praise his holy name!

—Psalm 97:11, 12, NLT

IT IS NOT WEALTH or intellect that gives happiness; it is true moral worth and a sense of duty performed. You may have the overcomer's reward and stand before the throne of Christ to sing His praises in the day when He assembles His saints; but your robes must be cleansed in the blood of the Lamb, and charity must cover you as a garment, and you be found spotless and without blemish.—*Testimonies for the Church*, vol. 4, 125.

"For he that will love life, and see good days, let him refrain his tongue from evil, and his lips that they speak no guile: let him eschew evil, and do good; let him seek peace, and ensue it. For the eyes of the Lord are over the righteous, and His ears are open unto their prayers: but the face of the Lord is against them that do evil." Those who have an experimental knowledge of this scripture are truly happy. They consider the approbation of Heaven of more worth than any earthly amusement; Christ in them the hope of glory will be health to the body and strength to the soul.—*Testimonies for the Church*, vol. 1, 566.

God has given me the responsibility of . . . proclaiming his entire message to you.
This message was kept secret for centuries . . . , but now it has been revealed
to God's people. For God wanted them to know that the riches and glory of Christ
are for you Gentiles, too. And this is the secret: Christ lives in you.
This gives you assurance of sharing his glory.

—Colossians 1:25–27, NLT

God Answers Our Prayers

"Until now you have asked nothing in My name.
Ask, and you will receive, that your joy may be full."
—John 16:24, NKJV

PRAY, BELIEVE, REJOICE. Sing praises to God because He has answered your prayers. Take Him at His word. "He is faithful that promised." Hebrews 10:23. Not one sincere supplication is lost. The channel is open; the stream is flowing.—*Testimonies for the Church*, vol. 7, 274.

The Lord has been waiting long to impart the greatest, truest joys to the heart. All those who look to Him with undivided hearts, He will greatly bless. Those who have thus looked to Him have caught more distinct views of Jesus as their sin bearer, their all-sufficient sacrifice, and have been hid in the cleft of the Rock, to behold the Lamb of God who taketh away the sins of the world.—*Counsels to Parents, Teachers, and Students*, 369.

The gifts of Him who has all power in heaven and earth are in store for the children of God. Gifts so precious that they come to us through the costly sacrifice of the Redeemer's blood; gifts that will satisfy the deepest craving of the heart, gifts lasting as eternity, will be received and enjoyed by all who will come to God as little children. Take God's promises as your own, plead them before Him as His own words, and you will receive fullness of joy.—*Thoughts From the Mount of Blessing*, 133.

Let us hold fast the confession of our hope without wavering,
for He who promised is faithful.
—Hebrews 10:23, NKJV

God Is Our Source of Wisdom

Joyful is the person who finds wisdom,
the one who gains understanding.
For wisdom is more profitable than silver,
and her wages are better than gold.
—Proverbs 3:13, 14, NLT

NEITHER BY SEARCHING the recesses of the earth nor in vain endeavors to penetrate the mysteries of God's being is wisdom found. It is found, rather, in humbly receiving the revelation that He has been pleased to give, and in conforming the life to His will.—*Testimonies for the Church*, vol. 8, 280.

Those who hunger for knowledge that they may bless their fellow men will themselves receive blessing from God. Through the study of His word their mental powers will be aroused to earnest activity. There will be an expansion and development of the faculties, and the mind will acquire power and efficiency.—*Christ's Object Lessons*, 334.

Let none think that there is no more knowledge for them to gain. The depth of human intellect may be measured; the works of human authors may be mastered; but the highest, deepest, broadest flight of the imagination cannot find out God. There is infinity beyond all that we can comprehend. We have seen only the glimmering of divine glory and of the infinitude of knowledge and wisdom; we have, as it were, been working on the surface of the mine, when rich golden ore is beneath the surface, to reward the one who will dig for it. The shaft must be sunk deeper and yet deeper in the mine, and the result will be glorious treasure. Through a correct faith, divine knowledge will become human knowledge.—*Christ's Object Lessons*, 113.

Our Father in heaven is the source of life, of wisdom, and of joy.—*Steps to Christ*, 9.

If you need wisdom, ask our generous God, and he will give it to you.
—James 1:5, NLT

His Wisdom Brings Joy

Her ways are ways of pleasantness,
and all her paths are peace.
She is a tree of life to those who lay hold of her;
those who hold her fast are called blessed.

—Proverbs 3:17, 18, ESV

THE WISE MAN SAYS that wisdom's "ways are ways of pleasantness, and all her paths are peace." Proverbs 3:17. Many cherish the impression that devotion to God is detrimental to health and to cheerful happiness in the social relations of life. But those who walk in the path of wisdom and holiness find that "godliness is profitable unto all things, having promise of the life that now is, and of that which is to come." 1 Timothy 4:8. They are alive to the enjoyment of life's real pleasures, while they are not troubled with vain regrets over misspent hours, nor with gloom or horror of mind, as the worldling too often is when not diverted by some exciting amusement.—*Counsels on Health*, 627.

True religion ennobles the mind, refines the taste, sanctifies the judgment, and makes its possessor a partaker of the purity and the holiness of heaven. It brings angels near and separates us more and more from the spirit and influence of the world. It enters into all the acts and relations of life and gives us the "spirit of a sound mind," and the result is happiness and peace.—*Counsels on Health*, 629.

They know the truth about God because he has made it obvious to them.
For ever since the world was created, people have seen the earth and sky.
Through everything God made, they can clearly see his invisible qualities—
his eternal power and divine nature. So they have no excuse for not knowing God.

—Romans 1:19, 20, NLT

MARCH 9

Joy to the World

Rejoicing With All Nature

Let the heavens rejoice, and let the earth be glad;
Let the sea roar, and all its fullness;
Let the field be joyful, and all that is in it.
Then all the trees of the woods will rejoice
before the LORD.

—Psalm 96:11–13, NKJV

GOD WOULD HAVE His children appreciate His works and delight in the simple, quiet beauty with which He has adorned our earthly home.—*Steps to Christ*, 85.

That Creator who planted the beautiful Eden for our first parents, and who has planted for us the lovely trees and flowers, and provided everything that is beautiful and glorious in nature for the human race to enjoy, designed that they should enjoy it. . . .

That God who has planted these noble trees and clothed them with their rich foliage, who has given us the brilliant and beautiful shades of the flowers, and whose lovely handiwork we see in all the realm of nature, does not design to make us unhappy; He does not design that we shall have no taste for, and take no pleasure in, these things. It is His design that we shall enjoy them and be happy in the charms of nature, which are of His own creating.—*Testimonies for the Church*, vol. 2, 588.

Let me enjoy the beauties of the kingdom of God. Let me delight in the paintings which His own fingers have colored. I may enjoy them. You may enjoy them. We may not worship them, but through them we may be directed to Him and behold His glory who made all these things for our enjoyment.—*Testimonies for the Church*, 592.

Nature Created for Our Joy

It is good to give thanks to the LORD,
And to sing praises to Your name, O Most High;
To declare Your lovingkindness in the morning,
And Your faithfulness every night,
On an instrument of ten strings,
On the lute,
And on the harp,
With harmonious sound.
For You, LORD, have made me glad through Your work;
I will triumph in the works of Your hands.
O LORD, how great are Your works!
Your thoughts are very deep.

—Psalm 92:1–5, NKJV

IN THE LOVELINESS of the things of nature you may learn more of the wisdom of God than the schoolmen know. On the lily's petals, God has written a message for you, written in language that your heart can read only as it unlearns the lessons of distrust and selfishness and corroding care. Why has He given you the singing birds and the gentle blossoms, but from the overflowing love of a Father's heart, that would brighten and gladden your path of life? All that was needed for existence would have been yours without the flowers and birds, but God was not content to provide what would suffice for mere existence. He has filled earth and air and sky with glimpses of beauty to tell you of His loving thought for you. The beauty of all created things is but a gleam from the shining of His glory. If He has lavished such infinite skill upon the things of nature, for your happiness and joy, can you doubt that He will give you every needed blessing?—*Thoughts From the Mount of Blessing*, 96.

A Delightful Land

"And all nations will call you blessed,
For you will be a delightful land,"
Says the L*ORD* *of hosts.*

—Malachi 3:12, NKJV

AS YOUR SENSES DELIGHT in the attractive loveliness of the earth, think of the world that is to come, that shall never know the blight of sin and death; where the face of nature will no more wear the shadow of the curse. Let your imagination picture the home of the saved, and remember that it will be more glorious than your brightest imagination can portray. In the varied gifts of God in nature we see but the faintest gleaming of His glory. It is written, "Eye hath not seen, nor ear heard, neither have entered into the heart of man, the things which God hath prepared for them that love Him." 1 Corinthians 2:9.

The poet and the naturalist have many things to say about nature, but it is the Christian who enjoys the beauty of the earth with the highest appreciation, because he recognizes his Father's handiwork and perceives His love in flower and shrub and tree. No one can fully appreciate the significance of hill and vale, river and sea, who does not look upon them as an expression of God's love to man.—*Steps to Christ*, 86, 87.

"You are under a curse, for your whole nation has been cheating me.
Bring all the tithes into the storehouse so there will be enough food in my Temple. . . .
Then all nations will call you blessed, for your land will be such a delight."

—Malachi 3:9, 10, 12, NLT

Nature Obeys His Will

Those who live at the ends of the earth
stand in awe of your wonders.
From where the sun rises to where it sets,
you inspire shouts of joy.
You take care of the earth and water it,
making it rich and fertile.
The river of God has plenty of water;
it provides a bountiful harvest of grain,
for you have ordered it so.

—Psalm 65:8, 9, NLT

THIS EARTH IS THE LORD'S. Here it may be seen that nature, animate and inanimate, obeys His will. . . .

How wonderfully, with what marvelous beauty, has everything in nature been fashioned. Everywhere we see the perfect works of the great Master Artist. The heavens declare His glory, and the earth, which is formed for the happiness of man, speaks to us of His matchless love. Its surface is not a monotonous plain, but grand old mountains rise to diversify the landscape. There are sparkling streams and fertile valleys, beautiful lakes, broad rivers, and the boundless ocean. God sends the dew and the rain to refresh the thirsty earth. The breezes, that promote health by purifying and cooling the atmosphere, are controlled by His wisdom. He has placed the sun in the heavens to mark the periods of day and night, and by its genial beams give light and warmth to the earth, causing vegetation to flourish.—*Testimonies for the Church*, vol. 5, 311, 312.

I call your attention to these blessings from the bounteous hand of God. . . . Our kind heavenly Father has given us so many things to promote our happiness. . . .

. . . He is the very fountain of love, the giver of blessings innumerable.—*Testimonies for the Church*, vol. 5, 312, 314.

Dear friends, let us continue to love one another, for love comes from God.
Anyone who loves is a child of God and knows God.
But anyone who does not love does not know God, for God is love.

—1 John 4:7, 8, NLT

MARCH 13

Joy to the World

The Sun of Righteousness Lights Our Day

Their line has gone out through all the earth,
And their words to the end of the world.
In them He has set a tabernacle for the sun,
Which is like a bridegroom coming out of his chamber,
And rejoices like a strong man to run its race.

—Psalm 19:4, 5, NKJV

WE NEED THE ENLIGHTENMENT of the Holy Spirit in order to discern the truths in God's word. The lovely things of the natural world are not seen until the sun, dispelling the darkness, floods them with its light. So the treasures in the word of God are not appreciated until they are revealed by the bright beams of the Sun of Righteousness. . . .

. . . As we study the Scriptures, we should pray for the light of God's Holy Spirit to shine upon the word, that we may see and appreciate its treasures.—*Christ's Object Lessons*, 113.

He whose heart has responded to the divine touch will be seeking for that which will increase his knowledge of God, and will refine and elevate the character. As a flower turns to the sun, that the bright rays may touch it with tints of beauty, so will the soul turn to the Sun of Righteousness, that heaven's light may beautify the character with the graces of the character of Christ.—*The Desire of Ages*, 468.

His love gives us the privilege of sitting together with Him in heavenly places. When the blessed light of the Sun of Righteousness shines into our hearts, and we rest in peace and joy in the Lord, then let us praise the Lord; praise Him who is the health of our countenance and our God. Let us praise Him, not in words only, but by the consecration to Him of all that we are and all that we have.—*Testimonies for the Church*, vol. 6, 479.

"And the day which is coming shall burn them up,"
Says the LORD of hosts,
"That will leave them neither root nor branch.
But to you who fear My name
The Sun of Righteousness shall arise
With healing in His wings;
And you shall go out
And grow fat like stall-fed calves "

—Malachi 4:1, 2, NKJV

Beholding Jesus

Truly the light is sweet,
And it is pleasant for the eyes to behold the sun.
—Ecclesiastes 11:7, NKJV

IF WE GAZE even a moment upon the sun in its meridian glory, when we turn away our eyes, the image of the sun will appear in everything upon which we look. Thus it is when we behold Jesus; everything we look upon reflects His image, the Sun of Righteousness. We cannot see anything else, or talk of anything else. His image is imprinted upon the eye of the soul and affects every portion of our daily life, softening and subduing our whole nature. By beholding, we are conformed to the divine similitude, even the likeness of Christ. To all with whom we associate we reflect the bright and cheerful beams of His righteousness. We have become transformed in character; for heart, soul, mind, are irradiated by the reflection of Him who loved us and gave Himself for us. . . .

. . . Jesus Christ is everything to us—the first, the last, the best in everything. Jesus Christ, His Spirit, His character, colors everything; it is the warp and the woof, the very texture of our entire being. The words of Christ are spirit and life. We cannot, then, center our thoughts upon self; it is no more we that live, but Christ that liveth in us, and He is the hope of glory. Self is dead, but Christ is a living Saviour. Continuing to look unto Jesus, we reflect His image to all around us. We cannot stop to consider our disappointments, or even to talk of them; for a more pleasant picture attracts our sight—the precious love of Jesus.—*Testimonies to Ministers and Gospel Workers*, 388, 389.

MARCH 15

Joy to the World

Rejoicing in the Power of God

"Have you given the horse its strength
or clothed its neck with a flowing mane?
Did you give it the ability to leap like a locust?
Its majestic snorting is terrifying!
It paws the earth and rejoices in its strength
when it charges out to battle."

—Job 39:19–21, NLT

THE SPASMODIC, FITFUL MOVEMENTS of some who claim to be Christians are well represented by the work of strong but untrained horses. When one pulls forward, another pulls back, and at the voice of their master one plunges ahead and the other stands immovable. If men will not move in concert in the great and grand work for this time, there will be confusion. It is not a good sign when men refuse to unite with their brethren and prefer to act alone. . . . If men wear the yoke of Christ, they can not pull apart; they will draw with Christ.

Some . . . pull with all the power that God has given them, but they have not yet learned that they should not pull alone. Instead of isolating themselves, let them draw in harmony with their fellow laborers. Unless they do this, their activity will work at the wrong time and in the wrong way. They will often work counter to that which God would have done, and thus their work is worse than wasted.—*Testimonies for the Church*, vol. 9, 258.

God is the embodiment of benevolence, mercy, and love. Those who are truly connected with Him cannot be at variance with one another. His Spirit ruling in the heart will create harmony, love, and unity.—*Testimonies for the Church*, vol. 5, 28.

Jesus has made it possible for you to accept His love and in happy co-operation with Him to work under its fragrant influence.—*Testimonies for the Church*, vol. 9, 50.

Happy in Useful Labor

Even so, I have noticed one thing, at least, that is good.
It is good for people to eat, drink, and enjoy their work
under the sun during the short life God has given them,
and to accept their lot in life.

—Ecclesiastes 5:18, NLT

THE HABIT OF ENJOYING useful labor, once formed, will never be lost.—*Testimonies for the Church*, vol. 3, 336.

He who is indolent and willingly ignorant places in his pathway that which will always be an obstruction. He refuses the culture that comes from honest toil. By failing to put forth a helping hand in behalf of humanity, he robs God. His career is very different from the career which God marked out for him; for to despise useful employment encourages the lower tastes and effectually paralyzes the most useful energies of the being.

Not a few, but thousands, of human beings exist only to consume the benefits which God in His mercy bestows on them. They forget to bring the Lord gratitude offerings for the riches He has intrusted to them in giving them the fruit of the earth. They forget that God desires them, by trading wisely on the talents lent them, to be producers as well as consumers. If they had a realization of the work the Lord desires them to do as His helping hand, they would not feel it a privilege to shun all responsibility and be waited on.

Real happiness is found only in being good and doing good. The purest, highest enjoyment comes to those who faithfully fulfill their appointed duties.—*Messages to Young People*, 210.

Labor Is a Blessing

For every man to whom God has given riches and wealth,
and given him power to eat of it, to receive his heritage
and rejoice in his labor–this is the gift of God.

–Ecclesiastes 5:19, NKJV

GOD APPOINTED LABOR as a blessing to man, to occupy his mind, to strengthen his body, and to develop his faculties. In mental and physical activity Adam found one of the highest pleasures of his holy existence. And when, as a result of his disobedience, he was driven from his beautiful home, and forced to struggle with a stubborn soil to gain his daily bread, that very labor, although widely different from his pleasant occupation in the garden, was a safeguard against temptation and a source of happiness. Those who regard work as a curse, attended though it be with weariness and pain, are cherishing an error. The rich often look down with contempt upon the working classes, but this is wholly at variance with God's purpose in creating man. What are the possessions of even the most wealthy in comparison with the heritage given to the lordly Adam? Yet Adam was not to be idle. Our Creator, who understands what is for man's happiness, appointed Adam his work. The true joy of life is found only by the working men and women.–*Patriarchs and Prophets*, 50.

Then to Adam He said, "Because you have heeded the voice of your wife,
and have eaten from the tree of which I commanded you, saying, 'You shall not eat of it':

"Cursed is the ground for your sake;
In toil you shall eat of it
All the days of your life.
Both thorns and thistles it shall bring forth for you,
And you shall eat the herb of the field.
In the sweat of your face you shall eat bread
Till you return to the ground,

For out of it you were taken;
For dust you are,
And to dust you shall return."

–Genesis 3:17–19, NKJV

God Gives Us the Fruit of Our Labor

"The LORD your God will make you abound in all the work of your hand, in the fruit of your body, in the increase of your livestock, and in the produce of your land for good. For the LORD will again rejoice over you for good as He rejoiced over your fathers."
—Deuteronomy 30:9, NKJV

HE WHO FED the multitude with five loaves and two small fishes is able today to give us the fruit of our labor. He who said to the fishers of Galilee, "Let down your nets for a draft," and who, as they obeyed, filled their nets till they broke, desires His people to see in this an evidence of what He will do for them today. The God who in the wilderness gave the children of Israel manna from heaven still lives and reigns. He will guide His people and give skill and understanding in the work they are called to do. He will give wisdom to those who strive to do their duty conscientiously and intelligently. He who owns the world is rich in resources, and will bless everyone who is seeking to bless others.

We need to look heavenward in faith. We are not to be discouraged because of apparent failure, nor should we be disheartened by delay. We should work cheerfully, hopefully, gratefully, believing that the earth holds in her bosom rich treasures for the faithful worker to garner, stores richer than gold or silver. The mountains and hills are changing; the earth is waxing old like a garment; but the blessing of God, which spreads for His people a table in the wilderness, will never cease.—*The Ministry of Healing*, 200.

"Our fathers ate the manna in the desert; as it is written, 'He gave them bread from heaven to eat.' " . . .

. . . "Your fathers ate the manna in the wilderness, and are dead." . . .
. . . "This is the bread which came down from heaven—not as your fathers ate the manna, and are dead. He who eats this bread will live forever."
—John 6:31, 49, 58, NKJV

Duty Well Done Brings Happiness

So I perceived that nothing is better
than that a man should rejoice in his own works,
for that is his heritage. For who can bring him to see
what will happen after him?

—Ecclesiastes 3:22, NKJV

THOSE WHO ARE ALWAYS BUSY, and go cheerfully about the performance of their daily tasks, are the most happy and healthy. The rest and composure of night brings to their wearied frames unbroken slumber. The Lord knew what was for man's happiness when He gave him work to do. The sentence that man must toil for his bread, and the promise of future happiness and glory, came from the same throne. Both are blessings. —*Testimonies the Church*, vol. 2, 529.

Let us remember that while the work we have to do may not be our choice, it is to be accepted as God's choice for us. Whether pleasing or unpleasing, we are to do the duty that lies nearest. "Whatsoever thy hand findeth to do, do it with thy might. . . ." Ecclesiastes 9:10. . . .

We are to look upon every duty, however humble, as sacred because it is a part of God's service. Our daily prayer should be, "Lord, help me to do my best. Teach me how to do better work. Give me energy and cheerfulness. Help me to bring into my service the loving ministry of the Saviour."—*The Ministry of Healing*, 472, 474.

Whatever your hand finds to do, do it with your might;
for there is no work or device or knowledge
or wisdom in the grave where you are going.

—Ecclesiastes 9:10, NKJV

The sleep of a laboring man is sweet,
Whether he eats little or much;
But the abundance of the rich will not permit him to sleep.

—Ecclesiastes 5:12, NKJV

Being Faithful in Every Detail

"Be careful not to sacrifice
your burnt offerings just anywhere you like.
You may do so only at the place the LORD will choose within
one of your tribal territories. There you must offer your burnt
offerings and do everything I command you. . . .
. . . You must eat these in the presence of the LORD your God
at the place he will choose. Eat them there with your children, your servants, and the Levites
who live in your towns, celebrating in the presence of the LORD your God in all you do."
—Deuteronomy 12:13, 14, 18, NLT

TO BECOME A TOILER, to continue patiently in well-doing which calls for self-denying labor, is a glorious work, which Heaven smiles upon. Faithful work is more acceptable to God than the most zealous and thought-to-be holiest worship. . . . Prayers, exhortation, and talk are cheap fruits, which are frequently tied on; but fruits that are manifested in good works, in caring for the needy, the fatherless, and widows, are genuine fruits, and grow naturally upon a good tree.—*Testimonies for the Church*, vol. 2, 24.

Success in this life, success in gaining the future life, depends upon a faithful, conscientious attention to the little things. Perfection is seen in the least, no less than in the greatest, of the works of God. The hand that hung the worlds in space is the hand that wrought with delicate skill the lilies of the field. And as God is perfect in His sphere, so we are to be perfect in ours. The symmetrical structure of a strong, beautiful character is built up by individual acts of duty. And faithfulness should characterize our life in the least as well as in the greatest of its details. Integrity in little things, the performance of little acts of fidelity and little deeds of kindness, will gladden the path of life; and when our work on earth is ended, it will be found that every one of the little duties faithfully performed has exerted an influence for good—an influence that can never perish. —*Patriarchs and Prophets*, 574.

"If you are faithful in little things, you will be faithful in large ones.
But if you are dishonest in little things, you won't be honest with greater responsibilities."
—Luke 16:10, NLT

Joy in the Harvest

The people who walk in darkness
will see a great light.
For those who live in a land of deep darkness,
a light will shine.
You will enlarge the nation of Israel,
and its people will rejoice.
They will rejoice before you
as people rejoice at the harvest.

—Isaiah 9:2, 3, NLT

GOD'S GREAT COVENANT declares that "while the earth remaineth, seedtime and harvest . . . shall not cease." Genesis 8:22. In the confidence of this promise the husbandman tills and sows. Not less confidently are we, in the spiritual sowing, to labor, trusting His assurance: "So shall My word be that goeth forth out of My mouth: it shall not return unto Me void, but it shall accomplish that which I please, and it shall prosper in the thing whereto I sent it." . . . Isaiah 55:11. . . .

The wheat develops, "first the blade, then the ear, after that the full corn in the ear." Mark 4:28. The object of the husbandman in the sowing of the seed and the culture of the plant, is the production of grain—bread for the hungry, and seed for future harvests. So the divine Husbandman looks for a harvest. He is seeking to reproduce Himself in the hearts and lives of His followers, that through them He may be reproduced in other hearts and lives.—*Education*, 105, 106.

The harvest of life is character, and it is this that determines destiny, both for this life and for the life to come. . . .

. . . Love, sympathy, and kindness yield fruitage of blessing, a harvest that is imperishable.—*Education*, 108, 109.

In the morning sow your seed,
And in the evening do not withhold your hand;
For you do not know which will prosper,
Either this or that,
Or whether both alike will be good.

—Ecclesiastes 11:6, NKJV

Labor Yields True Joy

When you eat the labor of your hands,
You shall be happy, and it shall be well with you.
—Psalm 128:2, NKJV

JESUS LIVED in a peasant's home, and faithfully and cheerfully acted His part in bearing the burdens of the household. . . . He learned a trade, and with His own hands worked in the carpenter's shop with Joseph. In the simple garb of a common laborer He walked the streets of the little town, going to and returning from His humble work. He did not employ His divine power to lessen His burdens or to lighten His toil.

As Jesus worked in childhood and youth, mind and body were developed. He did not use His physical powers recklessly, but in such a way as to keep them in health, that He might do the best work in every line. He was not willing to be defective, even in the handling of tools. He was perfect as a workman, as He was perfect in character. By His own example He taught that it is our duty to be industrious, that our work should be performed with exactness and thoroughness, and that such labor is honorable. The exercise that teaches the hands to be useful and trains the young to bear their share of life's burdens gives physical strength, and develops every faculty. All should find something to do that will be beneficial to themselves and helpful to others. God appointed work as a blessing, and only the diligent worker finds the true glory and joy of life.—*The Desire of Ages*, 72.

In the name of the Lord Jesus Christ, we command you, brothers and sisters,
to keep away from every believer who is idle and disruptive
and does not live according to the teaching you received from us. . . .
For even when we were with you, we gave you this rule:
"The one who is unwilling to work shall not eat."
—2 Thessalonians 3:6, 10, NIV

Food Provided by God

Out of the ground the L*ORD* *God made every tree grow*
that is pleasant to the sight and good for food.
The tree of life was also in the midst of the garden,
and the tree of the knowledge of good and evil.

—Genesis 2:9, NKJV

GOD HAS FURNISHED man with abundant means for the gratification of natural appetite. He has spread before him, in the products of the earth, a bountiful variety of food that is palatable to the taste and nutritious to the system. Of these our benevolent heavenly Father says that we may "freely eat." We may enjoy the fruits, the vegetables, the grains, without doing violence to the laws of our being. These articles, prepared in the most simple and natural manner, will nourish the body, and preserve its natural vigor without the use of flesh meats.—*Testimonies for the Church*, vol. 3, 50.

Persons who have accustomed themselves to a rich, highly stimulating diet have an unnatural taste, and they cannot at once relish food that is plain and simple. It will take time for the taste to become natural and for the stomach to recover from the abuse it has suffered. But those who persevere in the use of wholesome food will, after a time, find it palatable. Its delicate and delicious flavors will be appreciated, and it will be eaten with greater enjoyment than can be derived from unwholesome dainties.—*The Ministry of Healing*, 298.

The L*ORD* *God took the man and put him in the Garden of Eden*
to work it and take care of it. And the L*ORD* *God commanded the man,*
"You are free to eat from any tree in the garden;
but you must not eat from the tree of the knowledge of good and evil,
for when you eat from it you will certainly die."

—Genesis 2:15–17, NIV

We Should Relish Our Food

So go ahead. Eat your food with joy,
and drink your wine with a happy heart,
for God approves of this!

—Ecclesiastes 9:7, NLT

IT IS IMPORTANT that we relish the food we eat. If we cannot do this, but eat mechanically, we fail to be nourished and built up as we would be if we could enjoy the food we take into the stomach. We are composed of what we eat. In order to make a good quality of blood, we must have the right kind of food, prepared in a right manner.

It is a religious duty for those who cook to learn how to prepare healthful food in different ways, so that it may be eaten with enjoyment. . . . The eating has to do with the life. . . . It is highly essential that the art of cookery be considered one of the most important branches of education. . . . Knowledge of how to prepare food healthfully, especially bread, is no mean science.—*Testimonies for the Church*, vol. 1, 681, 682.

To the health and happiness of the whole family nothing is more vital than skill and intelligence on the part of the cook. By ill-prepared, unwholesome food she may hinder and even ruin both the adult's usefulness and the child's development. Or by providing food adapted to the needs of the body, and at the same time inviting and palatable, she can accomplish as much in the right as otherwise she accomplishes in the wrong direction. So, in many ways, life's happiness is bound up with faithfulness in common duties.—*Education*, 216.

So whether you eat or drink, or whatever you do, do it all for the glory of God.

—1 Corinthians 10:31, NLT

All Necessities of Life Assured

Those who are honest and fair,
who refuse to profit by fraud,
who stay far away from bribes,
who refuse to listen to those who plot murder,
who shut their eyes to all enticement to do wrong–
these are the ones who will dwell on high.
The rocks of the mountains will be their fortress.
Food will be supplied to them,
and they will have water in abundance.

–Isaiah 33:15, 16, NLT

EVERY DAY YOU ARE TO PRAY, "Give us this day our daily bread." Be not dismayed if you have not sufficient for tomorrow. You have the assurance of His promise, "So shalt thou dwell in the land, and verily thou shalt be fed." David says, "I have been young, and now am old; yet have I not seen the righteous forsaken, nor his seed begging bread." Psalm 37:3, 25.–*Thoughts From the Mount of Blessing*, 110.

That God who cared for Elijah will not pass by one of His self-sacrificing children. He who numbers the hairs of their head will care for them, and in time of famine they shall be satisfied. While the wicked are dying from hunger and pestilence, angels will shield the righteous and supply their wants. To him that "walketh righteously" is the promise: "Bread shall be given him; his waters shall be sure." "When the poor and needy seek water, and there is none, and their tongue faileth for thirst, I the Lord will hear them, I the God of Israel will not forsake them." Isaiah 33:15, 16; 41:17.–*The Great Controversy*, 629.

Even though the fig trees have no blossoms,
and there are no grapes on the vines;
even though the olive crop fails,
and the fields lie empty and barren;
even though the flocks die in the fields,
and the cattle barns are empty,
yet I will rejoice in the LORD!
I will be joyful in the God of my salvation!

–Habakkuk 3:17, 18, NLT

God Uses the Elements to Produce Food

You send rain on the mountains from your heavenly home,
and you fill the earth with the fruit of your labor.
You cause grass to grow for the livestock
and plants for people to use.
You allow them to produce food from the earth.
—Psalm 104:13, 14, NLT

God has bountifully provided for the sustenance and happiness of all His creatures; and if His laws were never violated, and all acted in harmony with the divine will, health, peace, and happiness, instead of misery and continual evil, would be experienced.—*Testimonies for the Church*, vol. 2, 368.

It is by the mighty power of the Infinite One that the elements of nature in earth and sea and sky are kept within bounds. And these elements He uses for the happiness of His creatures. "His good treasure" is freely expended "to give the rain . . . in his season, and to bless all the work" of man's hands. Deuteronomy 28:12.—*Prophets and Kings*, 134.

You make springs gush forth in the valleys;
they flow between the hills,
giving drink to every wild animal;
the wild asses quench their thirst.
By the streams the birds of the air have their habitation;
they sing among the branches. . . .
You cause the grass to grow for the cattle,
and plants for people to use,
to bring forth food from the earth,
and wine to gladden the human heart.
—Psalm 104:10–12, 14, 15, NRSV

The Joy of Israel

The people of Judah and Israel were as numerous
as the sand on the seashore;
they ate, they drank and they were happy.

—1 Kings 4:20, NIV

ISRAEL HAD HAD ABUNDANT OCCASION for rejoicing. The land to which the Lord had brought them was a land flowing with milk and honey. During the wilderness wandering, God had assured them that He was guiding them to a country where they need never suffer for lack of rain.—*Prophets and Kings*, 135.

God brought the Israelites from Egypt, that He might establish them in the land of Canaan, a pure, holy, and happy people. In the accomplishment of this object He subjected them to a course of discipline, both for their own good and for the good of their posterity. Had they been willing to deny appetite, in obedience to His wise restrictions, feebleness and disease would have been unknown among them. Their descendants would have possessed both physical and mental strength. They would have had clear perceptions of truth and duty, keen discrimination, and sound judgment. . . .

God might as easily have provided them with flesh as with manna, but a restriction was placed upon them for their good. It was His purpose to supply them with food better suited to their wants than the feverish diet to which many had become accustomed in Egypt. The perverted appetite was to be brought into a more healthy state, that they might enjoy the food originally provided for man—the fruits of the earth, which God gave to Adam and Eve in Eden.—*Patriarchs and Prophets*, 378.

The Joy of Hospitality

He told them to celebrate these days with feasting and gladness and by giving gifts of food to each other and presents to the poor. This would commemorate a time when the Jews gained relief from their enemies, when their sorrow was turned into gladness and their mourning into joy.

—Esther 9:22, NLT

GRATITUDE, REJOICING, benevolence, trust in God's love and care—these are health's greatest safeguard. To the Israelites they were to be the very keynote of life. —*The Ministry of Healing*, 281.

At their sacred feasts the Lord had directed that "the stranger, and the fatherless, and the widow, which are within thy gates, shall come, and shall eat, and be satisfied." Deuteronomy 14:29.—*Christ's Object Lessons*, 220.

These feasts were occasions of rejoicing, made sweeter and more tender by the hospitable welcome given to the stranger, the Levite, and the poor.—*The Ministry of Healing*, 281.

These gatherings were to be as object lessons to Israel. Being thus taught the joy of true hospitality, the people were throughout the year to care for the bereaved and the poor. And these feasts had a wider lesson. The spiritual blessings given to Israel were not for themselves alone. God had given the bread of life to them, that they might break it to the world.—*Christ's Object Lessons*, 220.

"At the end of every third year, bring the entire tithe of that year's harvest and store it in the nearest town. Give it to the Levites, who will receive no allotment of land among you, as well as to the foreigners living among you, the orphans, and the widows in your towns, so they can eat and be satisfied. Then the LORD your God will bless you in all your work."

—Deuteronomy 14:28, 29, NLT

Enjoying Good Food With Moderation

They worshiped together at the Temple each day,
met in homes for the Lord's Supper, and shared their meals
with great joy and generosity—all the while praising God
and enjoying the goodwill of all the people.
And each day the Lord added to their fellowship those
who were being saved.

—Acts 2:46, 47, NLT

EATING AND DRINKING in accordance with the laws of health promote virtuous actions. But if the stomach is abused by habits that have no foundation in nature, Satan takes advantage of the wrong that has been done and uses the stomach as an enemy of righteousness, creating a disturbance which affects the entire being.—*Counsels on Health*, 577.

God is not honored when the body is neglected or abused and is thus unfitted for His service. To care for the body by providing for it food that is relishable and strengthening is one of the first duties of the householder. It is far better to have less expensive clothing and furniture than to stint the supply of food.—*The Ministry of Healing*, 322.

Let the table be made inviting and attractive, as it is supplied with the good things which God has so bountifully bestowed. Let mealtime be a cheerful, happy time. As we enjoy the gifts of God, let us respond by grateful praise to the Giver.—*The Ministry of Healing*, 385.

When you sit down to eat with someone important,
keep in mind who he is. If you have a big appetite, restrain yourself.
Don't be greedy for the fine food he serves; he may be trying to trick you.

—Proverbs 23:1–3, GNT

Christ Our Guide

O LORD, *You are the portion of my inheritance and my cup;*
You maintain my lot.
The lines have fallen to me in pleasant places;
Yes, I have a good inheritance.
I will bless the LORD *who has given me counsel;*
My heart also instructs me in the night seasons.
I have set the LORD *always before me;*
Because He is at my right hand I shall not be moved.
—Psalm 16:5–8, NKJV

HAVE THERE NOT BEEN some bright spots in your experience? Have you not had some precious seasons when your heart throbbed with joy in response to the Spirit of God? When you look back into the chapters of your life experience do you not find some pleasant pages? Are not God's promises, like the fragrant flowers, growing beside your path on every hand? Will you not let their beauty and sweetness fill your heart with joy?—*Steps to Christ*, 117.

The road may be rough and the ascent steep; there may be pitfalls upon the right hand and upon the left; we may have to endure toil in our journey; when weary, when longing for rest, we may have to toil on; when faint, we may have to fight; when discouraged, we must still hope; but with Christ as our guide we shall not fail of reaching the desired haven at last. Christ Himself has trodden the rough way before us and has smoothed the path for our feet.

And all the way up the steep road leading to eternal life are well-springs of joy to refresh the weary.—*Thoughts From the Mount of Blessing*, 140.

LORD, *you alone are my inheritance, my cup of blessing.*
You guard all that is mine.
The land you have given me is a pleasant land.
What a wonderful inheritance!
—Psalm 16:5, 6, NLT

The Coming of the Lord Is Our Hope

The hope of the righteous will be gladness,
but the expectation of the wicked will perish.
—Proverbs 10:28, NKJV

THE COMING OF THE LORD has been in all ages the hope of His true followers. The Saviour's parting promise upon Olivet, that He would come again, lighted up the future for His disciples, filling their hearts with joy and hope that sorrow could not quench nor trials dim. Amid suffering and persecution, the "appearing of the great God and our Saviour Jesus Christ" was the "blessed hope."—*The Great Controversy*, 302.

From the day when the first pair turned their sorrowing steps from Eden, the children of faith have waited the coming of the Promised One to break the destroyer's power and bring them again to the lost Paradise.—*The Great Controversy*, 299.

To dwell forever in this home of the blest, to bear in soul, body, and spirit, not the dark traces of sin and the curse, but the perfect likeness of our Creator, and through ceaseless ages to advance in wisdom, in knowledge, and in holiness, ever exploring new fields of thought, ever finding new wonders and new glories, ever increasing in capacity to know and to enjoy and to love, and knowing that there is still beyond us joy and love and wisdom infinite—such is the object to which the Christian's hope is pointing. —*Counsels to Parents, Teachers, and Students*, 55.

APRIL 1

Joy Through Tribulation

Not to Be Exalted Above Measure

And lest I should be exalted above measure by the abundance of the revelations, a thorn in the flesh was given to me, a messenger of Satan to buffet me, lest I be exalted above measure. Concerning this thing I pleaded with the Lord three times that it might depart from me. And He said to me, "My grace is sufficient for you, for My strength is made perfect in weakness." Therefore most gladly I will rather boast in my infirmities, that the power of Christ may rest upon me.

—2 Corinthians 12:7–9, NKJV

While the Lord has not promised His people exemption from trials, He has promised that which is far better. He has said, "As thy days, so shall thy strength be." "My grace is sufficient for thee: for My strength is made perfect in weakness." Deuteronomy 33:25; 2 Corinthians 12:9. If you are called to go through the fiery furnace for His sake, Jesus will be by your side even as He was with the faithful three in Babylon. Those who love their Redeemer will rejoice at every opportunity of sharing with Him humiliation and reproach. The love they bear their Lord makes suffering for His sake sweet.—*Thoughts From the Mount of Blessing*, 30.

Through all our trials we have a never-failing Helper. He does not leave us alone to struggle with temptation, to battle with evil, and be finally crushed with burdens and sorrow. Though now He is hidden from mortal sight, the ear of faith can hear His voice saying, Fear not; I am with you. "I am He that liveth, and was dead; and, behold, I am alive forevermore." Revelation 1:18. I have endured your sorrows, experienced your struggles, encountered your temptations. I know your tears; I also have wept. The griefs that lie too deep to be breathed into any human ear, I know. Think not that you are desolate and forsaken. Though your pain touch no responsive chord in any heart on earth, look unto Me, and live.—*The Desire of Ages*, 483.

Strength Given to the Weak

That's why I take pleasure in my weaknesses,
and in the insults, hardships, persecutions,
and troubles that I suffer for Christ.
For when I am weak, then I am strong.
—2 Corinthians 12:10, NLT

THE LORD'S CARE is over all His creatures. He loves them all and makes no difference, except that He has the most tender pity for those who are called to bear life's heaviest burdens. God's children must meet trials and difficulties. But they should accept their lot with a cheerful spirit, remembering that for all that the world neglects to bestow, God Himself will make up to them in the best of favors.—*The Ministry of Healing*, 199.

In all ages of the church God's appointed messengers have exposed themselves to reproach and persecution for the truth's sake. But wherever God's people may be forced to go, even though, like the beloved disciple, they are banished to desert islands, Christ will know where they are and will strengthen and bless them, filling them with peace and joy.—*Testimonies for the Church*, vol. 9, 227.

He gives power to the weak
and strength to the powerless.
Even youths will become weak and tired,
and young men will fall in exhaustion.
But those who trust in the LORD will find new strength.
They will soar high on wings like eagles.
They will run and not grow weary.
They will walk and not faint.
—Isaiah 40:29–31, NLT

The Joy of Suffering for Others

I am now rejoicing in my suffering for your sake,
and in my flesh I am completing what is lacking in
Christ's afflictions for the sake of his body, that is, the church.
—Colossians 1:24, NRSV

THE APOSTLES COUNTED not their lives dear unto themselves, rejoicing that they were counted worthy to suffer shame for the name of Christ. Paul and Silas suffered the loss of all things. They suffered scourging, and were in no gentle manner thrown upon the cold floor of a dungeon in a most painful position, their feet elevated and fastened in the stocks. Did repinings and complaints then reach the ear of the jailer? Oh, no! From the inner prison, voices broke the silence of midnight with songs of joy and praise to God. These disciples were cheered by a deep and earnest love for the cause of their Redeemer, for which they suffered.

As the truth of God fills our hearts, absorbs our affections, and controls our lives, we also will count it joy to suffer for the truth's sake. No prison walls, no martyr's stake, can then daunt or hinder us in the great work.—*Testimonies for the Church*, vol. 3, 406.

The humble will see their God at work and be glad.
Let all who seek God's help be encouraged.
For the LORD hears the cries of the needy;
he does not despise his imprisoned people.
—Psalm 69:32, 33, NLT

Worthy to Suffer for Him

They called in the apostles and had them flogged.
Then they ordered them never again to speak in the name of Jesus,
and they let them go.
The apostles left the high council
rejoicing that God had counted them worthy
to suffer disgrace for the name of Jesus.

—Acts 5:40, 41, NLT

As men seek to come into harmony with God, they will find that the offense of the cross has not ceased. Principalities and powers and wicked spirits in high places are arrayed against all who yield obedience to the law of heaven. Therefore, so far from causing grief, persecution should bring joy to the disciples of Christ, for it is an evidence that they are following in the steps of their Master. . . .

In all ages Satan has persecuted the people of God. He has tortured them and put them to death, but in dying they became conquerors. They revealed in their steadfast faith a mightier One than Satan. Satan could torture and kill the body, but he could not touch the life that was hid with Christ in God. He could incarcerate in prison walls, but he could not bind the spirit. They could look beyond the gloom to the glory, saying, "I reckon that the sufferings of this present time are not worthy to be compared with the glory which shall be revealed in us." "Our light affliction, which is but for a moment, worketh for us a far more exceeding and eternal weight of glory." Romans 8:18; 2 Corinthians 4:17.—*Thoughts From the Mount of Blessing*, 29, 30.

And after you have suffered for a little while,
the God of all grace, who has called you to his eternal glory in Christ,
will himself restore, support, strengthen, and establish you.

—1 Peter 5:10, NRSV

An Opportunity for Great Joy

Dear brothers and sisters,
when troubles of any kind come your way,
consider it an opportunity for great joy.
For you know that when your faith is tested,
your endurance has a chance to grow.

—James 1:2, 3, NLT

THE BRIGHT AND CHEERFUL SIDE of our religion will be represented by all who are daily consecrated to God. We should not dishonor God by the mournful relation of trials that appear grievous. All trials that are received as educators will produce joy. The whole religious life will be uplifting, elevating, ennobling, fragrant with good words and works. The enemy is well pleased to have souls depressed, downcast, mourning and groaning; he wants just such impressions made as to the effect of our faith. But God designs that the mind shall take no low level. He desires every soul to triumph in the keeping power of the Redeemer.—*Testimonies for the Church*, vol. 6, 365.

The trial of faith is more precious than gold. All should learn that this is a part of the discipline in the school of Christ, which is essential to purify and refine them from the dross of earthliness. They must endure with fortitude the taunts and attacks of enemies, and overcome all obstacles that Satan may place in their path to hedge up the way.—*Testimonies for the Church*, vol. 5, 578.

Joyful are those you discipline, LORD,
those you teach with your instructions.
You give them relief from troubled times
until a pit is dug to capture the wicked.

—Psalm 94:12, 13, NLT

Endure Everything With Patience

So that you may lead lives worthy
of the Lord, fully pleasing to him,
as you bear fruit in every good work and as you grow
in the knowledge of God. May you be made strong
with all the strength that comes from his glorious power,
and may you be prepared to endure everything with patience.
—Colossians 1:10, 11, NRSV

IN THE RELIGIOUS LIFE of every soul who is finally victorious there will be scenes of terrible perplexity and trial; but his knowledge of the Scriptures will enable him to bring to mind the encouraging promises of God, which will comfort his heart and strengthen his faith in the power of the Mighty One.—*Testimonies for the Church*, vol. 5, 578.

In all ages God's appointed witnesses have exposed themselves to reproach and persecution for the truth's sake. . . .

These examples of human steadfastness bear witness to the faithfulness of God's promises—of His abiding presence and sustaining grace. They testify to the power of faith to withstand the powers of the world. It is the work of faith to rest in God in the darkest hour, to feel, however sorely tried and tempest-tossed, that our Father is at the helm. The eye of faith alone can look beyond the things of time to estimate aright the worth of the eternal riches.—*The Acts of the Apostles*, 575.

Then talk of the promises; talk of Jesus' willingness to bless. He does not forget us for one brief moment. When, notwithstanding disagreeable circumstances, we rest confidingly in His love, and shut ourselves in with Him, the sense of His presence will inspire a deep, tranquil joy.—*The Ministry of Healing*, 488.

And not only that, but we also boast in our sufferings,
knowing that suffering produces endurance,
and endurance produces character, and character produces hope.
—Romans 5:3, 4, NRSV

When His Spirit Works Through Us

But the fruit of the Spirit is love, joy, peace, patience,
kindness, goodness, faithfulness, gentleness, self-control;
against such things there is no law.

—Galatians 5:22, 23, ESV

"Charity suffereth long, and is kind; charity envieth not." The divine love ruling in the heart exterminates pride and selfishness. "Charity vaunteth not itself, is not puffed up." The purest joy springs from the deepest humiliation. The strongest and noblest characters rest upon the foundation of patience and love, and trusting submission to the will of God.

Charity "doth not behave itself unseemly, seeketh not her own, is not easily provoked, thinketh no evil." The heart in which love rules will not be filled with passion or revenge, by injuries which pride and self-love would deem unbearable. Love is unsuspecting, ever placing the most favorable construction upon the motives and acts of others. . . .

. . . Love not only bears with others' faults, but cheerfully submits to whatever suffering or inconvenience such forbearance makes necessary. This love "never faileth." It can never lose its value; it is the attribute of heaven. As a precious treasure it will be carried by its possessor through the portals of the city of God.

The fruit of the Spirit is love, joy, and peace. Discord and strife are the work of Satan and the fruit of sin. If we would as a people enjoy peace and love, we must put away our sins; we must come into harmony with God, and we shall be in harmony with one another. Let each ask himself: Do I possess the grace of love? Have I learned to suffer long and to be kind?—*Testimonies for the Church*, vol. 5, 168, 169.

For this very reason, make every effort to supplement your faith with virtue,
and virtue with knowledge, and knowledge with self-control,
and self-control with steadfastness, and steadfastness with godliness,
and godliness with brotherly affection, and brotherly affection with love.

—2 Peter 1:5–7, ESV

Trials Resulting in Growth

My brethren, take the prophets, who spoke in the name of the Lord, as an example of suffering and patience. Indeed we count them blessed who endure. You have heard of the perseverance of Job and seen the end intended by the Lord—that the Lord is very compassionate and merciful.

—James 5:10, 11, NKJV

PATIENCE AS WELL AS COURAGE has its victories. By meekness under trial, no less than by boldness in enterprise, souls may be won to Christ. The Christian who manifests patience and cheerfulness under bereavement and suffering, who meets even death itself with the peace and calmness of an unwavering faith, may accomplish for the gospel more than he could have effected by a long life of faithful labor. Often when the servant of God is withdrawn from active duty, the mysterious providence which our short-sighted vision would lament is designed by God to accomplish a work that otherwise would never have been done.—*The Acts of the Apostles*, 465.

Not in freedom from trial, but in the midst of it, is Christian character developed. Exposure to rebuffs and opposition leads the follower of Christ to greater watchfulness and more earnest prayer to the mighty Helper. Severe trial endured by the grace of God develops patience, vigilance, fortitude, and a deep and abiding trust in God. It is the triumph of the Christian faith that it enables its followers to suffer and be strong; to submit, and thus to conquer; to be killed all the day long, and yet to live; to bear the cross, and thus to win the crown of glory.—*The Acts of the Apostles*, 467.

Facing Trials With Joy

If you are reproached for the name of Christ,
blessed are you, for the Spirit of glory and of God rests upon you.
On their part He is blasphemed, but on your part He is glorified.
—1 Peter 4:14, NKJV

THE WORLD LOVES SIN, and hates righteousness, and this was the cause of its hostility to Jesus. All who refuse His infinite love will find Christianity a disturbing element. The light of Christ sweeps away the darkness that covers their sins, and the need of reform is made manifest. While those who yield to the influence of the Holy Spirit begin war with themselves, those who cling to sin war against the truth and its representatives.

Thus strife is created, and Christ's followers are accused as troublers of the people. But it is fellowship with God that brings them the world's enmity. They are bearing the reproach of Christ. They are treading the path that has been trodden by the noblest of the earth. Not with sorrow, but with rejoicing, should they meet persecution. Each fiery trial is God's agent for their refining. Each is fitting them for their work as colaborers with Him. Each conflict has its place in the great battle for righteousness, and each will add to the joy of their final triumph. Having this in view, the test of their faith and patience will be cheerfully accepted rather than dreaded and avoided. —*The Desire of Ages*, 306.

Since Christ suffered for us in the flesh,
arm yourselves also with the same mind,
for he who has suffered in the flesh
has ceased from sin.
—1 Peter 4:1, NKJV

APRIL 10

Joy Through Tribulation

How to Find Joy Here and Now and Forever

We then, as workers together with Him also
plead with you not to receive the grace of God in vain. . . .
. . . As sorrowful, yet always rejoicing; as poor, yet making many rich;
as having nothing, and yet possessing all things.

—2 Corinthians 6:1, 10, NKJV

WE ARE IN A WORLD of suffering. Difficulty, trial, and sorrow await us all along the way to the heavenly home. But there are many who make life's burdens doubly heavy by continually anticipating trouble. If they meet with adversity or disappointment they think that everything is going to ruin, that theirs is the hardest lot of all, that they are surely coming to want. Thus they bring wretchedness upon themselves and cast a shadow upon all around them. Life itself becomes a burden to them. But it need not be thus. It will cost a determined effort to change the current of their thought. But the change can be made. Their happiness, both for this life and for the life to come, depends upon their fixing their minds upon cheerful things. Let them look away from the dark picture, which is imaginary, to the benefits which God has strewn in their pathway, and beyond these to the unseen and eternal.—*The Ministry of Healing*, 247.

All who are pursuing the onward Christian course should have, and will have, an experience that is living, that is new and interesting. A living experience is made up of daily trials, conflicts, and temptations, strong efforts and victories, and great peace and joy gained through Jesus.—*Testimonies for the Church*, vol. 2, 579.

And since we are his children, we are his heirs.
In fact, together with Christ we are heirs of God's glory.
But if we are to share his glory, we must also share his suffering.

—Romans 8:17, NLT

All Things Work Together for Our Good

Sorrow is better than laughter,
For by a sad countenance the heart is made better.
—Ecclesiastes 7:3, NKJV

ALL OUR SUFFERINGS and sorrows, all our temptations and trials, all our sadness and griefs, all our persecutions and privations, in short, all things work together for our good. All experiences and circumstances are God's workmen whereby good is brought to us.—*The Ministry of Healing*, 488.

It may be that much work needs to be done in your character building, that you are a rough stone, which must be squared and polished before it can fill a place in God's temple. You need not be surprised if with hammer and chisel God cuts away the sharp corners of your character until you are prepared to fill the place He has for you. No human being can accomplish this work. Only by God can it be done. And be assured that He will not strike one useless blow. His every blow is struck in love, for your eternal happiness. He knows your infirmities and works to restore, not to destroy. —*Testimonies for the Church*, vol. 7, 264.

Now He who searches the hearts knows what the mind of the Spirit is,
because He makes intercession for the saints according to the will of God.
And we know that all things work together for good to those who love God,
to those who are the called according to His purpose.
—Romans 8:27, 28, NKJV

Persevere in Prayer

Rejoicing in hope, patient in tribulation,
continuing steadfastly in prayer.

—Romans 12:12, NKJV

HAPPY IS THE MAN whom God correcteth: . . . He maketh sore, and bindeth up: He woundeth, and His hands make whole. He shall deliver thee in six troubles: yea, in seven there shall no evil touch thee." Job 5:17–19. To every stricken one, Jesus comes with the ministry of healing. The life of bereavement, pain, and suffering may be brightened by precious revealings of His presence.

God would not have us remain pressed down by dumb sorrow, with sore and breaking hearts. He would have us look up and behold His dear face of love. The blessed Saviour stands by many whose eyes are so blinded by tears that they do not discern Him. He longs to clasp our hands, to have us look to Him in simple faith, permitting Him to guide us. His heart is open to our griefs, our sorrows, and our trials. He has loved us with an everlasting love and with loving-kindness compassed us about. We may keep the heart stayed upon Him and meditate upon His loving-kindness all the day. He will lift the soul above the daily sorrow and perplexity, into a realm of peace.

Think of this, children of suffering and sorrow, and rejoice in hope.—*Thoughts From the Mount of Blessing*, 12.

Be anxious for nothing, but in everything by prayer and supplication,
with thanksgiving, let your requests be made known to God;
and the peace of God, which surpasses all udnerstanding,
will guard your hearts and minds through Christ Jesus.

—Philippians 4:6, 7, NKJV

Bearing Our Burdens With Joy

Satisfy us in the morning with your steadfast love,
that we may rejoice and be glad all our days.
Make us glad for as many days as you have afflicted us,
and for as many years as we have seen evil.
Let your work be shown to your servants,
and your glorious power to their children.

—Psalm 90:14–16, ESV

LET ME ASSURE YOU that the struggles and conflicts which must be endured in the discharge of duty, the self-denials and sacrifices which must be made if we are faithful to Christ, are not created by Him. They are not imposed by arbitrary or unnecessary command; they do not come from the severity of the life which He requires us to lead in His service. Trials would exist in greater power and number were we to refuse obedience to Christ and become the servants of Satan and the slaves of sin.

Jesus invites us to come to Him and He will lift the weights from our weary shoulders and place upon us His yoke, which is easy, and His burden, which is light. The path in which He invites us to walk would never have cost us a pang had we always walked in it. It is when we stray from the path of duty that the way becomes difficult and thorny. The sacrifices which we must make in following Christ are only so many steps to return to the path of light, of peace and happiness.—*Testimonies for the Church*, vol. 4, 557, 558.

"Come to me, all who labor and are heavy laden,
and I will give you rest. Take my yoke upon you, and learn from me,
for I am gentle and lowly in heart, and you will find rest for your souls.
For my yoke is easy, and my burden is light."

—Matthew 11:28–30, ESV

Facing Trials Head-On

Make me hear joy and gladness,
That the bones You have broken may rejoice.

—Psalm 51:8, NKJV

IT IS TRUE that God loves us, that He is working for our happiness, and that, if His law had always been obeyed, we should never have known suffering; and it is no less true that, in this world, as the result of sin, suffering, trouble, burdens, come to every life. . . .

. . . This world is not a parade ground, but a battlefield. All are called to endure hardness, as good soldiers. . . .

The true way of dealing with trial is not be seeking to escape it, but by transforming it. This applies to all discipline, the earlier as well as the later. The neglect of the child's earliest training, and the consequent strengthening of wrong tendencies, makes his after education more difficult. . . . Painful it must be to the lower nature, crossing, as it does, the natural desires and inclinations; but the pain may be lost sight of in a higher joy.—*Education*, 295.

Our sorrows do not spring out of the ground. God "doth not afflict willingly nor grieve the children of men." Lamentations 3:33. When He permits trials and afflictions, it is "for our profit, that we might be partakers of His holiness." Hebrews 12:10. If received in faith, the trial that seems so bitter and hard to bear will prove a blessing. The cruel blow that blights the joys of earth will be the means of turning our eyes to heaven. How many there are who would never have known Jesus had not sorrow led them to seek comfort in Him!—*Thoughts From the Mount of Blessing*, 10.

O LORD, I will praise You;
Though You were angry with me,
Your anger is turned away, and You comfort me.

—Isaiah 12:1, NKJV

The Lord Is Tender and Patient

I will be glad and rejoice in Your mercy,
For you have considered my trouble;
You have known my soul in adversities.

—Psalm 31:7, NKJV

OH, HOW PRECIOUS is the sweet influence of the Spirit of God as it comes to depressed or despairing souls, encouraging the fainthearted, strengthening the feeble, and imparting courage and help to the tried servants of the Lord! Oh, what a God is ours, who deals gently with the erring and manifests His patience and tenderness in adversity, and when we are overwhelmed with some great sorrow!—*Patriarchs and Prophets*, 657.

The Lord permits trials in order that we may be cleansed from earthliness, from selfishness, from harsh, unchristlike traits of character. He suffers the deep waters of affliction to go over our souls in order that we may know Him and Jesus Christ whom He has sent, in order that we may have deep heart longings to be cleansed from defilement, and may come forth from the trial purer, holier, happier.—*Christ's Object Lessons*, 174.

"Now this is eternal life: that they know you, the only true God,
and Jesus Christ, whom you have sent."

—John 17:3, NIV

Who is a God like you,
who pardons sin and forgives the transgression
of the remnant of his inheritance?
You do not stay angry forever
but delight to show mercy.
You will again have compassion on us;
you will tread our sins underfoot
and hurl all our iniquities into the depths of the sea.

—Micah 7:18, 19, NIV

Do Not Despise God's Chastening

"Behold, happy is the man whom God corrects;
Therefore do not despise the chastening of the Almighty."

—Job 5:17, NKJV

MANY OF YOUR AFFLICTIONS have been visited upon you, in the wisdom of God, to bring you closer to the throne of grace. He softens and subdues His children by sorrows and trials. This world is God's workshop, where He fashions us for the courts of heaven. He uses the planing knife upon our quivering hearts until the roughness and irregularities are removed and we are fitted for our proper places in the heavenly building. Through tribulation and distress the Christian becomes purified and strengthened, and develops a character after the model that Christ has given.—*Testimonies for the Church*, vol. 4, 143.

The fact that we are called upon to endure trial shows that the Lord Jesus sees in us something precious which He desires to develop. If He saw in us nothing whereby He might glorify His name, He would not spend time in refining us. He does not cast worthless stones into His furnace. It is valuable ore that He refines.—*The Ministry of Healing*, 471.

Trust in the LORD with all you heart,
And lean not on your own understanding;
In all your ways acknowledge Him,
And He shall direct your paths.
Do not be wise in your own eyes;
Fear the LORD and depart from evil. . . .
My son, do not despise the chastening of the LORD,
Nor detest His correction;
For whom the LORD loves He corrects,
Just as a father the son in whom he delights.

—Proverbs 3:5–7, 11, 12, NKJV

Finding Joy in God's Law

Unless Your law had been my delight,
I would then have perished in my affliction.

—Psalm 119:92, NKJV

CHRIST'S TRUE DISCIPLES follow Him through sore conflicts, enduring self-denial and experiencing bitter disappointment; but this teaches them the guilt and woe of sin, and they are led to look upon it with abhorrence.—*The Act of the Apostles*, 590.

God has given us His holy precepts, because He loves mankind. To shield us from the results of transgression, He reveals the principles of righteousness. The law is an expression of the thought of God; when received in Christ, it becomes our thought. It lifts us above the power of natural desires and tendencies, above temptations that lead to sin. God desires us to be happy, and He gave us the precepts of the law that in obeying them we might have joy.—*The Desire of Ages*, 308.

Your justice is eternal,
and your instructions are perfectly true.
As pressure and stress bear down on me,
I find joy in your commands.
Your laws are always right;
help me to understand them so I may live.

—Psalm 119:142–144, NLT

The laws of the LORD are true;
each one is fair.
They are more desirable than gold,
even the finest gold.
They are sweeter than honey,
even honey dripping from the comb.

—Psalm 19:9–11, NLT

God Is Our Strength

I have spoken to you with great frankness; I take great pride in you.
I am greatly encouraged; in all our troubles
my joy knows no bounds.

—2 Corinthians 7:4, NIV

ALL WHO STAND UNSHRINKINGLY in the forefront of the battle must feel the special warfare of Satan against them. As they realize his attacks, they will flee to the Stronghold. They feel their need of special strength from God, and they labor in His strength; therefore the victories they gain do not exalt them, but lead them in faith to lean more securely upon the Mighty One. Deep and fervent gratitude to God is awakened in their hearts, and they are joyful in the tribulation which they experience while pressed by the enemy. These willing servants are gaining an experience and forming a character which will do honor to the cause of God.—*Testimonies for the Church*, vol. 2, 510.

Let me know that Jesus smiles upon me; let me know that he approves my actions and my course, and then let come what may, let afflictions be ever so great, I will be resigned to my lot and rejoice in the Lord.—"The Graces of the Spirit," *Review and Herald*, December 21, 1886, 785.

I often boast about you; I have great pride in you;
I am filled with consolation; I am overjoyed in all our affliction.

—2 Corinthians 7:4, NRSV

Comforting Others

Blessed be the God and Father of our Lord Jesus Christ,
the Father of mercies and God of all comfort, who comforts us
in all our affliction, so that we may be able to comfort those
who are in any affliction, with the comfort with which we ourselves
are comforted by God.

—2 Corinthians 1:3, 4, ESV

MANY WERE THE MESSAGES of comfort given the church by the prophets of old. "Comfort ye, comfort ye My people" (Isaiah 40:1), was Isaiah's commission from God; and with the commission were given wonderful visions that have been the believers' hope and joy through all the centuries that have followed. Despised of men, persecuted, forsaken, God's children in every age have nevertheless been sustained by His sure promises. By faith they have looked forward to the time when He will fulfill to His church the assurance, "I will make thee an eternal excellency, a joy of many generations." Isaiah 60:15.—*Prophets and Kings*, 722.

Then let us not mourn and grieve because in this life we are not free from disappointments and afflictions. If in the providence of God we are called upon to endure trials, let us accept the cross and drink the bitter cup, remembering that it is a Father's hand that holds it to our lips. Let us trust Him in the darkness as well as in the day. Can we not believe that He will give us everything that is for our good? "He that spared not His own Son, but delivered Him up for us all, how shall He not with Him also freely give us all things?" Even in the night of affliction how can we refuse to lift heart and voice in grateful praise, when we remember the love to us expressed by the cross of Calvary?—*Testimonies for the Church*, vol. 5, 315.

Sing, O heavens!
Be joyful, O earth!
And break out in singing, O mountains!
For the LORD has comforted His people,
And will have mercy on His afflicted.

—Isaiah 49:13, NKJV

Sorrow Turning Into Joy

"I tell you the truth, you will weep and mourn
over what is going to happen to me,
but the world will rejoice. You will grieve, but your grief
will suddenly turn to wonderful joy."

—John 16:20, NLT

WHEN THEY SHOULD SEE their Lord betrayed and crucified, the disciples would mourn and fast. In His last words to them in the upper chamber, He said, "A little while, and ye shall not see Me: and again, a little while, and ye shall see Me. Verily, verily, I say unto you, That ye shall weep and lament, but the world shall rejoice: and ye shall be sorrowful, but your sorrow shall be turned into joy." John 16:19, 20.

When He should come forth from the tomb, their sorrow would be turned to joy. After His ascension He was to be absent in person; but through the Comforter He would still be with them, and they were not to spend their time in mourning. This was what Satan wanted. He desired them to give the world the impression that they had been deceived and disappointed; but by faith they were to look to the sanctuary above, where Jesus was ministering for them; they were to open their hearts to the Holy Spirit, His representative, and to rejoice in the light of His presence.—*The Desire of Ages*, 277.

May the God of hope fill you with all joy and peace in believing,
that you may abound in hope by the power of the Holy Spirit.

—Romans 15:13, NKJV

Nevertheless I tell you the truth; it is expedient for you that I go away:
for if I go not away, the Comforter will not come unto you;
but if I depart, I will send him unto you. And when he is come,
he will reprove the world of sin, and of righteousness, and of judgment:
of sin, because they believe not on me; of righteousness, because I go to my Father,
and ye see me no more; of judgment, because the prince of this world is judged.

—John 16:7–11, KJV

Endless Joy

"Therefore you now have sorrow; but I will see you again and your heart will rejoice, and your joy no one will take from you."
—John 16:22, NKJV

GREAT DARKNESS was upon the face of the earth. The last hope of the disciples seemed swept away as Jesus died. Many of His followers witnessed the scene of His sufferings and death, and their cup of sorrow was full.—*Early Writings*, 177.

Lonely hours they spent in weeping over their disappointment. They had expected that Jesus would reign a temporal Prince, but their hopes died with Him. In their sorrow and disappointment, they doubted whether He had not deceived them. Even His mother wavered in her faith in Him as the Messiah.—*Early Writings*, 179.

Jesus arose from the dead, a triumphant conqueror. In solemn awe the angelic host gazed upon the scene. And as Jesus came forth from the sepulcher, those shining angels prostrated themselves to the earth in worship, and hailed Him with songs of victory and triumph.—*Early Writings*, 182.

Jesus remained with His disciples forty days, causing them joy and gladness of heart as He opened to them more fully the realities of the kingdom of God.—*Early Writings*, 189.

His anxious followers gladly listened to His teachings, eagerly feasting upon every word which fell from His holy lips. Now they certainly knew that He was the Saviour of the world. . . . Their hearts were warmed with love and exceeding joy, as Jesus told them that He would go and prepare mansions for them and come again and receive them, that they might be ever with Him.—*Early Writings*, 190.

"Let not your heart be troubled; you believe in God, believe also in Me.
In My Father's house are many mansions; if it were not so, I would have told you.
I go to prepare a place for you. And if I go and prepare a place for you,
I will come again and receive you to Myself;
that where I am, there you may be also."
—John 14:1–3, NKJV

From Sadness to Joy

Then shall the young women rejoice in the dance,
and the young men and the old shall be merry.
I will turn their mourning into joy,
I will comfort them, and give them gladness for sorrow.
—Jeremiah 31:13, NRSV

LET US LOOK to the monumental pillars, reminders of what the Lord has done to comfort us and to save us from the hand of the destroyer. Let us keep fresh in our memory all the tender mercies that God has shown us,—the tears He has wiped away, the pains He has soothed, the anxieties removed, the fears dispelled, the wants supplied, the blessings bestowed,—thus strengthening ourselves for all that is before us through the remainder of our pilgrimage.

We cannot but look forward to new perplexities in the coming conflict, but we may look on what is past as well as on what is to come, and say, "Hitherto hath the Lord helped us." "As thy days, so shall thy strength be." Deuteronomy 33:25. The trial will not exceed the strength that shall be given us to bear it. Then let us take up our work just where we find it, believing that whatever may come, strength proportionate to the trial will be given.

And by and by the gates of heaven will be thrown open to admit God's children, and from the lips of the King of glory the benediction will fall on their ears like richest music, "Come, ye blessed of My Father, inherit the kingdom prepared for you from the foundation of the world." Matthew 25:34.—*Steps to Christ*, 125.

The temptations in your life are no different from what others experience.
And God is faithful. He will not allow the temptation to be more than you can stand.
When you are tempted, he will show you a way out so that you can endure.
—1 Corinthians 10:13, NLT

Then Samuel took a stone and set it between Mizpah and Jeshanah,
and named it Ebenezer; for he said, "Thus far the LORD *has helped us."*
—1 Samuel 7:12, NRSV

Vitalizing Power

You have turned my mourning into joyful dancing.
You have taken away my clothes of mourning and clothed me with joy.
—Psalm 30:11, NLT

NOT ALL THIS WORLD bestows can heal a broken heart, or impart peace of mind, or remove care, or banish disease. Fame, genius, talent—all are powerless to gladden the sorrowful heart or to restore the wasted life. The life of God in the soul is man's only hope.

The love which Christ diffuses through the whole being is a vitalizing power. Every vital part—the brain, the heart, the nerves—it touches with healing. By it the highest energies of the being are roused to activity. It frees the soul from the guilt and sorrow, the anxiety and care, that crush the life forces. With it come serenity and composure. It implants in the soul, joy that nothing earthly can destroy,—joy in the Holy Spirit,—health-giving, life-giving joy.—*The Ministry of Healing*, 115.

When the Spirit of God takes possession of the heart, it transforms the life. Sinful thoughts are put away, evil deeds are renounced; love, humility, and peace take the place of anger, envy, and strife. Joy takes the place of sadness, and the countenance reflects the light of heaven. No one sees the hand that lifts the burden, or beholds the light descend from the courts above. The blessing comes when by faith the soul surrenders itself to God.—*The Desire of Ages*, 173.

And do not be conformed to this world,
but be transformed by the renewing of your mind,
that you may prove what is that good and acceptable and perfect will of God.
—Romans 12:2, NKJV

When There Is True Repentance

"The Spirit of the LORD God is upon Me,
Because the LORD has anointed Me
To preach good tidings to the poor;
He has sent Me to heal the brokenhearted, . . .
To comfort all who mourn, . . .
To give them beauty for ashes,
The oil of joy for mourning,
The garment of praise for the spirit of heaviness."
—Isaiah 61:1-3, NKJV

WHILE WE SORROW on account of sin, we are to rejoice in the precious privilege of being children of God.

We often sorrow because our evil deeds bring unpleasant consequences to ourselves; but this is not repentance. Real sorrow for sin is the result of the working of the Holy Spirit. The Spirit reveals the ingratitude of the heart that has slighted and grieved the Saviour, and brings us in contrition to the foot of the cross. By every sin Jesus is wounded afresh; and as we look upon Him whom we have pierced, we mourn for the sins that have brought anguish upon Him. Such mourning will lead to the renunciation of sin. . . .

. . . The tears of the penitent are only the raindrops that precede the sunshine of holiness. This sorrow heralds a joy which will be a living fountain in the soul. "Only acknowledge thine iniquity, that thou hast transgressed against the Lord thy God;" "and I will not cause Mine anger to fall upon you: for I am merciful, saith the Lord." Jeremiah 3:13, 12. "Unto them that mourn in Zion," He has appointed to give "beauty for ashes, the oil of joy for mourning, the garment of praise for the spirit of heaviness." Isaiah 61:3.—*The Desire of Ages*, 300.

"I will be his father, and he will be my son.
If he sins, I will correct and discipline him with the rod, like any father would do.
But my favor will not be taken from him as I took it from Saul,
whom I removed from your sight."
—2 Samuel 7:14, 15, NLT

Be Cheerful and Rejoice

Blessed are you who hunger now,
For you shall be filled.
Blessed are you who weep now,
For you shall laugh.

—Luke 6:21, NKJV

"WHEN MEN shall revile you, and persecute you," said Jesus, "rejoice, and be exceeding glad." And He pointed His hearers to the prophets who had spoken in the name of the Lord, as "an example of suffering affliction, and of patience." James 5:10. Abel, the very first Christian of Adam's children, died a martyr. Enoch walked with God, and the world knew him not. Noah was mocked as a fanatic and an alarmist. "Others had trial of cruel mockings and scourgings, yea, moreover of bonds and imprisonment." "Others were tortured, not accepting deliverance; that they might obtain a better resurrection." Hebrews 11:36, 35.—*Thoughts From the Mount of Blessing*, 33.

Remember that this earth is not heaven. Christ has declared: "In the world ye shall have tribulation: but be of good cheer; I have overcome the world." . . .

Jesus has not left you to be amazed at the trials and difficulties you meet. He has told you all about them, and He has told you also not to be cast down and oppressed when trials come. Look to Jesus, your Redeemer, and be cheerful and rejoice.—*Testimonies for the Church*, vol. 8, 127, 128.

"Fear not, for I am with you;
Be not dismayed, for I am your God.
I will strengthen you,
Yes, I will help you,
I will uphold you with My righteous right hand."

—Isaiah 41:10, NKJV

Danger in Prosperity

The blessing of the L*ORD brings wealth,*
without painful toil to it.

—Proverbs 10:22, NIV

IN THE MIDST of prosperity lurks danger. Throughout the ages, riches and honor have ever been attended with peril to humility and spirituality. It is not the empty cup that we have difficulty in carrying; it is the cup full to the brim that must be carefully balanced. Affliction and adversity may cause sorrow, but it is prosperity that is most dangerous to spiritual life. Unless the human subject is in constant submission to the will of God, unless he is sanctified by the truth, prosperity will surely arouse the natural inclination to presumption. . . .

Whenever pride and ambition are indulged, the life is marred, for pride, feeling no need, closes the heart against the infinite blessings of Heaven. He who makes self-glorification his aim will find himself destitute of the grace of God, through whose efficiency the truest riches and the most satisfying joys are won. But he who gives all and does all for Christ will know the fulfillment of the promise, "The blessing of the Lord, it maketh rich, and He addeth no sorrow with it." Proverbs 10:22. With the gentle touch of grace the Saviour banishes from the soul unrest and unholy ambition, changing enmity to love and unbelief to confidence. When He speaks to the soul, saying, "Follow Me," the spell of the world's enchantment is broken. At the sound of His voice the spirit of greed and ambition flees from the heart, and men arise, emancipated, to follow Him.—*Prophets and Kings*, 59, 60.

"The L*ORD sends poverty and wealth;*
he humbles and he exalts."

—1 Samuel 2:7, NIV

Partakers of the Divine Nature

No discipline seems pleasant at the time, but painful.
Later on, however, it produces a harvest of righteousness
and peace for those who have been trained by it.
—Hebrews 12:11, NIV

THE TRIALS TO WHICH Christians are subjected in sorrow, adversity, and reproach are the means appointed of God to separate the chaff from the wheat. Our pride, selfishness, evil passions, and love of worldly pleasure must all be overcome; therefore God sends us afflictions to test and prove us, and show us that these evils exist in our characters. We must overcome through His strength and grace, that we may be partakers of the divine nature, having escaped the corruption that is in the world through lust. "For our light affliction," says Paul, "which is but for a moment, worketh for us a far more exceeding and eternal weight of glory; while we look not at the things which are seen, but at the things which are not seen: for the things which are seen are temporal; but the things which are not seen are eternal." Afflictions, crosses, temptations, adversity, and our varied trials are God's workmen to refine us, sanctify us, and fit us for the heavenly garner.—*Testimonies for the Church*, vol. 3, 115.

The precious Saviour will send help just when we need it. The way to heaven is consecrated by His footprints. Every thorn that wounds our feet has wounded His. Every cross that we are called to bear He has borne before us. The Lord permits conflicts, to prepare the soul for peace.—*The Great Controversy*, 633.

Through these he has given us his very great and precious promises,
so that through them you may participate in the divine nature,
having escaped the corruption in the world caused by evil desires.
—2 Peter 1:4, NIV

A Share in Christ's Glory

Beloved, do not be surprised
at the fiery ordeal that is taking place among you
to test you, as though something strange were happening to you.
But rejoice insofar as you are sharing Christ's sufferings,
so that you may also be glad and shout for joy when his glory is revealed.
—1 Peter 4:12, 13, NRSV

Follow your Saviour through evil as well as good report; count it all joy, and a sacred honor, to bear the cross of Christ. Jesus loves you. He died for you.—*Testimonies for the Church*, vol. 2, 237.

The Majesty of heaven, the King of glory, left His riches, His splendor, His honor and glory, and, in order to save sinful man, condescended to a life of humility, poverty, and shame; "who for the joy that was set before Him endured the cross, despising the shame." Oh, why are we so sensitive to trial and reproach, to shame and suffering, when our Lord has given us such an example? Who would wish to enter into the joy of their Lord while they were unwilling to partake of His sufferings? What! the servant unwilling to bear the humility and shame and reproach which the Master bore unselfishly for him! the servant shrinking from a life of humility and sacrifice which is for his own eternal happiness, by which he may finally obtain an exceedingly great, an eternal reward! The language of my heart is: Let me be a partaker with Christ of His sufferings, that I may finally share with Him the glory.—*Testimonies for the Church*, vol. 2, 490.

He is the reflection of God's glory. . . .
When he had made purification for sins,
he sat down at the right hand of the Majesty on high.
—Hebrews 1:3, NRSV

Fiery Trials

Being protected by the power of God through faith
for a salvation ready to be revealed in the last time.
In this you rejoice, even if now for a little while
you have had to suffer various trials.

—1 Peter 1:5, 6, NRSV

IN THIS LIFE we must meet fiery trials and make costly sacrifices, but the peace of Christ is the reward. There has been so little self-denial, so little suffering for Christ's sake, that the cross is almost entirely forgotten. We must be partakers with Christ of His sufferings if we would sit down in triumph with Him on His throne. So long as we choose the easy path of self-indulgence and are frightened at self-denial, our faith will never become firm, and we cannot know the peace of Jesus nor the joy that comes through conscious victory. The most exalted of the redeemed host that stand before the throne of God and the Lamb, clad in white, know the conflict of overcoming, for they have come up through great tribulation.—*Testimonies for the Church*, vol. 5, 215.

In this you rejoice, even if now for a little while
you have had to suffer various trials, so that the genuineness of your faith—
being more precious than gold that, though perishable, is tested by fire—
may be found to result in praise and glory and honor
when Jesus Christ is revealed. Although you have not seen him,
you love him; and even though you do not see him now,
you believe in him and rejoice with an indescribable and glorious joy,
for you are receiving the outcome of your faith, the salvation of your souls.

—1 Peter 1:6–9, NRSV

I want to know Christ and experience the mighty power
that raised him from the dead. I want to suffer with him, sharing in his death.

—Philippians 3:10, NLT

Instead, be very glad—for these trials make you partners with Christ
in his suffering, so that you will have the wonderful joy
of seeing his glory when it is revealed to all the world.

—1 Peter 4:13, NLT

Our Heavenly Reward

"Blessed are you when they revile you and persecute you,
and say all kinds of evil against you falsely for My sake.
Rejoice and be exceedingly glad, for great is your reward in heaven,
for so they persecuted the prophets who were before you."
—Matthew 5:11, 12, NKJV

GREAT IS THE REWARD in heaven of those who are witnesses for Christ through persecution and reproach. While the people are looking for earthly good, Jesus points them to a heavenly reward. But He does not place it all in the future life; it begins here. The Lord appeared of old time to Abraham and said, "I am thy shield, and thy exceeding great reward." Genesis 15:1. This is the reward of all who follow Christ. Jehovah Immanuel—He "in whom are hid all the treasures of wisdom and knowledge," in whom dwells "all the fullness of the Godhead bodily" (Colossians 2:3, 9)—to be brought into sympathy with Him, to know Him, to possess Him, as the heart opens more and more to receive His attributes; to know His love and power, to possess the unsearchable riches of Christ, to comprehend more and more "what is the breadth, and length, and depth, and height; and to know the love of Christ, which passeth knowledge, that ye might be filled with all the fullness of God" (Ephesians 3:18, 19)—"this is the heritage of the servants of the Lord, and their righteousness is of Me, saith the Lord." Isaiah 54:17.

It was this joy that filled the hearts of Paul and Silas when they prayed and sang praises to God at midnight in the Philippian dungeon. Christ was beside them there, and the light of His presence irradiated the gloom with the glory of the courts above. From Rome, Paul wrote, unmindful of his fetters as he saw the spread of the gospel, "I therein do rejoice, yea, and will rejoice." Philippians 1:18. And the very words of Christ upon the mount are re-echoed in Paul's message to the Philippian church, in the midst of their persecutions, "Rejoice in the Lord alway: and again I say, Rejoice." Philippians 4:4.—*Thoughts From the Mount of Blessing*, 34, 35.

MAY 1

Cheerfulness and Contentment

He Has Forgiven My Sins

Behold, they brought to Him a paralytic lying on a bed.
When Jesus saw their faith, He said to the paralytic,
"Son, be of good cheer; your sins are forgiven you."
—Matthew 9:2, NKJV

THIS PARALYTIC had lost all hope of recovery. His disease was the result of a sinful life, and his sufferings were embittered by remorse. . . .

His great desire was relief from the burden of sin. He longed to see Jesus and receive the assurance of forgiveness and peace with heaven. Then he would be content to live or to die, according to God's will. . . .

. . . He besought his friends to carry him on his bed to Jesus, and this they gladly undertook to do. But so dense was the crowd that had assembled in and about the house where the Saviour was, that it was impossible for the sick man and his friends to reach Him. . . .

Again and again the bearers of the paralytic tried to push their way through the crowd, but in vain. The sick man looked about him in unutterable anguish. How could he relinquish hope when the longed-for help was so near? At his suggestion his friends bore him to the top of the house and, breaking up the roof, let him down at the feet of Jesus.

The discourse was interrupted. The Saviour looked upon the mournful countenance and saw the pleading eyes fixed upon Him. Well He knew the longing of that burdened soul. It was Christ who had brought conviction to his conscience when he was yet at home. . . . It was Christ who had drawn the sufferer to Himself. Now, in words that fell like music on the listener's ear, the Saviour said, "Son, be of good cheer; thy sins be forgiven thee." Matthew 9:2.

The burden of guilt rolls from the sick man's soul. He cannot doubt. . . . Hope takes the place of despair, and joy of oppressive gloom. The man's physical pain is gone, and his whole being is transformed. Making no further request, he lay in peaceful silence, too happy for words.—*The Ministry of Healing*, 73–76.

MAY 2
Cheerfulness and Contentment

We Are His Witnesses

The following night the Lord stood by him, and said,
"Be of good cheer, Paul: for as you have testified for Me in Jerusalem,
so you must also bear witness at Rome."

—Acts 23:11, NKJV

THE PEOPLE OF GOD are His representatives upon the earth, and He intends that they shall be lights in the moral darkness of this world. Scattered all over the country, in the towns, cities, and villages, they are God's witnesses, the channels through which He will communicate to an unbelieving world the knowledge of His will and the wonders of His grace. It is His plan that all who are partakers of the great salvation shall be missionaries for Him. The piety of the Christian constitutes the standard by which worldlings judge the gospel. Trials patiently borne, blessings gratefully received, meekness, kindness, mercy, and love, habitually exhibited, are the lights that shine forth in the character before the world, revealing the contrast with the darkness that comes of the selfishness of the natural heart.—*Patriarchs and Prophets*, 134.

It is our duty to be very jealous for the glory of God and to bring no evil report, even by the sadness of the countenance or by ill-advised words, as if the requirements of God were a restriction upon our liberty. Even in this world of sorrow, disappointment, and sin the Lord desires us to be cheerful, and strong in His strength. The whole person is privileged to bear a decided testimony in every line. In features, in temper, in words, in character, we are to witness that the service of God is good.—*Testimonies for the Church*, vol. 6, 365.

"Do not tremble; do not be afraid.
Did I not proclaim my purposes for you long ago?
You are my witnesses—is there any other God?
No! There is no other Rock—not one!"

—Isaiah 44:8, NLT

God Always Keeps His Promises

*"Therefore take heart, men,
for I believe God that it will be just as it was told me."*
—Acts 27:25, NKJV

Some are always fearing, and borrowing trouble. . . . Their minds are continually dwelling upon something disagreeable which they fear may come; or some difficulty may really exist which, though small, blinds their eyes to the many things that demand gratitude. The difficulties they encounter, instead of driving them to God, the only source of their help, separate them from Him because they awaken unrest and repining.

Do we well to be thus unbelieving? Why should we be ungrateful and distrustful? Jesus is our friend; all heaven is interested in our welfare. We should not allow the perplexities and worries of everyday life to fret the mind and cloud the brow. If we do we shall always have something to vex and annoy. We should not indulge a solicitude that only frets and wears us, but does not help us to bear trials.

You may be perplexed in business; your prospects may grow darker and darker, and you may be threatened with loss; but do not become discouraged; cast your care upon God, and remain calm and cheerful. Pray for wisdom to manage your affairs with discretion, and thus prevent loss and disaster. Do all you can on your part to bring about favorable results. Jesus has promised His aid, but not apart from our effort. When, relying upon our Helper, you have done all you can, accept the result cheerfully.—*Steps to Christ*, 121, 122.

True Happiness Comes Only From God

You have put gladness in my heart,
More than in the season that their grain and wine increased.
—Psalm 4:7, NKJV

THE CHRISTIAN SHOULD not set too high a value, or depend too much, upon a happy flight of feeling. These feelings are not always true guides. It should be the study of every Christian to serve God from principle, and not be ruled by feeling. By so doing, faith will be brought into exercise, and will increase.—*Testimonies for the Church*, vol. 1, 161.

Feeling is not faith; the two are distinct. Faith is ours to exercise, but joyful feeling and the blessing are God's to give.—*Early Writings*, 72.

If the Christian lives a humble, self-sacrificing life, peace and joy in the Lord will be the result.—*Testimonies for the Church*, vol. 1, 161.

Happiness drawn from earthly sources is as changeable as varying circumstances can make it; but the peace of Christ is a constant and abiding peace. It does not depend upon any circumstances in life, on the amount of worldly goods or the number of earthly friends. Christ is the fountain of living water, and happiness drawn from Him can never fail.—*Thoughts From the Mount of Blessing*, 16.

Rejoice always, pray without ceasing, in everything give thanks;
for this is the will of God in Christ Jesus for you.
—1 Thessalonians 5:16–18, NKJV

Jesus answered and said to her, "Whoever drinks of this water will thirst again,
but whoever drinks of the water that I shall give him will never thirst.
But the water that I shall give him will become in him a fountain of water
springing up into everlasting life."
—John 4:13, 14, NKJV

Communion With the Lord Brings Gladness

I know the L*ORD is always with me.*
I will not be shaken, for he is right beside me.
No wonder my heart is glad, and I rejoice.
My body rests in safety.

—Psalm 16:8, 9, NLT

IF WE KEEP THE LORD ever before us, allowing our hearts to go out in thanksgiving and praise to Him, we shall have a continual freshness in our religious life. Our prayers will take the form of a conversation with God as we would talk with a friend. He will speak His mysteries to us personally. Often there will come to us a sweet joyful sense of the presence of Jesus. Often our hearts will burn within us as He draws nigh to commune with us as He did with Enoch. When this is in truth the experience of the Christian, there is seen in his life a simplicity, a humility, meekness, and lowliness of heart, that show to all with whom he associates that he has been with Jesus and learned of Him.

In those who possess it, the religion of Christ will reveal itself as a vitalizing, pervading principle, a living, working, spiritual energy. There will be manifest the freshness and power and joyousness of perpetual youth. The heart that receives the word of God is not as a pool that evaporates, not like a broken cistern that loses its treasure. It is like the mountain stream fed by unfailing springs, whose cool, sparkling waters leap from rock to rock, refreshing the weary, the thirsty, the heavy laden.—*Christ's Object Lessons*, 129, 130.

With weeping they shall come,
and with consolations I will lead them back,
I will let them walk by brooks of water,
in a straight path in which they shall not stumble.

—Jeremiah 31:9, NRSV

Be Glad for Salvation

May all who seek you
rejoice and be glad in you;
may those who long for your saving help always say,
"The LORD *is great!"*

—Psalm 40:16, NIV

WITHOUT A CONNECTION with God no one can possibly be happy. Fallen man is to learn that our Heavenly Father cannot be satisfied until His love embraces the repentant sinner, transformed through the merits of the spotless Lamb of God. . . .

Jesus Christ laid hold on humanity, that with His human arm He might encircle the race, while with His divine arm He grasped the throne of the Infinite. He planted His cross midway between earth and heaven, and said, "I, if I be lifted up from the earth, will draw all men unto Me." The cross was to be the center of attraction.

It was to speak to all men, and draw them across the gulf that sin had made, to unite finite man with the infinite God. . . . Those whose sins are forgiven, who love Jesus, will be united with Him. They will bear the yoke of Christ. This yoke is not to hamper them, not to make their religious life one of unsatisfying toil. No; the yoke of Christ is to be the very means by which the Christian life is to become one of pleasure and joy. The Christian is to be joyful in contemplation of that which the Lord has done in giving His only-begotten Son to die for the world, "that whosoever believeth in Him should not perish, but have everlasting life."—*Messages to Young People*, 137, 138.

"Take my yoke upon you. Let me teach you,
because I am humble and gentle at heart,
and you will find rest for your souls."

—Matthew 11:29, NLT

Life, Righteousness, and Honor

Light shines on the godly,
and joy on those whose hearts are right.
May all who are godly rejoice in the LORD
and praise his holy name!

—Psalm 97:11, 12, NLT

RIGHTEOUSNESS HAS ITS ROOT in godliness. No human being is righteous any longer than he has faith in God and maintains a vital connection with Him. As a flower of the field has its root in the soil; as it must receive air, dew, showers, and sunshine, so must we receive from God that which ministers to the life of the soul.—*Testimonies for the Church*, vol. 7, 194.

Not by painful struggles or wearisome toil, not by gift or sacrifice, is righteousness obtained; but it is freely given to every soul who hungers and thirsts to receive it. —*Thoughts From the Mount of Blessing*, 18.

Righteousness is love, and love is the light and the life of God. The righteousness of God is embodied in Christ. We receive righteousness by receiving Him.—*Thoughts From the Mount of Blessing*, 18.

Many . . . build barriers between themselves and Jesus, so that His love cannot flow into their hearts, and then they complain that they do not see the Sun of Righteousness. Let them forget self and live for Jesus, and the light of heaven will bring gladness to their souls.—*Counsels to Parents, Teachers, and Students*, 232.

He who follows righteousness and mercy
finds life, righteousness, and honor.

—Proverbs 21:21, NKJV

So it is God who decides to show mercy.
We can neither choose it nor work for it.

—Romans 9:16, NLT

"Blessed are those who hunger and thirst for righteousness,
For they shall be filled."

—Matthew 5:6, NKJV

Reasons for Praise and Gladness

He brought his people out with joy,
his chosen ones with singing.
He gave them the lands of the nations,
and they took possession of the wealth of the peoples,
that they might keep his statutes
and observe his laws.
Praise the LORD*!*

—Psalm 105:43–45, NRSV

GOD SURROUNDED ISRAEL with every facility, gave them every privilege, that would make them an honor to His name and a blessing to surrounding nations. If they would walk in the ways of obedience, He promised to make them "high above all nations which He hath made, in praise, and in name, and in honor." "All people of the earth," He said, "shall hear that thou art called by the name of the Lord; and they shall be afraid of thee." The nations which shall hear all these statutes shall say, "Surely this great nation is a wise and understanding people." Deuteronomy 26:19; 28:10; Deuteronomy 4:6).—*Education*, 40.

We are exhorted to call to "remembrance the former days. . . ." Hebrews 10:32. For His people in this generation the Lord has wrought as a wonder-working God. —*Testimonies for the Church*, vol. 6, 364.

He has done for His chosen people that which should inspire every heart with thanksgiving, and it grieves Him that so little praise is offered. He desires to have a stronger expression from His people, showing that they know they have reason for joy and gladness.—*Testimonies for the Church*, vol. 6, 364.

O LORD, *you are my God;*
I will exalt you, I will praise your name;
for you have done wonderful things,
plans formed of old, faithful and sure.

—Isaiah 25:1, NRSV

He Longs to Make His Children Glad

"In the past he permitted all the nations to go their own ways,
but he never left them without evidence of himself and his goodness.
For instance, he sends you rain and good crops
and gives you food and joyful hearts."

—Acts 14:16, 17, NLT

NATURE TESTIFIES that One infinite in power, great in goodness, mercy, and love, created the earth, and filled it with life and gladness. . . .

. . . In earth and sea and sky, with their marvelous tint and color, varying in gorgeous contrast or blended in harmony, we behold His glory. The everlasting hills tell us of His power. The trees that wave their green banners in the sunlight, and the flowers in their delicate beauty, point to their Creator. The living green that carpets the brown earth tells of God's care for the humblest of His creatures. . . .

All things tell of His tender, fatherly care and of His desire to make His children happy.—*The Ministry of Healing*, 411, 412.

It is through His power that summer and winter, seedtime and harvest, day and night follow each other in their regular succession. It is by His word that vegetation flourishes, that the leaves appear and the flowers bloom. Every good thing we have, each ray of sunshine and shower of rain, every morsel of food, every moment of life, is a gift of love.—*Thoughts From the Mount of Blessing*, 74.

Whatever is good and perfect is a gift coming down to us from God our Father,
who created all the lights in the heavens. He never changes or casts a shifting shadow.

—James 1:17, NLT

"You are worthy, O Lord our God,
to receive glory and honor and power.
For you created all things,
and they exist because you created what you pleased."

—Revelation 4:11, NLT

Good Words Gladden the Heart

Anxiety in the heart of man causes depression,
But a good word makes it glad.

—Proverbs 12:25, NKJV

LET US NOT GATHER TOGETHER all the unpleasant pictures—the iniquities and corruptions and disappointments, the evidences of Satan's power—to hang in the halls of our memory, to talk over and mourn over until our souls are filled with discouragement. . . .

There are, thank God, brighter and more cheering pictures which the Lord has presented to us. Let us group together the blessed assurances of His love as precious treasures, that we may look upon them continually. The Son of God leaving His Father's throne, clothing His divinity with humanity, that He might rescue man from the power of Satan; His triumph in our behalf, opening heaven to man, revealing to human vision the presence chamber where Deity unveils His glory; the fallen race uplifted from the pit of ruin into which sin had plunged them, and brought again into connection with the infinite God, and, having endured the divine test through faith in our Redeemer, clothed in the righteousness of Christ and exalted to His throne—these are the pictures with which God bids us gladden the chambers of the soul.—*Testimonies for the Church*, vol. 5, 744, 745.

"The LORD your God in your midst,
The Mighty One, will save;
He will rejoice over you with gladness,
He will quiet you with His love,
He will rejoice over you with singing."

—Zephaniah 3:17, NKJV

Finally, brethren, whatever things are true,
whatever things are noble, whatever things are just,
whatever things are pure, whatever things are lovely,
whatever things are of good report, if there is any virtue
and if there is anything praiseworthy—meditate on these things.

—Philippians 4:8, NKJV

Happiness and Contentment Found in Godliness

Well, religion does make us very rich,
if we are satisfied with what we have.

—1 Timothy 6:6, GNT

FAITH IN GOD'S LOVE and overruling providence lightens the burdens of anxiety and care. It fills the heart with joy and contentment in the highest or the lowliest lot. Religion tends directly to promote health, to lengthen life, and to heighten our enjoyment of all its blessings. It opens to the soul a never-failing fountain of happiness. Would that all who have not chosen Christ might realize that He has something vastly better to offer them that they are seeking for themselves. Man is doing the greatest injury and injustice to his own soul when he thinks and acts contrary to the will of God.—*Patriarchs and Prophets*, 600.

In order to be happy, we must strive to attain to that character which Christ exhibited. One marked peculiarity of Christ was His self-denial and benevolence. He came not to seek His own. He went about doing good, and this was His meat and drink. We may, by following the example of the Saviour, be in holy communion with Him, and by daily seeking to imitate His character and follow His example, we shall be a blessing to the world and shall secure for ourselves contentment here and an eternal reward hereafter.—*Testimonies for the Church*, vol. 4, 227.

Looking unto Jesus, the author and finisher of our faith,
who for the joy that was set before Him endured the cross,
despising the shame, and has sat down
at the right hand of the throne of God.

—Hebrews 12:2, NKJV

Riches Are Not Necessary

Now godliness with contentment is great gain.
For we brought nothing into this world, and it is certain
we can carry nothing out. And having food and clothing,
with these we shall be content.

—1 Timothy 6:6–8, NKJV

MANY ARE DETERMINED to be rich; this is their study, and in their zeal eternal considerations are overlooked. They are blinded by Satan and make themselves believe that it is for good purposes they desire this gain; they strain their consciences, deceive themselves, and are constantly coveting riches. Such have erred from the faith and pierced themselves through with many sorrows. They have sacrificed their noble, elevated principles, given up their faith for riches, and, if not disappointed in their object, they are disappointed in the happiness which they supposed riches would bring. . . .

The apostle Paul shows the only true use for riches, and bids Timothy charge the rich to do good, that they be rich in good works, ready to distribute, willing to communicate; for in so doing they are laying up in store for themselves a good foundation against the time to come. . . . Godliness with contentment is great gain. Here is the true secret of happiness, and real prosperity of soul and body.—*Testimonies for the Church*, vol. 1, 541, 542.

Command those who are rich in this present age not to be haughty,
nor to trust in uncertain riches but in the living God,
who gives us richly all things to enjoy.

—1 Timothy 6:17, NKJV

The Secret to True Happiness

How I praise the Lord that you are concerned about me again. . . .
Not that I was ever in need, for I have learned how to be content with whatever I have. I know how to live on almost nothing or with everything. I have learned the secret of living in every situation, whether it is with a full stomach or empty, with plenty or little.
—Philippians 4:10–12, NLT

Oh, that we could be satisfied with less heart longings, less striving for things difficult to obtain . . . , while that which God values above jewels, the meek and quiet spirit, is not cherished. . . . It is better to endure cheerfully every inconvenience than to part with peace and contentment.—*Testimonies for the Church*, vol. 4, 622.

There are restless ones who, were they to go to a new place to live, would still be dissatisfied, because the spirit of disaffection is in their hearts, and a change of place does not bring a change of heart. Their characters have not been refined and ennobled by the Spirit of Christ. They need to learn the lesson of contentment.—*Fundamentals of Christian Education*, 495.

Those who are drinking at the fountain of life will not, like the worldling, manifest a longing desire for change and pleasure. In their deportment and character will be seen the rest and peace and happiness that they have found in Jesus by daily laying their perplexities and burdens at His feet. They will show that there is contentment and even joy in the path of obedience and duty.—*Testimonies for the Church*, vol. 4, 432.

Blessed is the man who endures temptation; for when he has been approved,
he will receive the crown of life which the Lord has promised to those who love Him.
—James 1:12, NKJV

The Love for Jesus and of Riches Are Incompatible

"What should we do?" asked some soldiers.
John replied, "Don't extort money or make false accusations.
And be content with your pay."

—Luke 3:14, NLT

THE SELFISH, MONEY-LOVING MAN lives only to secure for himself the riches, honors, and pleasures of this world. He loses the eternal world from his reckoning.—*Christ's Object Lessons*, 101.

If men love their riches better than they love their fellow men, better than they love God or the truths of His word, if their hearts are on their riches, they cannot have eternal life. . . . Like the young man in the Bible, many go away sorrowful because they cannot have their riches and a treasure in heaven, too. They cannot have both; and they venture to risk their chance of eternal life for a worldly possession. . . .

. . . The love of Jesus and of riches cannot dwell in the same heart. The love of God so far surpasses the love of riches that the possessor breaks away from his riches and transfers his affections to God. Through love he is then led to minister to the wants of God's cause. It is his highest pleasure to make a right disposition of his Lord's goods.—*Testimonies for the Church*, vol. 1, 172.

Don't wear yourself out trying to get rich.
Be wise enough to know when to quit.
In the blink of an eye wealth disappears,
for it will sprout wings
and fly away like an eagle.

—Proverbs 23:4, 5, NLT

The Hope That Brings True Joy

Let your conduct be without covetousness;
be content with such things as you have.
For He himself has said, "I will never leave you
nor forsake you."

—Hebrews 13:5, NKJV

CULTIVATE A CONTENTED, cheerful spirit.—*Testimonies for the Church*, vol. 2, 434.

The world is full of dissatisfied spirits who overlook the happiness and blessings within their reach, and are continually seeking for happiness and satisfaction that they do not realize. They are constantly on the stretch for some expected, far-off good greater than they possess, and are ever in a state of disappointment.—*Testimonies for the Church*, 640.

They have not God, they have not the hope which reaches to that within the veil, which is as an anchor to the soul both sure and steadfast. All who possess this hope will purify themselves even as He is pure. Such are free from restless longings, repinings, and discontent; they are not continually looking for evil and brooding over borrowed trouble. But we see many who are having a time of trouble beforehand; anxiety is stamped upon every feature; they seem to find no consolation, but have a continual fearful looking for of some dreadful evil.

Such dishonor God, and bring the religion of Christ into disrepute. They have not true love for God. . . . Their affections have become morbid. But vain amusements will never correct the minds of such. They need the transforming influence of the Spirit of God in order to be happy.—*Testimonies for the Church*, vol. 1, 566.

Though the fig tree may not blossom,
Nor fruit be on the vines;
Though the labor of the olive may fail,
And the fields yield no food;
Though the flock may be cut off from the fold,
And there be no herd in the stalls—
Yet I will rejoice in the LORD,
I will joy in the God of my salvation.

—Habakkuk 3:17, 18, NKJV

Selfishness and Greed Breed Discontent

Those who belong to Christ Jesus
have nailed the passions and desires of their sinful nature
to his cross and crucified them there.

—Galatians 5:24, NLT

THE HEART IN HARMONY with God is lifted above the annoyances and trials of this life. But a heart where the peace of Christ is not, is unhappy, full of discontent. . . . A life of selfishness is a life of evil. . . . Passions kept warm and fierce by Satan's promptings are a bitter fountain, ever sending forth bitter streams to poison the life of others. —*Testimonies for the Church*, vol. 5, 488.

Those who yield to Satan's power gain no happiness thereby. They are never contented or at rest. They are dissatisfied, querulous and irritable, unthankful and rebellious.—*Testimonies for the Church*, vol. 4, 207.

The principle of worldlings is to get all they can of the perishable things of this life. Selfish love of gain is the ruling principle in their lives. But the purest joy is not found in riches nor where covetousness is always craving, but where contentment reigns and where self-sacrificing love is the ruling principle. There are thousands who are passing their lives in indulgence and whose hearts are filled with repining. They are victims of selfishness and discontent in the vain effort to satisfy their minds with indulgence. But unhappiness is stamped upon their very countenances, and behind them is a desert, because their course is not fruitful in good works.—*Testimonies for th eChurch*, vol. 3, 382.

A stone is heavy and sand is weighty,
but the resentment caused by a fool is even heavier.
Anger is cruel, and wrath is like a flood,
but jealousy is even more dangerous.

—Proverbs 27:3, 4, NLT

Content With What the Lord Gives

" 'And do you seek great things for yourself?
Do not seek them; for behold, I will bring adversity on all flesh,' "
says the LORD. *" 'But I will give your life to you as a prize*
in all places, wherever you go.' "

—Jeremiah 45:5, NKJV

THE WIDE, DEEP RIVER, that offers a highway for the traffic and travel of nations, is valued as a world-wide benefit; but what of the little rills that help to form this noble stream? Were it not for them, the river would disappear. Upon them its very existence depends. So men called to lead in some great work are honored as if its success were due to them alone; but that success required the faithful co-operation of humbler workers almost without number—workers of whom the world knows nothing. Tasks uncommended, labor without recognition, is the lot of most of the world's toilers. And in such a lot many are filled with discontent. They feel that life is wasted. But the little rill that makes its noiseless way through grove and meadow, bearing health and fertility and beauty, is as useful in its way as the broad river. And in contributing to the river's life, it helps achieve that which alone it could never have accomplished.

The lesson is one needed by many. Talent is too much idolized, and station too much coveted. There are too many who will do nothing unless they are recognized as leaders; too many who must receive praise, or they have no interest to labor. What we need to learn is faithfulness in making the utmost use of the powers and opportunities we have, and contentment in the lot to which Heaven assigns us.—*Education*, 116, 117.

A Merry Heart Has a Feast From God Each Day

All the days of the afflicted are evil,
but he who is of a merry heart has a continual feast.
—Proverbs 15:15, NKJV

WE MAY HAVE a feast of good things every day, for God can open the whole treasure of heaven to us.—*Testimonies to Ministers and Gospel Workers*, 119.

No human agent can supply that which will satisfy the hunger and thirst of the soul. But Jesus says, . . . "I am the bread of life: he that cometh to Me shall never hunger; and he that believeth on Me shall never thirst." John 6:35.—*Thoughts From the Mount of Blessing*, 18.

What food is to the body, Christ must be to the soul. Food cannot benefit us unless we eat it, unless it becomes a part of our being. So Christ is of no value to us if we do not know Him as a personal Saviour. A theoretical knowledge will do us no good. We must feed upon Him, receive Him into the heart, so that His life becomes our life. His love, His grace, must be assimilated.—*The Desire of Ages*, 389.

Let church members bear in mind that the fact that their names are registered on the church books will not save them. They must show themselves approved of God, workmen that need not be ashamed. Day by day they are to build their characters in accordance with Christ's directions. They are to abide in Him, constantly exercising faith in Him. Thus they will grow up to the full stature of men and women in Christ—wholesome, cheerful, grateful Christians, led by God into clearer and still clearer light.—*Testimonies for the Church*, vol. 9, 48.

The Lord Helps and Heals

A cheerful heart is a good medicine,
but a broken spirit saps a person's strength.
—Proverbs 17:22, NLT

THE RELATION THAT EXISTS between the mind and the body is very intimate. When one is affected, the other sympathizes. The condition of the mind affects the health to a far greater degree than many realize. Many of the diseases from which men suffer are the result of mental depression. Grief, anxiety, discontent, remorse, guilt, distrust, all tend to break down the life forces and to invite decay and death. . . .

Courage, hope, faith, sympathy, love, promote health and prolong life. A contented mind, a cheerful spirit, is health to the body and strength to the soul. "A merry [rejoicing] heart doeth good like a medicine." Proverbs 17:22.—*The Ministry of Healing*, 241.

Christ is the wellspring of life. That which many need is to have a clearer knowledge of Him; they need to be patiently and kindly, yet earnestly, taught how the whole being may be thrown open to the healing agencies of heaven. When the sunlight of God's love illuminates the darkened chambers of the soul, restless weariness and dissatisfaction will cease, and satisfying joys will give vigor to the mind and health and energy to the body.—*The Ministry of Healing*, 247.

Being cheerful keeps you healthy.
It is slow death to be gloomy all the time.
—Proverbs 17:22, GNT

Christian Grace

So I commend enjoyment, for there is nothing better for people under the sun than to eat, and drink, and enjoy themselves, for this will go with them in their toil through the days of life that God gives them under the sun.

—Ecclesiastes 8:15, NRSV

SOME PRESERVE a cold, chilling reserve, an iron dignity, that repels those who are brought within their influence. This spirit is contagious; it creates an atmosphere that is withering to good impulses and good resolves; it chokes the natural current of human sympathy, cordiality, and love; and under its influence people become constrained, and their social and generous attributes are destroyed for want of exercise.—*Testimonies for the Church*, vol. 4, 63.

You have a duty to perform, which is to make yourself cheerful, and to cultivate unselfishness in your feelings until it will be your greatest pleasure to make all around you happy. . . . You need to soften your hearts and be imbued with the Spirit of Christ, that you may, while living in an atmosphere of cheerfulness and benevolence, help those about you to be healthy and happy also. You have imagined that cheerfulness was not in accordance with the religion of Christ. This is a mistake. We may have true Christian dignity and at the same time be cheerful and pleasant in our deportment. Cheerfulness without levity is one of the Christian graces.—*Testimonies for the Church*, vol. 4, 61, 62.

Rejoice always, pray without ceasing, give thanks in all circumstances; for this is the will of God in Christ Jesus for you.

—1 Thessalonians 5:16–18, NRSV

Life's Greatest Joy

"There will be joy and songs of thanksgiving,
and I will multiply my people, not diminish them;
I will honor them, not despise them."

—Jeremiah 30:19, NLT

MANY PROFESSED CHRISTIANS do not correctly represent the Christian religion. They appear gloomy, as if under a cloud. They often speak of the great sacrifices they have made to become Christians. They appeal to those who have not accepted Christ, representing by their own example and conversation that they must give up everything which would make life pleasant and joyful. They throw a pall of darkness over the blessed Christian hope. The impression is given that God's requirements are a burden even to the willing soul, and that everything that would give pleasure, or that would delight the taste, must be sacrificed.—*Messages to Young People*, 363.

Obedience to our Saviour does not detract from our happiness and true pleasure in this life.—*Testimonies for the Church*, vol. 3,374.

Whatever Christ asks us to renounce, He offers in its stead something better. . . . When once the gaze is fixed upon Him, the life finds its center. . . . Duty becomes a delight and sacrifice a pleasure. To honor Christ, to become like Him, to work for Him, is the life's highest ambition and its greatest joy.—*Education*, 296.

Rejoice in hope, be patient in suffering, persevere in prayer.

—Romans 12:12, NRSV

MAY 22
Cheerfulness and Contentment

A Pleasure for God

"God will not cast away the blameless,
Nor will He uphold the evildoers.
He will yet fill your mouth with laughing,
And your lips with rejoicing."

—Job 8:20, 21, NKJV

YOU WILL EVER FIND with the true Christian a marked cheerfulness, a holy, happy confidence in God, a submission to His providences, that is refreshing to the soul. —*Testimonies for the Church*, vol. 3, 377.

Said Christ: "If any man will come after Me, let him deny himself, and take up his cross, and follow Me." We are not to make crosses for ourselves, by wearing sackcloth, by pinching our bodies, or by denying ourselves wholesome, nourishing food. We are not to shut ourselves in monasteries, away from the world, and do no good to our fellow beings, thinking this is the cross of Christ; neither are we required to expose health and life unnecessarily, nor to go mourning up the hill of Christian life, feeling it a sin to be cheerful, contented, happy, and joyful. These are all self-made crosses, but not the cross of Christ.—*Testimonies for the Church*, vol. 4, 626.

Christians who gather up gloom and sadness to their souls, and murmur and complain, are giving to others a false representation of God and the Christian life. They give the impression that God is not pleased to have His children happy, and in this they bear false witness against our heavenly Father.—*Steps to Christ*, 116.

Always be joyful. Never stop praying. Be thankful in all circumstances,
for this is God's will for you who belong to Christ Jesus.

—1 Thessalonians 5:16–18, NLT

He Rejoices When a Prodigal Returns

The father said to his servants,
"Bring out the best robe and put it on him,
and put a ring on his hand and sandals on his feet.
And bring the fatted calf here and kill it, and let us eat and be merry."
—Luke 15:22, 23, NKJV

LITTLE DID THE GAY, thoughtless youth, as he went out from his father's gate, dream of the ache and longing left in that father's heart. When he danced and feasted with his wild companions, little did he think of the shadow that had fallen on his home. And now as with weary and painful steps he pursues the homeward way, he knows not that one is watching for his return. But while he is yet "a great way off" the father discerns his form. Love is of quick sight. Not even the degradation of the years of sin can conceal the son from the father's eyes. He "had compassion, and ran, and fell on his neck" in a long, clinging, tender embrace.

The father will permit no contemptuous eye to mock at his son's misery and tatters. He takes from his own shoulders the broad, rich mantle, and wraps it around the son's wasted form. . . . The father holds him close to his side, and brings him home. No opportunity is given him to ask a servant's place. He is a son, who shall be honored with the best the house affords, and whom the waiting men and women shall respect and serve.

The father said to his servants, "Bring forth the best robe, and put it on him; and put a ring on his hand, and shoes on his feet; and bring hither the fatted calf, and kill it; and let us eat and be merry; for this my son was dead, and is alive again; he was lost, and is found. And they began to be merry."—*Christ's Object Lessons*, 203, 204.

"Likewise, I say to you,
there is joy in the presence of the angels of God
over one sinner who repents."
—Luke 15:10, NKJV

Enter Into the Joy of Others

"For this son of mine was dead and has now returned to life.
He was lost, but now he is found." So the party began.

—Luke 15:24, NLT

IN HIS RESTLESS YOUTH the prodigal looked upon his father as stern and severe. How different his conception of him now! So those who are deceived by Satan look upon God as hard and exacting. . . . His law they regard as a restriction upon men's happiness, a burdensome yoke from which they are glad to escape. But he whose eyes have been opened by the love of Christ will behold God as full of compassion. He does not appear as a tyrannical, relentless being, but as a father longing to embrace his repenting son. The sinner will exclaim with the Psalmist, "Like as a father pitieth his children, so the Lord pitieth them that fear Him." Psalm 103:13.—*Christ's Object Lessons*, 204.

The very first reaching out of the heart after God is known to Him. Never a prayer is offered, however faltering, never a tear is shed, however secret, never a sincere desire after God is cherished, however feeble, but the Spirit of God goes forth to meet it. Even before the prayer is uttered or the yearning of the heart made known, grace from Christ goes forth to meet the grace that is working upon the human soul.—*Christ's Object Lessons*, 206.

Arise and go to your Father. He will meet you a great way off.—*Christ's Object Lessons*, 206.

He will bring you into His banqueting house, and His banner over you shall be love. (Song of Solomon 2:4).—*Christ's Object Lessons*, 206.

And heaven and earth shall unite in the Father's song of rejoicing: "For this My son was dead, and is alive again; he was lost, and is found."—*Christ's Object Lessons*, 207.

"I will answer them before they even call to me.
While they are still talking about their needs,
I will go ahead and answer their prayers!"

—Isaiah 65:24, NLT

Cheerfulness Reflects the Beauty of the Soul

A glad heart makes a happy face;
a broken heart crushes the spirit.

—Proverbs 15:13, NLT

ALL MAY POSSESS a cheerful countenance, a gentle voice, a courteous manner, and these are elements of power.—*Education*, 240.

The human countenance itself is a mirror of the soul, read by others, and having a telling influence upon them for good or evil.—*Testimonies for the Church*, vol. 3, 522.

The faces of those who are benevolent and sympathetic will shine with the luster of true goodness, while those who do not cherish kindly thoughts and unselfish motives express in their faces the sentiments cherished in their hearts.—*Testimonies for the Church*, vol. 4, 63.

Christ abiding in the heart shines out in the faces of those who love Him and keep His commandments. Truth is written there. The sweet peace of heaven is revealed. There is expressed a habitual gentleness, a more than human love.—*Christ's Object Lessons*, 102.

Love imparts to its possessor grace, propriety, and comeliness of deportment. Love illuminates the countenance and subdues the voice; it refines and elevates the entire man. It brings him into harmony with God, for it is a heavenly attribute.—*Testimonies for the Church*, vol. 4, 559.

If you want to enjoy life
and see many happy days,
keep your tongue from speaking evil
and your lips from telling lies.
Turn away from evil and do good.
Search for peace, and work to maintain it.

—1 Peter 3:10, 11, NLT

MAY 26
Cheerfulness and Contentment

Making Duty and Drudgery Noble

If your gift is to encourage others, be encouraging.
If it is giving, give generously. If God has given you leadership ability, take the responsibility seriously. And if you have a gift for showing kindness to others, do it gladly.
—Romans 12:8, NLT

WHEN WE ARE TRULY consecrated to God, His love will abide in our hearts by faith, and we will cheerfully do our duty in accordance with the will of God.—*Testimonies to Ministers and Gospel Workers*, 399.

True service links the lowliest of God's servants on earth with the highest of His servants in the courts above.—*Messages to Young People*, 72.

Even though your work may seem to be a drudgery, you may ennoble it by the way in which you do it. Do it as unto the Lord. Do it cheerfully, and with heaven-born dignity. It is the noble principles which are brought into the work that make it wholly acceptable in the Lord's sight.—*Messages to Young People*, 72.

We must sow beside all waters, keeping our souls in the love of God, working while it is day, and using the means the Lord has given us to do whatever duty comes next. Whatever our hands find to do, we are to do it with cheerfulness; whatever sacrifice we are called upon to make, we are to make it cheerfully.—*Testimonies to Ministers and Gospel Workers*, 423.

And whatever you do, do it heartily, as to the Lord and not to men,
knowing that from the Lord you will receive
the reward of the inheritance; for you serve the Lord Christ.
—Colossians 3:23, 24, NKJV

The Joy in Being Able to Give

So let each one give as he purposes in his heart,
not grudgingly or of necessity; for God loves a cheerful giver.
—2 Corinthians 9:7, NKJV

GOD DESIGNS that the exercise of benevolence shall be purely voluntary. . . . "God loveth a cheerful giver." He is not pleased to have His treasury replenished with forced supplies. The loyal hearts of His people, rejoicing in the saving truth for this time, will, through love and gratitude to Him for this precious light, be earnest and anxious to aid with their means in sending the truth to others. The very best manner in which to give expression to our love for our Redeemer is to make offerings to bring souls to the knowledge of the truth. The plan of redemption was entirely voluntary on the part of our Redeemer, and it is the purpose of Christ that all our benevolence should be freewill offerings.—*Testimonies for the Church*, vol. 3, 413.

Spiritual prosperity is closely bound up with Christian liberality. The followers of Christ should rejoice in the privilege of revealing in their lives the beneficence of their Redeemer. As they give to the Lord they have the assurance that their treasure is going before them to the heavenly courts. Would men make their property secure? Let them place it in the hands that bear the marks of the crucifixion. Would they enjoy their substance? Let them use it to bless the needy and suffering. Would they increase their possessions? Let them heed the divine injunction, "Honor the Lord with thy substance, and with the first fruits of all thine increase: so shall thy barns be filled with plenty, and thy presses shall burst out with new wine." Proverbs 3:9, 10. Let them seek to retain their possessions for selfish purposes, and it will be to their eternal loss. But let their treasure be given to God, and from that moment it bears His inscription. It is sealed with His immutability.—*The Acts of the Apostles*, 344.

The Earthly and Heavenly Church

"Thus says the LORD of hosts:
'The fast of the fourth month,
The fast of the fifth,
The fast of the seventh,
And the fast of the tenth,
Shall be joy and gladness and cheerful feasts
For the house of Judah.
Therefore love truth and peace.' "

—Zechariah 8:19, NKJV

OUR MEETINGS SHOULD be made intensely interesting. They should be pervaded with the very atmosphere of heaven.—*Testimonies for the Church*, vol. 5, 609.

They should be treated with the greatest solemnity and reverence, yet all the pleasantness possible should be brought into them. They should not be prolonged till they become wearisome, for the impression thus made upon the minds of the youth will cause them to associate religion with all that is dry and uninteresting; and many will be led to cast their influence on the side of the enemy, who, if properly taught, would become a blessing to the world and to the church. . . . The social meetings and all other religious exercises should be so planned and managed that they will be not only profitable, but so pleasant as to be positively attractive.—*Testimonies for the Church*, vol. 6, 174.

The church of God below is one with the church of God above. Believers on the earth and the beings in heaven who have never fallen constitute one church. Every heavenly intelligence is interested in the assemblies of the saints who on earth meet to worship God. In the inner court of heaven they listen to the testimony of the witnesses for Christ in the outer court on earth, and the praise and thanksgiving from the worshipers below is taken up in the heavenly anthem, and praise and rejoicing sound through the heavenly courts because Christ has not died in vain for the fallen sons of Adam. While angels drink from the fountainhead, the saints on earth drink of the pure streams flowing from the throne, the streams that make glad the city of our God.—*Testimonies for the Church*, vol. 6, 366.

The Joy of an Everlasting Friendship

But immediately Jesus spoke to them, saying,
"Be of good cheer! It is I; do not be afraid."
—Matthew 14:27, NKJV

CHRISTIANS SHOULD BE the most cheerful and happy people that live. They may have the consciousness that God is their father and their everlasting friend. . . .

. . . All who have indeed become acquainted, by experimental knowledge, with the love and tender compassion of our Heavenly Father will impart light and joy wherever they may be. Their presence and influence will be to their associates as the fragrance of sweet flowers, because they are linked to God and heaven, and the purity and exalted loveliness of heaven are communicated through them to all that are brought within their influence.—*Messages to Young People*, 363.

Our Saviour was deeply serious and intensely in earnest, but never gloomy or morose. The life of those who imitate Him will be full of earnest purpose; they will have a deep sense of personal responsibility. Levity will be repressed; there will be no boisterous merriment, no rude jesting; but the religion of Jesus gives peace like a river. It does not quench the light of joy; it does not restrain cheerfulness nor cloud the sunny, smiling face.—*Steps to Christ*, 120.

"The LORD bless you and keep you;
The LORD make His face shine upon you,
And be gracious to you;
The LORD lift up His countenance upon you,
And give you peace."
—Numbers 6:24–26, NKJV

MAY 30
Cheerfulness and Contentment

In Christ's Overcoming Power

"These things I have spoken to you, that in Me you may have peace.
In the world you will have tribulation; but be of good cheer,
I have overcome the world."

—John 16:33, NKJV

So long as we are in the world, we shall meet with adverse influences. There will be provocations to test the temper; and it is by meeting these in a right spirit that the Christian graces are developed. If Christ dwells in us, we shall be patient, kind, and forbearing, cheerful amid frets and irritations. Day by day and year by year we shall conquer self, and grow into a noble heroism. This is our allotted task; but it cannot be accomplished without help from Jesus, resolute decision, unwavering purpose, continual watchfulness, and unceasing prayer. Each one has a personal battle to fight. Not even God can make our characters noble or our lives useful, unless we become co-workers with Him. Those who decline the struggle lose the strength and joy of victory.—*Gospel Workers*, 477.

True happiness will be the result of every self-denial, every crucifixion of self. One victory won, the next is more easily gained. . . . God . . . wants all to be saved. Man has light and opportunities, and if he will improve them he may overcome. . . .

When a man is earnestly engaged day by day in overcoming the defects in his character, he is cherishing Christ in his soul-temple; the light of Christ is in him. Under the bright beams of the light of Christ's countenance his entire being becomes elevated and ennobled. He has the peace of heaven in his soul.—*Testimonies for the Church*, vol. 4, 345, 346.

I have fought the good fight, I have finished the race, I have kept the faith.
Finally, there is laid up for me the crown of righteousness,
which the Lord, the righteous Judge, will give to me on that Day,
and not to me only but also to all who have loved His appearing.

—2 Timothy 4:7, 8, NKJV

No Dread, No Fear

"Don't be afraid, for I am with you.
Don't be discouraged, for I am your God.
I will strengthen you and help you.
I will hold you up with my victorious right hand."

—Isaiah 41:10, NLT

IS JESUS TRUE? Does He mean what He says? Answer decidedly, Yes, every word. Then if you have settled this, by faith claim every promise that He has made, and receive the blessing; for this acceptance by faith gives life to the soul. You may believe that Jesus is true to you, even though you feel yourself to be the weakest and most unworthy of His children.—*Testimonies to Ministers and Gospel Workers*, 517.

Words cannot describe the peace and joy possessed by him who takes God at His word. Trials do not disturb him, slights do not vex him. Self is crucified. Day by day his duties may become more taxing, his temptations stronger, his trials more severe; but he does not falter; for he receives strength equal to his need.—*Messages to Young People*, 98.

Christ knows the strength of your temptations and the strength of your power to resist. His hand is always stretched out in pitying tenderness to every suffering child. To the tempted, discouraged one he says, Child for whom I suffered and died, cannot you trust Me? "As thy days, so shall thy strength be."—*Messages to Young People*, 97.

Peace comes with dependence on divine power. . . .

. . . Be cheerful, and praise the Lord for His loving-kindness. That which you cannot understand, commit to Him. He loves you and pities your every weakness.—*Testimonies to Ministers and Gospel Workers*, 518.

Nothing is apparently more helpless, yet really more invincible, than the soul that feels its nothingness and relies wholly on the merits of the Saviour. By prayer, by the study of His word, by faith in His abiding presence, the weakest of human beings may live in contact with the living Christ, and He will hold them by a hand that will never let go.—*The Ministry of Healing*, 182.

JUNE 1
Christian Fellowship

Christian Fellowship and Brotherly Love

Therefore, my dear brothers and sisters, stay true to the Lord.
I love you and long to see you, dear friends,
for you are my joy and the crown I receive for my work.
—Philippians 4:1, NLT

CHRIST HAD BIDDEN the first disciples love one another as He had loved them. Thus they were to bear testimony to the world that Christ was formed within, the hope of glory. "A new commandment I give unto you," He had said, "That ye love one another; as I have loved you, that ye also love one another." John 13:34. At the time when these words were spoken, the disciples could not understand them; but after they had witnessed the sufferings of Christ, after His crucifixion and resurrection, and ascension to heaven, and after the Holy Spirit had rested on them at Pentecost, they had a clearer conception of the love of God and of the nature of that love which they must have for one another. . . .

. . . They rejoiced in the sweetness of communion with saints. They were tender, thoughtful, self-denying, willing to make any sacrifice for the truth's sake. In their daily association with one another, they revealed the love that Christ had enjoined upon them. By unselfish words and deeds they strove to kindle this love in other hearts.—*The Acts of the Apostles*, 547.

We proclaim to you what we ourselves have actually
seen and heard so that you may have fellowship with us.
And our fellowship is with the Father and with his Son, Jesus Christ.
We are writing these things so that you may fully share our joy.
—1 John 1:3, 4, NLT

Living in Harmony With Our Brothers and Sisters

Fulfill my joy by being like-minded, having the same love, being of one accord, of one mind.

—Philippians 2:2, NKJV

God designs that His people shall be a unit, that they shall see eye to eye and be of the same mind and of the same judgment.—*Testimonies for the Church*, vol. 3, 361.

The religion of Christ does not require us to lose our identity of character, but merely to adapt ourselves, in some measure, to the feelings and ways of others. Many people may be brought together in a unity of religious faith whose opinions, habits, and tastes in temporal matters are not in harmony; but if they have the love of Christ glowing in their bosoms, and are looking forward to the same heaven as their eternal home, they may have the sweetest and most intelligent communion together, and a unity the most wonderful.—*Testimonies for the Church*, vol. 4, 65.

Let us be determined to be in unity with our brethren. This duty God has placed upon us. We shall make their hearts glad by following their counsel, and make ourselves strong through the influence that this will give us.—*Testimonies to Ministers and Gospel Workers*, 500.

How good and pleasant it is
when God's people live together in unity!

—Psalm 133:1, NIV

Therefore if you have any encouragement from being united with Christ,
if any comfort from his love, if any common sharing in the Spirit,
if any tenderness and compassion, then make my joy complete
by being like-minded, having the same love,
being one in spirit and of one mind.

—Philippians 2:1, 2, NIV

Your Happiness Is My Happiness

And if one member suffers, all the members suffer with it;
or if one member is honored, all the members rejoice with it.
—1 Corinthians 12:26, NKJV

CHRISTIANITY IS A SYSTEM which, received and obeyed, would spread peace, harmony, and happiness throughout the earth. The religion of Christ will unite in close brotherhood all who accept its teachings. It was the mission of Jesus to reconcile men to God, and thus to one another.—*The Great Controversy*, 46.

Let your hearts be true to Jesus. Although you may feel that you are the least of all saints, yet you are members of Christ's body, and through Him you are identified with all His human agencies and with the excellence and power of the heavenly intelligences. None of us liveth to himself. To each is assigned a post of duty, not for his own narrow, selfish interests, but that the influence of each may be a strength to all.—*Testimonies for the Church*, vol. 7, 296.

God's church is the court of holy life, filled with varied gifts and endowed with the Holy Spirit. The members are to find their happiness in the happiness of those whom they help and bless.—*The Acts of the Apostles*, 12.

Let love be without hypocrisy. Abhor what is evil. Cling to what is good.
Be kindly affetionate to one another with brotherly love,
in honor giving preference to one another.
—Romans 12:9, 10, NKJV

Let Us Make Others Happy

Being confident of this, I know that I shall remain
and continue with you all for your progress and joy of faith.
—Philippians 1:25, NKJV

FROM THE ANOINTED ONES that stand in God's presence the fullness of divine light and love and power is imparted to His people, that they may impart to others light and joy and refreshing. Those who are thus enriched are to enrich others with the treasure of God's love.—*Prophets and Kings*, 594.

Religion is founded upon love to God, which also leads us to love one another. It is full of gratitude, humility, long-suffering. It is self-sacrificing, forbearing, merciful, and forgiving. It sanctifies the whole life and extends its influence over others.

Those who love God cannot harbor hatred or envy. When the heavenly principle of eternal love fills the heart, it will flow out to others, not merely because favors are received of them, but because love is the principle of action and modifies the character, governs the impulses, controls the passions, subdues enmity, and elevates and ennobles the affections. This love is not contracted so as merely to include "me and mine," but is as broad as the world and as high as heaven, and is in harmony with that of the angel workers. This love cherished in the soul sweetens the entire life and sheds a refining influence on all around. Possessing it, we cannot but be happy, let fortune smile or frown.—*Testimonies for the Church*, vol. 4, 223.

I pray that out of his glorious riches he may strengthen you
with power through his Spirit in your inner being,
so that Christ may dwell in your hearts through faith.
And I pray that you, being rooted and establish in love, may have power.
—Ephesians 3:16–18, NIV

JUNE 5

Christian Fellowship

Fellowship and Solidarity

I long to see you again, for I remember your tears as we parted.
And I will be filled with joy when we are together again.

—2 Timothy 1:4, NLT

WE SUSTAIN A LOSS when we neglect the privilege of associating together to strengthen and encourage one another in the service of God. The truths of His word lose their vividness and importance in our minds. Our hearts cease to be enlightened and aroused by their sanctifying influence, and we decline in spirituality. In our association as Christians we lose much by lack of sympathy with one another. He who shuts himself up to himself is not filling the position that God designed he should. . . .

If Christians would associate together, speaking to each other of the love of God and of the precious truths of redemption, their own hearts would be refreshed and they would refresh one another.—*Steps to Christ*, 101.

We are all children of one Father, dependent upon one another for happiness. The claims of God and of humanity are upon us. It is the proper cultivation of the social elements of our nature that brings us into sympathy with our brethren and affords us happiness in our efforts to bless others.—*Patriarchs and Prophets*, 541.

Recalling your tears, I long to see you so that I may be filled with joy.
I am reminded of your sincere faith, a faith that lived
first in your grandmother Lois and your mother Eunice
and now, I am sure, lives in you.

—2 Timothy 1:4, 5, NRSV

Praying for Others

Always in every prayer of mine making request for you all with joy, for your fellowship in the gospel from the first day until now.

—Philippians 1:4, 5, NKJV

PRAYER IS COMMUNION with God, the Fountain of wisdom, the Source of strength, and peace, and happiness. . . . Paul exhorts believers to "pray without ceasing," in everything, by prayer and supplication, with thanksgiving, making known their requests to God. "Pray one for another" James says. . . . 1 Thessalonians 5:17; James 5:16. —*Testimonies for the Church*, vol. 7, 42.

Learn to exercise faith in presenting your neighbors before the throne of grace and pleading with God to touch their hearts.—*Testimonies for the Church*, vol. 8, 245.

Souls are to be sought for, prayed for, labored for. Earnest appeals are to be made. Fervent prayers are to be offered. Our tame, spiritless petitions are to be changed into petitions of intense earnestness. God's word declares: The effectual fervent prayer of a righteous man availeth much.—*Testimonies for the Church*, vol. 7, 12.

The minister is not to rule imperiously over the flock entrusted to his care, but to be their ensample, and to show them the way to heaven. Following the example of Christ, he should intercede with God for the people of his care till he sees that his prayers are answered.—*Testimonies for the Church*, vol. 4, 267.

In all my prayers for all of you, I always pray with joy because of your partnership in the gospel from the first day until now.

—Philippians 1:4, 5, NIV

Encouraging Fellow Believers

The brothers and sisters in Rome had heard we were coming,
and they came to meet us at the Forum on the Appian Way.
Others joined us at The Three Taverns. When Paul saw them,
he was encouraged and thanked God.

—Acts 28:15, NLT

IT WAS WITH A HEAVY HEART that Paul went forward to his long-expected visit to the world's metropolis. How different the circumstances from those he had anticipated! How was he, fettered and stigmatized, to proclaim the gospel? . . .

At last the travelers reach Appii Forum, forty miles from Rome. As they make their way through the crowds that throng the great thoroughfare, the gray-haired old man, chained with a group of hardened-looking criminals, receives many a glance of scorn and is made the subject of many a rude, mocking jest.

Suddenly a cry of joy is heard, and a man springs from the passing throng and falls upon the prisoner's neck, embracing him with tears and rejoicing, as a son would welcome a long-absent father. Again and again is the scene repeated. . . .

As the warmhearted disciples eagerly flock around their father in the gospel, the whole company is brought to a standstill. The soldiers are impatient of delay, yet they have not the heart to interrupt this happy meeting; for they, too, have learned to respect and esteem their prisoner. . . .

Few realize the significance of those words of Luke, that when Paul saw his brethren, "he thanked God, and took courage." In the midst of the weeping, sympathizing company of believers, who were not ashamed of his bonds, the apostle praised God aloud. The cloud of sadness that had rested upon his spirit was swept away. . . . With firmer step and joyful heart he continued on his way.—*The Acts of the Apostles*, 448, 449.

And I want you to know, my dear brothers and sisters, that everything that has happened to me
here has helped to spread the Good News. For everyone here, including
the whole palace guard, knows that I am in chains because of Christ.
And because of my imprisonment, most of the believers here
have gained confidence and boldly speak God's message without fear.

—Philippians 1:12–14, NLT

Wonderful and Pleasant Heavenly Harmony

How wonderful and pleasant it is
when brothers live together in harmony!

—Psalm 133:1, NLT

THERE ARE MYSTERIOUS LINKS that bind souls together, so that the heart of one answers to the heart of another. One catches the ideas, the sentiments, the spirit, of another. This association may be a blessing or a curse.—*Messages to Young People*, 411.

Christian sociability is altogether too little cultivated by God's people. . . .

. . . Those who shut themselves up within themselves, who are unwilling to be drawn upon to bless others by friendly associations, lose many blessings; for by mutual contact minds receive polish and refinement; by social intercourse acquaintances are formed and friendships contracted which result in a unity of heart and an atmosphere of love which is pleasing in the sight of heaven.—*Messages to Young People*, 405.

Behold, how good and how pleasant it is
For brethren to dwell together in unity!
It is like the precious oil upon the head,
Running down on the beard,
The beard of Aaron,
Running down on the edge of his garments.
It is like the dew of Hermon,
Descending upon the mountains of Zion;
For there the LORD commanded the blessing—
Life forevermore.

—Psalm 133:1–3, NKJV

JUNE 9
Christian Fellowship

Shared Happiness

"And you shall rejoice in your feast,
you and your son and your daughter,
your male servant and your female servant and the Levite,
the stranger and the fatherless and the widow,
who are within your gates."
—Deuteronomy 16:14, NKJV

THE ISRAELITES, in all their festivities, included the poor, the stranger, and the Levite, who was both the assistant of the priest in the sanctuary, and a religious teacher and missionary. These were regarded as the guests of the people, to share their hospitality on all occasions of social and religious rejoicing, and to be tenderly cared for in sickness or in need. It is such as these whom we should make welcome to our homes. How much such a welcome might do to cheer and encourage the missionary nurse or the teacher, the care-burdened, hard-working mother, or the feeble and aged, so often without a home, and struggling with poverty and many discouragements. . . .

. . . The warmth of a genial welcome, a place at your fireside, a seat at your home table, the privilege of sharing the blessing of the hour of prayer, would to many of these be like a glimpse of heaven.

Our sympathies are to overflow the boundaries of self and the enclosure of family walls. There are precious opportunities for those who will make their homes a blessing to others. . . .

. . . If we would show an interest in the youth, invite them to our homes, and surround them with cheering, helpful influences, there are many who would gladly turn their steps into the upward path.—*The Ministry of Healing*, 352, 354.

Keep loving each other as brothers and sisters.
Don't forget to show hospitality to strangers,
for some who have done this have entertained angels without realizing it!
—Hebrews 13: 1, 2, NLT

Confidence and Unity

Therefore I rejoice that I have confidence in you in everything.
—2 Corinthians 7:16, NKJV

When men will show confidence in their fellowmen they will come much nearer to possessing the mind of Christ. . . .

. . . Jesus found access to minds by the pathway of their most familiar associations. . . .

Jesus assumed humanity that He might meet humanity. He brings men under the transforming power of truth by meeting them where they are. He gains access to the heart by securing sympathy and confidence, making all feel that His identification with their nature and interest is complete.—*Testimonies to Ministers and Gospel Workers*, 189, 190.

Let us cherish a spirit of confidence in the wisdom of our brethren. . . . Connected with the service of God, we must individually realize that we are parts of a great whole. . . .

Workers for Christ are to strive for unity. We are the children of the same family, and have one heavenly Father. Let us not put on garments of heaviness, and cherish doubts and a lack of confidence in our brethren. We should not hurt our souls by gathering the thistles and the thorns, but instead we should gather the roses and the lilies and the pinks, and express their fragrance in our words and acts.—*Testimonies to Ministers and Gospel Workers*, 500, 502.

When there is harmonious action among the individual members of the church, when there is love and confidence manifested by brother to brother, there will be proportionate force and power in our work for the salvation of men.—*Testimonies to Ministers and Gospel Workers*, 188.

I do not say this to condemn you; I have said before
that you have such a place in our hearts that we would live or die with you.
I have spoken to you with great frankness; I take great pride in you.
I am greatly encouraged; in all our troubles my joy knows no bounds. . . .
. . . I am glad I can have complete confidence in you.
—2 Corinthians 7:3, 4, 16, NIV

Promoting the Welfare of Others

Therefore we have been comforted in your comfort.
And we rejoiced exceedingly more for the joy of Titus,
because his spirit has been refreshed by you all.
—2 Corinthians 7:13, NKJV

THE WARMTH OF TRUE FRIENDSHIP, the love that binds heart to heart, is a foretaste of the joys of heaven.—*The Ministry of Healing*, 360.

Every soul is surrounded by an atmosphere of its own—an atmosphere, it may be, charged with the life-giving power of faith, courage, and hope, and sweet with the fragrance of love. Or it may be heavy and chill with the gloom of discontent and selfishness, or poisonous with the deadly taint of cherished sin. By the atmosphere surrounding us, every person with whom we come in contact is consciously or unconsciously affected.—*Christ's Object Lessons*, 339.

The life of Christ was an ever-widening, shoreless influence, an influence that bound Him to God and to the whole human family. Through Christ, God has invested man with an influence that makes it impossible for him to live to himself. Individually we are connected with our fellow men, a part of God's great whole, and we stand under mutual obligations. No man can be independent of his fellow men; for the well-being of each affects others. It is God's purpose that each shall feel himself necessary to others' welfare, and seek to promote their happiness.—*Christ's Object Lessons*, 339.

We have been greatly encouraged by this.
In addition to our own encouragement, we were especially delighted
to see how happy Titus was about the way
all of you welcomed him and set his mind at ease.
—2 Corinthians 7:13, NLT

Refreshing Others Through Christ

That I may come to you with joy by the will of God,
and may be refreshed together.
—Romans 15:32, NKJV

All who profess to be children of God should bear in mind that as missionaries they will be brought into contact with all classes of minds. There are the refined and the coarse, the humble and the proud, the religious and the skeptical, the educated and the ignorant, the rich and the poor. These varied minds cannot be treated alike; yet all need kindness and sympathy. By mutual contact our minds should receive polish and refinement. We are dependent upon one another, closely bound together by the ties of human brotherhood.

"Heaven forming each on other to depend,
A master or a servant or a friend,
Bids each on other for assistance call,
Till one man's weakness grows the strength of all."

It is through the social relations that Christianity comes in contact with the world. Every man or woman who has received the divine illumination is to shed light on the dark pathway of those who are unacquainted with the better way. Social power, sanctified by the Spirit of Christ, must be improved in bringing souls to the Saviour. Christ is not to be hid away in the heart as a coveted treasure, sacred and sweet, to be enjoyed solely by the possessor. We are to have Christ in us as a well of water, springing up into everlasting life, refreshing all who come in contact with us.—*The Ministry of Healing*, 495, 496.

Support and Understanding

So the anger of the LORD was kindled against Moses, and He said:
"Is not Aaron the Levite your brother? I know that he can speak well.
And look, he is also coming out to meet you.
When he sees you, he will be glad in his heart."
—Exodus 4:14, NKJV

THE DESIRE FOR LOVE and sympathy is implanted in the heart by God Himself. Christ, in His hour of agony in Gethsemane, longed for the sympathy of His disciples. . . . Paul, though apparently indifferent to hardship and suffering, yearned for sympathy and companionship.—*The Acts of the Apostles*, 491.

While we should cultivate sociability, let it not be merely for amusement, but for a higher purpose.—*Gospel Workers*, 125.

All our associations with our fellow mortals should be with reference to their eternal interest and to our own.—*Testimonies for the Church*, vol. 4, 236.

We may associate together . . . and do all to the glory of God. . . .

. . . From all these pleasant associations, we want to be gathering new strength to become better men and women. From every source possible we want to gather new courage, new strength, new power, that we may elevate our lives to purity and holiness, and not come down upon the low level of this world.—*Testimonies for the Church*, vol. 2, 586, 587.

Then the LORD's anger burned against Moses and he said,
"What about your brother, Aaron the Levite? I know he can speak well.
He is already on his way to meet you, and he will be glad to see you."
—Exodus 4:14, NIV

The Marks of a True Friend

"I am distressed for you, my brother Jonathan;
greatly beloved were you to me;
your love to me was wonderful,
passing the love of women."

—2 Samuel 1:26, NRSV

THE FRIENDSHIP OF JONATHAN for David was . . . of God's providence, to preserve the life of the future ruler of Israel.—*Patriarchs and Prophets*, 649.

Jonathan, by birth heir to the throne, yet knowing himself set aside by the divine decree; to his rival the most tender and faithful of friends, shielding David's life at the peril of his own; steadfast at his father's side through the dark days of his declining power, and at his side falling at the last—the name of Jonathan is treasured in heaven, and it stands on earth a witness to the existence and the power of unselfish love. —*Education*, 157.

"Saul and Jonathan, beloved and lovely!
In life and in death they were not divided;
they were swifter than eagles;
they were stronger than lions.

"You daughters of Israel, weep over Saul,
who clothed you luxuriously in scarlet,
who put ornaments of gold on your apparel.

"How the mighty have fallen
in the midst of the battle!

"Jonathan lies slain on your high places.
I am distressed for you, my brother Jonathan;
very pleasant have you been to me;
your love to me was extraordinary,
surpassing the love of women."

—2 Samuel 1:26, ESV

JUNE 15
Christian Fellowship

Rejoicing Together

Rejoice with those who rejoice,
and weep with those who weep.

—Romans 12:15, NKJV

GOD HAS SO CONSTITUTED US that even the strongest desire sympathy.—*Gospel Workers*, 209.

Men cannot love God supremely and their neighbor as themselves, and be as cold as icebergs. Not only do they rob God of the love due Him, but they rob their neighbor as well. Love is a plant of heavenly growth, and it must be fostered and nourished. Affectionate hearts, truthful, loving words, will make happy families and exert an elevating influence upon all who come within the sphere of their influence.—*Testimonies for the Church*, vol. 4, 548.

The wonderful example of Christ, the matchless tenderness with which He entered into the feelings of others, weeping with those who wept, rejoicing with those who rejoiced, must have a deep influence upon the character of all who follow Him in sincerity. By kindly words and acts they will try to make the path easy for weary feet. . . .

All around us are afflicted souls. Here and there, everywhere, we may find them. Let us search out these suffering ones and speak a word in season to comfort their hearts. Let us ever be channels through which shall flow the refreshing waters of compassion. —*The Ministry of Healing*, 157, 158.

"For so the Lord has commanded us:
'I have set you as a light to the Gentiles,
That you should be for salvation to the ends of the earth.' "

—Acts 13:47, NKJV

Little Things That Bring Joy

And her neighbors and relatives heard
that the Lord had shown great mercy to her,
and they rejoiced with her.

—Luke 1:58, ESV

FRIENDLY SYMPATHY and real feelings of tender interest for others would bring to your souls blessings that you have never yet experienced and would bring you into close relation to our Redeemer, whose advent to the world was for the purpose of doing good and whose life we are to copy.—*Testimonies for the Church*, vol. 3, 526.

The love and interest of Christ's followers must be as broad as the world. Those who live merely for "me and mine" will fail of heaven.—*Testimonies for the Church*, vol. 3, 529.

We should have words and deeds of tender consideration for others. We can manifest a thousand little attentions in friendly words and pleasant looks, which will be reflected upon us again. Thoughtless Christians manifest by their neglect of others that they are not in union with Christ. It is impossible to be in union with Christ and yet be unkind to others and forgetful of their rights. Many long intensely for friendly sympathy. God has given each of us an identity of our own, which cannot be merged in that of another; but our individual characteristics will be much less prominent if we are indeed Christ's and His will is ours. Our lives should be consecrated to the good and happiness of others, as was our Saviour's. We should be self-forgetful, ever looking out for opportunities, even in little things, to show gratitude for the favors we have received of others, and watching for opportunities to cheer others and lighten and relieve their sorrows and burdens by acts of tender kindness and little deeds of love. These thoughtful courtesies, that, commencing in our families, extend outside the family circle, help make up the sum of life's happiness; and the neglect of these little things makes up the sum of life's bitterness and sorrow.—*Testimonies for the Church*, vol. 3, 539.

Joyfully Putting Others First

Yes, and if I am being poured out as a drink offering
on the sacrifice and service of your faith,
I am glad and rejoice with you all. For the same reason
you also be glad and rejoice with me.

—Philippians 2:17, 18, NKJV

GOD DOES NOT ACCEPT the most splendid service unless self is laid upon the altar, a living, consuming sacrifice.—*Testimonies for the Church*, vol. 7, 248.

Not one nook or corner of the soul is to be a hiding place for selfishness. God desires that heaven's plan shall be carried out, and heaven's divine order and harmony prevail, in every family, in every church, in every institution. Did this love leaven society, we should see the outworking of noble principles of Christian refinement and courtesy, and in Christian charity toward the purchase of the blood of Christ.—*Testimonies for the Church*, vol. 8, 139.

It was to give in His own life an illustration of unselfishness that Jesus came in the form of humanity. And all who accept this principle are to be workers together with Him in demonstrating it in practical life.—*Education*, 154.

We cannot be happy while we are wrapped up in our interest for ourselves. . . . If we injure others, we injure ourselves also. If we bless others, we also bless ourselves; for the influence of every good deed is reflected upon our own hearts.—*Testimonies for the Church*, vol. 4, 71.

In order to be happy ourselves, we must live to make others happy. It is well for us to yield our possessions, our talents, and our affections in grateful devotion to Christ, and in that way find happiness here and immortal glory hereafter.—*Testimonies for the Church*, vol. 3, 250.

Put Yourself in My Place

That is why I wrote to you as I did,
so that when I do come, I won't be grieved by the very ones
who ought to give me the greatest joy. Surely you all know
that my joy comes from your being joyful.
—2 Corinthians 2:3, NLT

IN YOUR ASSOCIATION WITH OTHERS, put yourself in their place. Enter into their feelings, their difficulties, their disappointments, their joys, and their sorrows. Identify yourself with them, and then do to them as, were you to exchange places with them, you would wish them to deal with you. This is the true rule of honesty. It is another expression of the law. "Thou shalt love thy neighbor as thyself." Matthew 22:39. And it is the substance of the teaching of the prophets. It is a principle of heaven, and will be developed in all who are fitted for its holy companionship.

The golden rule is the principle of true courtesy, and its truest illustration is seen in the life and character of Jesus. Oh, what rays of softness and beauty shone forth in the daily life of our Saviour! What sweetness flowed from His very presence! The same spirit will be revealed in His children. Those with whom Christ dwells will be surrounded with a divine atmosphere. Their white robes of purity will be fragrant with perfume from the garden of the Lord. Their faces will reflect light from His, brightening the path for stumbling and weary feet.—*Thoughts From the Mount of Blessing*, 134, 135.

"Teacher, which is the most important commandment in the law of Moses?"
Jesus replied, " 'You must love the LORD your God with all your heart,
all your soul, and all your mind.' This is the first and greatest commandment.
A second is equally important: 'Love your neighbor as yourself.'
The entire law and all the demands of the prophets
are based on these two commandments."
—Matthew 22:36–40, NLT

JUNE 19
Christian Fellowship

Words and Acts of Kindness

The heartfelt counsel of a friend
is as sweet as perfume and incense.

—Proverbs 27:9, NLT

CHRISTIANS SHOULD BE CAREFUL in regard to their words. . . . The conversation should be upon spiritual and divine things. . . . If the association with Christian friends is chiefly devoted to the improvement of the mind and heart, there will be no after regrets, and they can look back on the interview with a pleasant satisfaction.—*Testimonies for the Church*, vol. 2, 186.

In all our associations it should be remembered that in the experience of others there are chapters sealed from mortal sight. On the pages of memory are sad histories that are sacredly guarded from curious eyes. There stand registered long, hard battles with trying circumstances, perhaps troubles in the home life, that day by day weaken courage, confidence, and faith. Those who are fighting the battle of life at great odds may be strengthened and encouraged by little attentions that cost only a loving effort. To such the strong, helpful grasp of the hand by a true friend is worth more than gold or silver. Words of kindness are as welcome as the smile of angels.—*The Ministry of Healing*, 158.

Perfume and incense bring joy to the heart,
and the pleasantness of a friend
springs from their heartfelt advice.

—Proverbs 27:9, NIV

Searching for the Lost

"And when he comes home,
he calls together his friends and his neighbors,
saying to them, 'Rejoice with me, for I have found
my sheep that was lost.' "

—Luke 15:6, ESV

THANK GOD, He has presented to our imagination no picture of a sorrowful shepherd returning without the sheep. The parable does not speak of failure but of success and joy in the recovery.—*Christ's Object Lessons*, 188.

And when the straying one is found, does he command it to follow him? Does he threaten or beat it, or drive it before him, thinking of the discomfort and anxiety that he has suffered on its account? No; he lays the exhausted sheep on his shoulder, and with cheerful gratitude that his search has not been in vain, he returns to the fold. His gratitude finds expression in songs of rejoicing. And "when he cometh home, he calleth together his friends and neighbors, saying unto them, Rejoice with me; for I have found my sheep which was lost."

So when the lost sinner is found by the Good Shepherd, heaven and earth unite in rejoicing and thanksgiving. For "joy shall be in heaven over one sinner that repenteth, more than over ninety and nine just persons, which need no repentance" [Luke 5:6, 7].—*Gospel Workers,* section 6, p. 182.

This illustrates the blessed, joyful work of laboring for the erring. The church that engages successfully in this work is a happy church.—*Testimonies for the Church*, vol. 2, 22.

Those who live to please the Spirit will harvest everlasting life from the Spirit.
So let's not get tired of doing what is good. At just the right time
we will reap a harvest of blessing if we don't give up. Therefore, whenever we have
the opportunity, we should do good to everyone—especially to those in the family of faith.
—Galatians 6:8–10, NLT

JUNE 21
Christian Fellowship

The Return of the Lost

"When she has found it,
she calls together her friends and neighbors, saying,
'Rejoice with me, for I have found the coin that I had lost.' "

—Luke 15:9, NRSV

IN THE EAST the houses of the poor usually consisted of but one room, often windowless and dark. The room was rarely swept, and a piece of money falling on the floor would be speedily covered by the dust and rubbish. In order that it might be found, even in the daytime, a candle must be lighted, and the house must be swept diligently.

The wife's marriage portion usually consisted of pieces of money, which she carefully preserved as her most cherished possession, to be transmitted to her own daughters. The loss of one of these pieces would be regarded as a serious calamity, and its recovery would cause great rejoicing, in which the neighboring women would readily share.—*Christ's Object Lessons*, 192, 193.

"Likewise, I say unto you, there is joy in the presence of the angels of God over one sinner that repenteth." If the angels of God rejoice over the erring who see and confess their wrongs and return to the fellowship of their brethren, how much more should the followers of Christ, who are themselves erring, and who every day need the forgiveness of God and of their brethren, feel joy over the return of a brother or a sister who has been deceived by the sophistry of Satan.—*Testimonies for the Church*, vol. 3, 100.

Let them praise his name with dancing,
making melody to him with tambourine and lyre.
For the LORD takes pleasure in his people;
he adorns the humble with victory.

—Psalm 149:3, 4, NRSV

The Key to Marital Bliss

Live joyfully with the wife whom you love
all the days of your vain life which He has given you under the sun,
all your days of vanity; for that is your portion in life,
and in the labor which you perform under the sun.
—Ecclesiastes 9:9, NKJV

THE SPIRIT THAT CHRIST manifests toward us is the spirit that husband and wife are to manifest toward each other. "As Christ also hath loved us," "walk in love." "As the church is subject unto Christ, so let the wives be to their own husbands in everything. Husbands, love your wives, even as Christ also loved the church, and gave Himself for it." Ephesians 5:2, 24, 25.

Neither the husband nor the wife should attempt to exercise over the other an arbitrary control. Do not try to compel each other to yield to your wishes. You cannot do this and retain each other's love. Be kind, patient, and forbearing, considerate, and courteous. By the grace of God you can succeed in making each other happy, as in your marriage vow you promised to do.—*The Ministry of Healing*, 361.

Home should be a place where cheerfulness, courtesy, and love abide; and where these graces dwell, there will abide happiness and peace. Troubles may invade, but these are the lot of humanity. Let patience, gratitude, and love keep sunshine in the heart, though the day may be ever so cloudy. In such homes angels of God abide.—*The Ministry of Healing*, 393.

But among the Lord's people, women are not independent of men,
and men are not independent of women. For although the first woman came from man,
every other man was born from a woman, and everything comes from God.
—1 Corinthians 11:11, 12, NLT

JUNE 23
Christian Fellowship

Mutual Love and Support

Let your fountain be blessed,
And rejoice with the wife of your youth.

—Proverbs 5:18, NKJV

LET THE HUSBAND aid his wife by his sympathy and unfailing affection. If he wishes to keep her fresh and gladsome, so that she will be as sunshine in the home, let him help her bear her burdens. His kindness and loving courtesy will be to her a precious encouragement, and the happiness he imparts will bring joy and peace to his own heart.—*The Ministry of Healing*, 374.

Let the husband and wife study each other's happiness, never failing in the small courtesies and little kindly acts that cheer and brighten the life.—*The Ministry of Healing*, 393.

Though difficulties, perplexities, and discouragements may arise, let neither husband nor wife harbor the thought that their union is a mistake or a disappointment. Determine to be all that it is possible to be to each other. Continue the early attentions. In every way encourage each other in fighting the battles of life. . . . Let there be mutual love, mutual forbearance. Then marriage, instead of being the end of love, will be as it were the very beginning of love.—*The Ministry of Healing*, 360.

"Haven't you read the Scriptures?" Jesus replied. "They record that from the beginning 'God made them male and female.' " And he said, " 'This explains why a man leaves his father and mother and is joined to his wife, and the two are united into one.' Since they are no longer two but one, let no one split apart what God has joined togerther."

—Matthew 19:4–6, NLT

Obedient Children Bring Joy

A wise son makes a glad father,
But a foolish man despises his mother.
—Proverbs 15:20, NKJV

CHILDREN WHO ARE CHRISTIANS will prefer the love and approbation of their God-fearing parents above every earthly blessing. They will love and honor their parents. It should be one of the principal studies of their lives how to make their parents happy.—*Messages to Young People*, 335.

Children, God has seen fit to intrust you to the care of your parents, for them to instruct and discipline, and thus act their part in forming your character for heaven. And yet it rests with you to say whether you will develop a good Christian character by making the best of the advantages you have had from godly, faithful, praying parents. Notwithstanding all the anxiety and faithfulness of parents in behalf of their children, they alone cannot save them. There is a work for the children to do. Every child has an individual case to attend to.

Believing parents, you have a responsible work before you, to guide the footsteps of your children, even in their religious experience. When they truly love God, they will bless and reverence you for the care which you have manifested for them, and for your faithfulness in restraining their desires and subduing their wills.—*Messages to Young People*, 338.

They will love the Lord Jesus, and it will be their delight to please Him. They will not be impatient if reproved; but will make glad the heart of father and mother by their kindness, their patience, their willingness to do all they can in helping to bear the burdens of daily life.—*Messages to Young People*, 333.

"Listen, O Israel! The LORD is our God, the LORD alone.
And you must love the LORD your God with all your heart,
all your soul, and all your strength. And you must commit yourselves
wholeheartedly to these commands that I am giving you today.
Repeat them again and again to your children. Talk about them
when you are at home and when you are on the road,
when you are going to bed and when you are getting up."
—Deuteronomy 6:4–7, NLT

From the Cradle

She is clothed with strength and dignity,
and she laughs without fear of the future.
When she speaks, her words are wise,
and she gives instructions with kindness. . . .
Her children stand and bless her.
Her husband praises her:
"There are many virtuous and
capable women in the world,
but you surpass them all!"

—Proverbs 31:25–29, NLT

THE MOTHER SHOULD CULTIVATE a cheerful, contented, happy disposition. Every effort in this direction will be abundantly repaid in both the physical well-being and the moral character of her children.—*The Ministry of Healing*, 374.

There is a God above, and the light and glory from His throne rests upon the faithful mother as she tries to educate her children to resist the influence of evil. No other work can equal hers in importance. She has not, like the artist, to paint a form of beauty upon canvas, nor, like the sculptor, to chisel it from marble. She has not, like the author, to embody a noble thought in words of power, nor, like the musician, to express a beautiful sentiment in melody. It is hers, with the help of God, to develop in a human soul the likeness of the divine.—*The Ministry of Healing*, 377.

Teach them to enjoy the beauties of nature and in useful employments to exercise systematically all the powers of body and mind. Bring them up to have sound constitutions and good morals, to have sunny dispositions and sweet tempers. Impress upon their tender minds the truth that God does not design that we should live for present gratification merely, but for our ultimate good. Teach them that to yield to temptation is weak and wicked; to resist, noble and manly. These lessons will be as seed sown in good soil, and they will bear fruit that will make your hearts glad.—*The Ministry of Healing*, 386.

The Greatest Inheritance for Our Children

The father of the righteous will greatly rejoice,
And he that begets a wise child will delight in him.
Let your father and your mother be glad,
And let her who bore you rejoice.
—Proverbs 23:24, 25, NKJV

WHAT THE PARENTS ARE, that, to a great extent, the children will be.—*The Ministry of Healing*, 371.

Great is the honor and the responsibility placed upon fathers and mothers, in that they are to stand in the place of God to their children. Their character, their daily life, their methods of training, will interpret His words to the little ones. Their influence will win or repel the child's confidence in the Lord's assurances. . . .

Happy are the parents whose lives are a true reflection of the divine, so that the promises and commands of God awaken in the child gratitude and reverence; the parents whose tenderness and justice and long-suffering interpret to the child the love and justice and long-suffering of God; and who, by teaching the child to love and trust and obey them, are teaching him to love and trust and obey his Father in heaven. Parents who impart to a child such a gift have endowed him with a treasure more precious than the wealth of all the ages—a treasure as enduring as eternity.—*The Ministry of Healing*, 375.

But as for you, continue in what you have learned and firmly believed,
knowing from whom you learned it, and how from childhood
you have known the sacred writing that are able to instruct you
for salvation through faith in Christ Jesus.
—2 Timothy 3:14, 15, NRSV

JUNE 27
Christian Fellowship

The Sweetest Hour of the Day

"You shall rejoice before the LORD *your God,*
you and your sons and your daughters,
your male and female servants,
and the Levite who is within your gates,
since he has no portion nor inheritance with you."
—Deuteronomy 12:12, NKJV

FATHERS AND MOTHERS, however pressing your business, do not fail to gather your family around God's altar. Ask for the guardianship of holy angels in your home. Remember that your dear ones are exposed to temptations. Daily annoyances beset the path of young and old. Those who would live patient, loving, cheerful lives must pray. Only by receiving constant help from God can we gain the victory over self. —*The Ministry of Healing*, 393.

The hours of morning and evening worship should be the sweetest and most helpful of the day. Let it be understood that into these hours no troubled, unkind thoughts are to intrude; that parents and children assemble to meet with Jesus, and to invite into the home the presence of holy angels. Let the services be brief and full of life, adapted to the occasion, and varied from time to time. Let all join in the Bible reading and learn and often repeat God's law. . . . Let the little ones take part in prayer, and let them join in song, if it be but a single verse.—*Education*, 186.

Sing to God, sing praises to His name;
Extol Him who rides on the clouds,
By His name YAH,
And rejoice before Him.

—Psalm 68:4, NKJV

The Virtues That the Father Should Enforce

For the LORD *corrects those he loves,*
just as a father corrects a child in whom he delights.
—Proverbs 3:12, NLT

THE FATHER SHOULD ENFORCE in his family the sterner virtues—energy, integrity, honesty, patience, courage, diligence, and practical usefulness. And what he requires of his children he himself should practice, illustrating these virtues in his own manly bearing.

But, fathers, do not discourage your children. Combine affection with authority, kindness and sympathy with firm restraint. Give some of your leisure hours to your children; become acquainted with them; associate with them in their work and in their sports, and win their confidence. Cultivate friendship with them, especially with your sons. In this way you will be a strong influence for good.

The father should do his part toward making home happy. Whatever his cares and business perplexities, they should not be permitted to overshadow his family; he should enter his home with smiles and pleasant words.—*The Ministry of Healing*, 391, 392.

Give thanks to the LORD *and proclaim his greatness.*
Let the whole world know what he has done.
Sing to him; yes, sing his praises.
Tell everyone about his wonderful deeds.
Exult in his holy name;
rejoice, you who worship the LORD.
Search for the LORD *and for his strength;*
continually seek him.
—Psalm 105:1–4, NLT

JUNE 29
Christian Fellowship

Christ Will Rejoice Over His Bride

For as a young man marries a young woman,
so shall your builder marry you,
and as the bridegroom rejoices over the bride,
so shall your God rejoice over you.

—Isaiah 62:5, NRSV

God celebrated the first marriage. Thus the institution has for its originator the Creator of the universe. "Marriage is honorable" (Hebrews 13:4); it was one of the first gifts of God to man, and it is one of the two institutions that, after the Fall, Adam brought with him beyond the gates of Paradise. When the divine principles are recognized and obeyed in this relation, marriage is a blessing; it guards the purity and happiness of the race, it provides for man's social needs, it elevates the physical, the intellectual, and the moral nature.—*Patriarchs and Prophets*, 46.

He who gave Eve to Adam as a helpmeet, performed His first miracle at a marriage festival. In the festal hall where friends and kindred rejoiced together, Christ began His public ministry. Thus He sanctioned marriage, recognizing it as an institution that He Himself had established. He ordained that men and women should be united in holy wedlock, to rear families whose members, crowned with honor, should be recognized as members of the family above.

Christ honored the marriage relation by making it also a symbol of the union between Him and His redeemed ones. He Himself is the Bridegroom; the bride is the church, of which, as His chosen one, He says, "Thou art all fair, My love; there is no spot in thee." Song of Solomon 4:7.—*The Ministry of Healing*, 356.

You have captured my heart. . . .
You hold it hostage with one glance of your eyes. . . .
Your love delights me,
my treasure, my bride.

—Song of Solomon 4:9, 10, NLT

The Union of Christ and His Church

"Let us be glad and rejoice
and let us give honor to him.
For the time has come for the wedding feast of the Lamb,
and his bride has prepared herself. . . ."

And the angel said to me, "Write this:
Blessed are those who are invited to the wedding feast of the Lamb."
And he added, "These are true words that come from God."
—Revelation 19:7, 9, NLT

IN BOTH THE OLD AND THE NEW TESTAMENT, the marriage relation is employed to represent the tender and sacred union that exists between Christ and His people.—*The Desire of Ages*, 151.

A Jewish marriage was an impressive occasion, and its joy was not displeasing to the Son of man.—*The Desire of Ages*, 150.

To the mind of Jesus the gladness of the wedding festivities pointed forward to the rejoicing of that day when He shall bring home His bride to the Father's house, and the redeemed with the Redeemer shall sit down to the marriage supper of the Lamb. He says, "As the bridegroom rejoiceth over the bride, so shall thy God rejoice over thee." "Thou shalt no more be termed Forsaken; . . . but thou shalt be called My Delight; . . . for the Lord delighteth in thee." "He will rejoice over thee with joy; He will rest in His love, He will joy over thee with singing." Isaiah 62:5, 4, margin; Zephaniah 3:17. When the vision of heavenly things was granted to John the apostle, he wrote: "I heard as it were the voice of a great multitude, and as the voice of many waters, and as the voice of mighty thunderings, saying, Alleluia: for the Lord God omnipotent reigneth. Let us be glad and rejoice, and give honor to Him: for the marriage of the Lamb is come, and His wife hath made herself ready." "Blessed are they which are called unto the marriage supper of the Lamb," Revelation 19:6, 7, 9.—*The Desire of Ages*, 150, 151.

JULY 1
The Joy of Service

A Joyous Partnership With God

"[He] says of Cyrus, 'He is My shepherd,
And he shall perform all My pleasure,
Saying to Jerusalem, "You shall be built,"
And to the temple, "Your foundation shall be laid." ' "
—Isaiah 44:28, NKJV

GOD WORKS BY whom He will. He sometimes selects the humblest instrument to do the greatest work, for His power is revealed through the weakness of men. We have our standard, and by it we pronounce one thing great and another small; but God does not estimate according to our rule. We are not to suppose that what is great to us must be great to God, or that what is small to us must be small to Him. It does not rest with us to pass judgment on our talents or to choose our work. We are to take up the burdens that God appoints, bearing them for His sake, and ever going to Him for rest. Whatever our work, God is honored by wholehearted, cheerful service. He is pleased when we take up our duties with gratitude, rejoicing that we are accounted worthy to be co-laborers with Him.—*Christ's Object Lessons*, 363.

Christ accepts, oh, so gladly, every human agency that is surrendered to Him. He brings the human into union with the divine, that He may communicate to the world the mysteries of incarnate love. Talk it, pray it, sing it; proclaim abroad the message of His glory, and keep pressing onward to the regions beyond.—*Thoughts From the Mount of Blessing*, 44.

Creating Opportunities

"Behold! My Servant whom I uphold,
My Elect One in whom My soul delights!
I have put My Spirit upon Him;
He will bring forth justice to the Gentiles."

—Isaiah 42:1, NKJV

TO JESUS, WHO EMPTIED Himself for the salvation of lost humanity, the Holy Spirit was given without measure. So it will be given to every follower of Christ when the whole heart is surrendered for His indwelling. Our Lord Himself has given the command, "Be filled with the Spirit" (Ephesians 5:18), and this command is also a promise of its fulfillment. It was the good pleasure of the Father that in Christ should "all the fullness dwell," and "in Him ye are made full." Colossians 1:19, R.V.; 2:10, R.V.—*Thoughts From the Mount of Blessing*, 20.

God wants you to work, not with self-disparagement nor in discouragement, but with the strongest faith and hope, with cheerfulness and joy, representing Christ to the world. The religion of Jesus is joy, peace, and happiness. As we search the Scriptures, and see the infinite condescension of the Father in giving Jesus to the world that all who believe in Him may have everlasting life, every power of our being should be called into activity, to give praise and honor and glory to Him for His unspeakable love to the children of men.—*Testimonies for the Church*, vol. 5, 579.

Let us work now as we have never worked before. . . . We are to improve every opportunity of drawing souls to Christ. . . .

The work to be carried on by the people of God is declared in the words of Inspiration: . . . "Behold My servant, whom I uphold; Mine elect, in whom My soul delighteth; I have put My Spirit upon Him. He shall bring forth judgment to the Gentiles. . . . He shall not fail nor be discouraged, till He have set judgment in the earth: and the isles shall wait for His law." Isaiah 42:1–4.—*Testimonies for the Church*, vol. 9, 62, 64.

Healing More Than Lecturing

"Behold, I send My messenger,
And he will prepare the way before Me.
And the Lord, whom you seek,
Will suddenly come to His temple,
Even the Messenger of the covenant,
In whom you delight.
Behold, He is coming,"
Says the LORD of hosts.

—Malachi 3:1, NKJV

NEVER WAS THERE such an evangelist as Christ. He was the Majesty of heaven, but He humbled Himself to take our nature, that He might meet men where they were. To all people, rich and poor, free and bond, Christ, the Messenger of the covenant, brought the tidings of salvation. . . . He went from city to city, from town to town, preaching the gospel and healing the sick—the King of glory in the lowly garb of humanity.—*The Ministry of Healing*, 22.

He was always patient and cheerful, and the afflicted hailed Him as a messenger of life and peace. He saw the needs of men and women, children and youth, and to all He gave the invitation, "Come unto Me."

During His ministry, Jesus devoted more time to healing the sick than to preaching. His miracles testified to the truth of His words, that He came not to destroy, but to save. Wherever He went, the tidings of His mercy preceded Him. Where He had passed, the objects of His compassion were rejoicing in health and making trial of their new-found powers. Crowds were collecting around them to hear from their lips the works that the Lord had wrought. His voice was the first sound that many had ever heard, His name the first word they had ever spoken, His face the first they had ever looked upon. Why should they not love Jesus and sound His praise? As He passed through the towns and cities He was like a vital current, diffusing life and joy.—*The Ministry of Healing*, 19.

A Good Soldier of Christ

Endure suffering along with me, as a good soldier of Christ Jesus.
Soldiers don't get tied up in the affairs of civilian life,
for then they cannot please the officer who enlisted them.
—2 Timothy 2:3, 4, NLT

A GENUINE CHRISTIAN will labor only to please God, having an eye single to His glory and enjoying the reward of doing His will. . . .

. . . Love for souls for whom Christ died will lead to a denial of self and a willingness to make any sacrifice in order to be co-workers with Christ in the salvation of souls. —*Testimonies for the Church*, vol. 2, 548, 549.

The strength of an army is measured largely by the efficiency of the men in the ranks. A wise general instructs his officers to train every soldier for active service. He seeks to develop the highest efficiency on the part of all. . . . He counts on loyal and untiring service from every man in his army. . . .

And so it is in the army of Prince Immanuel. Our General, who has never lost a battle, expects willing, faithful service from everyone who has enlisted under His banner.—*Testimonies for the Church*, vol. 9, 116.

No man can succeed in the service of God unless his whole heart is in the work and he counts all things but loss for the excellency of the knowledge of Christ. No man who makes any reserve can be the disciple of Christ, much less can he be His colaborer. When men appreciate the great salvation, the self-sacrifice seen in Christ's life will be seen in theirs. Wherever He leads the way, they will rejoice to follow.—*The Desire of Ages*, 273.

The Latter Rain Will Be More Abundant Than the Former Rain

Be glad then, you children of Zion,
And rejoice in the Lord *your God;*
For He has given you the former rain faithfully,
And He will cause the rain to come down for you—
The former rain,
And the latter rain in the first month.

—Joel 2:23, NKJV

The Spirit came upon the waiting, praying disciples with a fullness that reached every heart. The Infinite One revealed Himself in power to His church. It was as if for ages this influence had been held in restraint, and now Heaven rejoiced in being able to pour out upon the church the riches of the Spirit's grace. And under the influence of the Spirit, words of penitence and confession mingled with songs of praise for sins forgiven. Words of thanksgiving and of prophecy were heard. All heaven bent low to behold and to adore the wisdom of matchless, incomprehensible love. Lost in wonder, the apostles exclaimed, "Herein is love." They grasped the imparted gift. And what followed? The sword of the Spirit, newly edged with power and bathed in the lightnings of heaven, cut its way through unbelief. Thousands were converted in a day.—*The Acts of the Apostles*, 38.

The disciples were astonished and overjoyed at the greatness of the harvest of souls.—*The Acts of the Apostles*, 44.

These scenes are to be repeated, and with greater power. The outpouring of the Holy Spirit on the day of Pentecost was the former rain, but the latter rain will be more abundant. The Spirit awaits our demand and reception.—*Christ's Object Lessons*, 121.

When the Day of Pentecost had fully come, they were all with one accord in one place. And suddenly there came a sound from heaven, as of a rushing mighty wind, and it filled the whole house where they were sitting. Then there appeared to them divided tongues, as of fire, and one sat upon each of them. And they were all filled with the Holy Spirit and began to speak with other tongues, as the Spirit gave them utterance.

—Acts 2:1–4, NKJV

Serving Gladly Every Day

Serve the LORD *with gladness;*
Come before His presence with singing.
Know that the LORD, *He is God;*
It is He who has made us, and not we ourselves;
We are His people and the sheep of His pasture.

—Psalm 100:2, 3, NKJV

THERE IS COMFORT AND JOY in the service of Christ.—*The Ministry of Healing*, 487.

He desires us to serve Him in newness of life, with gladness every day.—*Christ's Object Lessons*, 299.

The exceeding rewards for right-doing, the enjoyment of heaven, the society of the angels, the communion and love of God and His Son, the elevation and extension of all our powers throughout eternal ages—are these not mighty incentives and encouragements to urge us to give the heart's loving service to our Creator and Redeemer?—*Steps to Christ*, 21.

All the varied capabilities that men possess—of mind and soul and body—are given them by God, to be so employed as to reach the highest possible degree of excellence. But this cannot be a selfish and exclusive culture; for the character of God, whose likeness we are to receive, is benevolence and love. Every faculty, every attribute, with which the Creator has endowed us is to be employed for His glory and for the uplifting of our fellow men. And in this employment is found its purest, noblest, and happiest exercise.—*Patriarchs and Prophets*, 595.

"Heal the sick, cleanse the lepers, raise the dead, cast out demons.
Freely you have received, freely give."

—Matthew 10:8, NKJV

Ready to Spend and Be Spent

I will very gladly spend and be spent for your souls;
though the more abundantly I love you,
the less I am loved.

—2 Corinthians 12:15, NKJV

HOWEVER TRYING THEIR LABOR, the true workers do not regard it as drudgery. They are ready to spend and to be spent; but it is a cheerful work, done with a glad heart. Joy in God is expressed through Jesus Christ. Their joy is the joy set before Christ—"to do the will of Him that sent Me, and to finish His work." John 4:34. They are in co-operation with the Lord of glory. This thought sweetens all toil, it braces the will, it nerves the spirit for whatever may befall. Working with unselfish heart, ennobled by being partakers of Christ's sufferings, sharing His sympathies, and co-operating with Him in His labor, they help to swell the tide of His joy and bring honor and praise to His exalted name.

This is the spirit of all true service for God. . . .

And however short our service or humble our work, if in simple faith we follow Christ, we shall not be disappointed of the reward. . . . Blessed will be the recompense of grace to those who have wrought for God in the simplicity of faith and love.—*Christ's Object Lessons*, 402, 403, 404.

"But take careful heed to do the commandment and the law
which Moses the servant of the LORD commanded you,
to love the LORD your God, to walk in all His ways,
to keep His commandments, to hold fast to Him,
and to serve Him with all your heart and with all your soul."

—Joshua 22:5, NKJV

Finding Joy in Any Sacrifice for Him

What thanks can we render to God for you,
for all the joy with which we rejoice for your sake before our God,
night and day praying exceedingly that we may see your face
and perfect what is lacking in your faith?
—1 Thessalonians 3:9, 10, NKJV

LOVE TO JESUS will be manifested in a desire to work as He worked for the blessing and uplifting of humanity. It will lead to love, tenderness, and sympathy toward all the creatures of our heavenly Father's care.

The Saviour's life on earth was not a life of ease and devotion to Himself, but He toiled with persistent, earnest, untiring effort for the salvation of lost mankind. . . .

So those who are the partakers of the grace of Christ will be ready to make any sacrifice, that others for whom He died may share the heavenly gift. They will do all they can to make the world better for their stay in it.—*Steps to Christ*, 77, 78.

But if you call God your Father you acknowledge yourselves His children, to be guided by His wisdom and to be obedient in all things, knowing that His love is changeless. You will accept His plan for your life. As children of God, you will hold His honor, His character, His family, His work, as the objects of your highest interest. It will be your joy to recognize and honor your relation to your Father and to every member of His family. You will rejoice to do any act, however humble, that will tend to His glory or to the well-being of your kindred.—*Thoughts From the Mount of Blessing*, 105.

I have been crucified with Christ; it is no longer I who live,
but Christ lives in me; and the life which I now live in the flesh
I live by faith in the Son of God, who loved me and gave Himself for me.
—Galatians 2:20, NKJV

JULY 9
The Joy of Service

Let Us Not Build Walls of Separation

"You did not serve the L*ORD your God*
with joy and gladness of heart, for the abundance of everything."
—Deuteronomy 28:47, NKJV

GOD CHOSE ISRAEL to reveal His character to men. He desired them to be as wells of salvation in the world. To them were committed the oracles of heaven, the revelation of God's will. . . .

But the people of Israel lost sight of their high privileges as God's representatives. They forgot God and failed to fulfill their holy mission. The blessings they received brought no blessing to the world. All their advantages they appropriated for their own glorification. They shut themselves away from the world in order to escape temptation. The restrictions that God had placed upon their association with idolaters as a means of preventing them from conforming to the practices of the heathen, they used to build up a wall of separation between themselves and all other nations. They robbed God of the service He required of them, and they robbed their fellow men of religious guidance and a holy example. . . .

The Jewish leaders thought themselves too wise to need instruction, too righteous to need salvation, too highly honored to need the honor that comes from Christ. The Saviour turned from them to entrust to others the privileges they had abused and the work they had slighted.—*The Acts of the Apostles*, 14, 16.

"Go ye into all the world, and preach the gospel to every creature" (Mark 16:15), is Christ's command to His followers. Not that all are called to be ministers or missionaries in the ordinary sense of the term; but all may be workers with Him in giving the "glad tidings" to their fellow men. To all, great or small, learned or ignorant, old or young, the command is given.—*Education*, 264.

Treating Christ's Servants Well

Receive him therefore in the Lord with all gladness,
and hold such men in esteem.
—Philippians 2:29, NKJV

THE MISSION OF CHRIST'S SERVANTS is a high honor, and a sacred trust. "He that receiveth you," He says, "receiveth Me, and he that receiveth Me receiveth Him that sent Me." No act of kindness shown to them in His name will fail to be recognized and rewarded. And in the same tender recognition He includes the feeblest and lowliest of the family of God: "Whosoever shall give to drink unto one of these little ones"—those who are as children in their faith and their knowledge of Christ—"a cup of cold water only in the name of a disciple, verily I say unto you, he shall in nowise lose his reward."—*The Desire of Ages*, 357.

To all who, in time of trial and want, give sympathy and assistance to others more needy, God has promised great blessing. He has not changed. . . . No less sure now than when spoken by our Saviour is the promise, "He that receiveth a prophet in the name of a prophet shall receive a prophet's reward." Matthew 10:41.

"Be not forgetful to entertain strangers: for thereby some have entertained angels unawares." Hebrews 13:2. These words have lost none of their force through the lapse of time. Our heavenly Father still continues to place in the pathway of His children opportunities that are blessings in disguise; and those who improve these opportunities find great joy.—*Prophets and Kings*, 131, 132.

"And the King will answer and say to them,
'Assuredly, I say to you, inasmuch as you did it
to one of the least of these My brethren, you did it to Me.' "
—Matthew 25:40, NKJV

The Greatest Joy

"What man of you, having an hundred sheep,
if he loses one of them, does not leave the ninety-nine in the wilderness, and go after the one which is lost until he finds it?
And when he has found it, he lays it on his shoulders, rejoicing.
And when he comes home, he calls together his friends and neighbors, saying to them, 'Rejoice with me, for I have found my sheep which was lost!' "

—Luke 15:4–6, NKJV

THE PARABLE OF THE STRAYING SHEEP should be treasured as a motto in every household. The divine Shepherd leaves the ninety and nine, and goes out into the wilderness to seek the one that is lost. There are thickets, quagmires, and dangerous crevices in the rocks, and the Shepherd knows that if the sheep is in any of these places, a friendly hand must help it out. As He hears its bleating afar off, He encounters any and every difficulty that He may save His sheep that is lost. When He discovers the lost one, He does not greet it with reproaches. He is only glad that He has found it alive. With firm yet gentle hand He parts the briers or takes it from the mire; tenderly He lifts it to His shoulders and bears it back to the fold. The pure, sinless Redeemer bears the sinful, the unclean.

The Sin Bearer carries the befouled sheep; yet so precious is His burden that He rejoices, singing: "I have found My sheep which was lost." Luke 15:6. . . .

. . . We must bear in mind the great joy manifested by the Shepherd at the recovery of the lost. He calls upon His neighbors: "Rejoice with Me; for I have found My sheep which was lost." And all heaven echoes the note of joy. The Father Himself joys over the rescued one with singing. What a holy ecstasy of joy is expressed in this parable! That joy it is your privilege to share.

Are you, who have this example before you, co-operating with Him who is seeking to save the lost? Are you colaborers with Christ?—*Testimonies for the Church*, vol. 6, 124, 125.

Exalting Christ

But that doesn't matter. Whether their motives are false or genuine,
the message about Christ is being preached either way,
so I rejoice. And I will continue to rejoice.
—Philippians 1:18, NLT

THE DUTY AND DELIGHT of all service is to uplift Christ before the people. This is the end of all true labor. Let Christ appear; let self be hidden behind Him.—*Testimonies for the Church*, vol. 9, 147.

The heart of the true Christian is imbued with true love, with a most earnest hunger for souls. He is not at rest until he is doing all that is in his power to seek and to save that which is lost. Time and strength are spent; toilsome work is not shunned. Others must be given the truth which has brought to his own soul such gladness and peace and joy in the Holy Ghost.

When the truly converted soul enjoys the love of God, he will feel his obligation to yoke up with Christ and work in harmony with Him. The Spirit of Christ rests upon him. He reveals the Saviour's love, pity, and compassion, because he is one with Christ. He yearns to bring others to Jesus. His heart is melted with tenderness as he sees the peril of the souls that are out of Christ. He watches for souls as one that must give an account. With invitations and pleadings mingled with assurances of the promises of God, he seeks to win souls to Christ; and it is registered in the books of record. He is a laborer together with God.—*Testimonies to Ministers and Gospel Workers*, 122.

Be diligent to present yourself approved to God,
a worker who does not need to be ashamed,
rightly dividing the word of truth.
—2 Timothy 2:15, NKJV

Making Others Happy

Not that we lord it over your faith,
but we work with you for your joy,
for you stand firm in your faith.

—2 Corinthians 1:24, ESV

HE WHO IS FOLLOWING the divine guidance has found the only true source of saving grace and real happiness, and has gained the power of imparting happiness to all around him.—*Messages to Young People*, 264.

You are not placed on earth merely to delve for self, to dig and build, to toil and spin, but to make life bright and joyous and beautiful with the love of Christ—like the flowers, to gladden other lives by the ministry of love.—*Thoughts From the Mount of Blessing*, 97.

There is nothing, save the selfish heart of man, that lives unto itself. No bird that cleaves the air, no animal that moves upon the ground, but ministers to some other life. There is no leaf of the forest, or lowly blade of grass, but has its ministry. Every tree and shrub and leaf pours forth that element of life without which neither man nor animal could live; and man and animal, in turn, minister to the life of tree and shrub and leaf. . . . The sun sheds its light to gladden a thousand worlds. The ocean, itself the source of all our springs and fountains, receives the streams from every land, but takes to give.—*The Desire of Ages*, 20.

Seeking to make yourself happy . . . is poor work, unprofitable business.—*Testimonies for the Church*, vol. 2, 56.

The greatest happiness experienced will be in doing others good, in making others happy. Such happiness will be lasting.—*Testimonies for the Church*, vol. 1, 161.

Watchful of Opportunities to Bring Joy

"I helped those without hope, and they blessed me.
And I caused the widows' hearts to sing for joy."

—Job 29:13, NLT

GOD CALLS NOT ONLY for our gifts for the needy, but for our cheerful countenance, our hopeful words, our kindly handclasp. When Christ healed the sick, He laid His hands upon them. So should we come in close touch with those whom we seek to benefit.

There are many from whom hope has departed. Bring back the sunshine to them. Many have lost their courage. Speak to them words of cheer. Pray for them. There are those who need the bread of life. Read to them from the word of God. Upon many is a soul sickness which no earthly balm can reach nor physician heal. Pray for these souls, bring them to Jesus. Tell them that there is a balm in Gilead and a Physician there.—*Christ's Object Lessons*, 418.

We should lose no opportunity of performing deeds of mercy, of tender forethought and Christian courtesy, for the burdened and the oppressed. If we can do no more, we may speak words of courage and hope to those who are unacquainted with God, and who can be approached most easily by the avenue of sympathy and love.

Rich and abundant are the promises made to those who are watchful of opportunities to bring joy and blessing into the lives of others.—*Prophets and Kings*, 327.

Finally, all of you should be of one mind.
Sympathize with each other. Love each other as brothers and sisters.
Be tenderhearted, and keep a humble attitude.

—1 Peter 3:8, NLT

Showing Respect to Ministers and Leaders

Obey those who rule over you,
and be submissive, for they watch out for your souls,
as those who must give account. Let them do so with joy
and not with grief, for that would be unprofitable for you.

—Hebrews 13:17, NKJV

THE FIFTH COMMANDMENT requires children not only to yield respect, submission, and obedience to their parents, but also to give them love and tenderness, to lighten their cares, to guard their reputation, and to succor and comfort them in old age. It also enjoins respect for ministers and rulers and for all others to whom God has delegated authority.—*Patriarchs and Prophets*, 308.

Men and women are to be brought under the influence of true, earnest, wholehearted workers, who labor for souls as they that must give an account. All who are baptized into a measure of the apostolic spirit will be constrained to become God's missionaries. If they will be true, firm in the faith, if they will not sell their Lord for gain, but will ever acknowledge the divine supremacy and superintendence, God will prepare the way before them and will greatly bless them. He will help them to represent His goodness, love, and mercy. And the glory of the Lord will be their rearward. There will be joy in the heavenly courts, and joy, pure, heavenly joy, will fill the hearts of the workers.—*Testimonies for the Church*, vol. 9, 58.

"He changes times and seasons,
deposes kings and sets up kings;
he gives wisdom to the wise
and knowledge to those who have understanding.
He reveals deep and hidden things;
he knows what is in the darkness,
and light dwells with him."

—Daniel 2:21, 22, NRSV

We Should Be Sources of Joy

How I praise the Lord that you are concerned about me again.
I know you have always been concerned for me,
but you didn't have the chance to help me.
—Philippians 4:10, NLT

DIVINE WISDOM HAS APPOINTED, in the plan of salvation, the law of action and reaction, making the work of beneficence, in all its branches, twice blessed. He that gives to the needy blesses others, and is blessed himself in a still greater degree. God could have reached His object in saving sinners without the aid of man; but He knew that man could not be happy without acting a part in the great work in which he would be cultivating self-denial and benevolence.—*Testimonies for the Church*, vol. 3, 382.

God positively enjoins upon all His followers a duty to bless others with their influence and means, and to seek that wisdom of Him which will enable them to do all in their power to elevate the thoughts and affections of those who come within their influence. In doing for others, a sweet satisfaction will be experienced, an inward peace which will be a sufficient reward. When actuated by a high and noble desire to do others good, they will find true happiness in a faithful discharge of life's manifold duties. This will bring more than an earthly reward; for every faithful, unselfish performance of duty is noticed by the angels and shines in the life record. In heaven none will think of self, nor seek their own pleasure; but all, from pure, genuine love, will seek the happiness of the heavenly beings around them. If we wish to enjoy heavenly society in the earth made new, we must be governed by heavenly principles here.—*Testimonies for the Church*, vol. 2, 132.

Joy for a Change of Heart

*I am not sorry that I sent that severe letter to you,
though I was sorry at first, for I know it was painful
to you for a little while. Now I am glad I sent it,
not because it hurt you, but because the pain caused you
to repent and change your ways.It was the kind of sorrow
God wants his people to have, so you were not harmed
by us in any way.*

—2 Corinthians 7:8, 9, NLT

PAUL . . . HAD HOPED to meet Titus at Troas and to learn from him how the words of counsel and reproof sent to the Corinthian brethren had been received, but in this he was disappointed. "I had no rest in my spirit," he wrote concerning this experience, "because I found not Titus my brother." He therefore left Troas and crossed over to Macedonia, where, at Philippi he met Timothy. . . .

This faithful messenger brought the cheering news that a wonderful change had taken place among the Corinthian believers. Many had accepted the instruction contained in Paul's letter and had repented of their sins. Their lives were no longer a reproach to Christianity, but exerted a powerful influence in favor of practical godliness.

Filled with joy, the apostle sent another letter to the Corinthian believers, expressing his gladness of heart because of the good work wrought in them: "Though I made you sorry with a letter, I do not repent, though I did repent." . . . "Now I rejoice," he continued, "not that ye were made sorry, but that ye sorrowed to repentance." . . .

For some time Paul had been carrying a burden of soul for the churches—a burden so heavy that he could scarcely endure it. . . .

But now one cause of anxiety was removed. At the tidings of the acceptance of his letter to the Corinthians, Paul broke forth into words of rejoicing. . . .

. . . He felt that Satan was not to triumph over the work of God in Corinth, and in words of praise he poured forth the gratitude of his heart.—*The Acts of the Apostles*, 323–326.

Happiness Found in Serving Others

Knowing this, I am convinced that I will remain alive
so I can continue to help all of you grow and experience
the joy of your faith. And when I come to you again, you will have even more reason to take
pride in Christ Jesus because of what
he is doing through me.

—Philippians 1:25, 26, NLT

THE SPIRIT OF UNSELFISH LABOR for others gives depth, stability, and Christlike loveliness to the character, and brings peace and happiness to its possessor. The aspirations are elevated. There is no room for sloth or selfishness. Those who thus exercise the Christian graces will grow and will become strong to work for God. They will have clear spiritual perceptions, a steady, growing faith, and an increased power in prayer. The Spirit of God, moving upon their spirit, calls forth the sacred harmonies of the soul in answer to the divine touch. Those who thus devote themselves to unselfish effort for the good of others are most surely working out their own salvation.—*Steps to Christ*, 80.

Seize every opportunity to contribute to the happiness of those around you, sharing with them your affection. Words of kindness, looks of sympathy, expressions of appreciation, would to many a struggling, lonely one be as a cup of cold water to a thirsty soul. A word of cheer, an act of kindness, would go far to lighten the burdens that are resting heavily upon weary shoulders. It is in unselfish ministry that true happiness is found.—*Testimonies for the Church*, vol. 7, 49.

"What does the LORD your God require of you,
but to fear the LORD your God, to walk in all His ways and to love Him,
to serve the LORD your God with all your heart and with all your soul,
and to keep the commandments of the LORD and His statutes
which I command you today for your good?"

—Deuteronomy 10:12, 13, NKJV

The Happy Christian Makes Others Happy

Let each of us please his neighbor
for his good, leading to edification.
For even Christ did not please Himself; but as it is written,
"The reproaches of those who reproached You fell on Me."
—Romans 15:2, 3, NKJV

IT IS THE NATURE OF CHRISTIANITY to make happy families and happy society. Discord, selfishness, and strife will be put away from every man and woman who possesses the true spirit of Christ.—*Testimonies for the Church*, vol. 4, 520.

God's standard of man is elevated to the highest meaning of the term, and if he acts up to his God-given manhood he will promote happiness in this life, which will lead to glory and an eternal reward in the life to come.

The members of the human family are entitled to the name of men and women only when they employ their talents, in every possible way, for the good of others. The life of Christ is before us as a pattern.—*Testimonies for the Church*, vol. 4, 520.

Those who feel no special pleasure in seeking to be a blessing to others, in working, even at a sacrifice, to do them good, cannot have the spirit of Christ or of heaven; for they have no union with the work of heavenly angels and cannot participate in the bliss that imparts elevated joy to them. Christ has said: "Joy shall be in heaven over one sinner that repenteth, more than over ninety and nine just persons, which need no repentance." If the joy of angels is to see sinners repent, will it not be the joy of sinners, saved by the blood of Christ, to see others repent and turn to Christ through their instrumentality? In working in harmony with Christ and the holy angels we shall experience a joy that cannot be realized aside from this work.—*Testimonies for the Church*, vol. 3, 381.

Working With God Brings Happiness

Be merciful to me, O Lord,
For I cry to You all day long.
Rejoice the soul of Your servant,
For to You, O Lord, I lift up my soul.
For You, Lord, are good, and ready to forgive,
And abundant in mercy to all those who call upon You.
—Psalm 86:3–5, NKJV

THE FACES OF MEN AND WOMEN who walk and work with God express the peace of heaven. They are surrounded with the atmosphere of heaven. For these souls the kingdom of God has begun. They have Christ's joy, the joy of being a blessing to humanity. They have the honor of being accepted for the Master's use; they are trusted to do His work in His name.—*The Desire of Ages*, 312.

God might have committed the message of the gospel, and all the work of loving ministry, to the heavenly angels. He might have employed other means for accomplishing His purpose. But in His infinite love He chose to make us co-workers with Himself, with Christ and the angels, that we might share the blessing, the joy, the spiritual uplifting, which results from this unselfish ministry.—*Steps to Christ*, 79.

In proportion as the love of Christ fills our hearts and controls our lives, covetousness, selfishness, and love of ease will be overcome, and it will be our pleasure to do the will of Christ, whose servants we claim to be. Our happiness will then be proportionate to our unselfish works, prompted by the love of Christ.—*Testimonies for the Church*, vol. 3, 382.

For a time is coming when people will no longer listen to sound and wholesome teaching.
They will . . . look for teachers who will tell them whatever their itching ears want to hear.
They will reject the truth and chase after myths.
But you should keep a clear mind in every situation.
Don't be afraid of suffering for the Lord. Work at telling others the Good News,
and fully carry out the ministry God has given you.
—2 Timothy 4:3–5, NLT

The Joy Found in Worship

Serve the L*ORD with fear,*
And rejoice with trembling.

—Psalm 2:11, NKJV

WHATEVER COMES, let it not enfeeble your moral courage and cause your religion to degenerate into a heartless form. The loving Jesus is ready to bless abundantly; but we need to obtain an experience in faith, in earnest prayer, and in rejoicing in the love of God. Shall any of us be weighed in the balances and be found wanting? We must watch ourselves, watch the least unholy promptings of our nature, lest we become traitors to the high responsibilities God has bestowed upon us as His human agencies.—*Testimonies for the Church*, vol. 5, 532.

Every living Christian will be a disinterested worker for God. The Lord has given us a knowledge of His will that we may become channels of light to others. If Christ is abiding in us, we cannot help working for Him. It is impossible to retain the favor of God and enjoy the blessing of a Saviour's love, and yet be indifferent to the danger of those who are perishing in their sins. "Herein is My Father glorified, that ye bear much fruit."—*Testimonies for the Church*, vol. 5, 238.

The world's Redeemer did not design that His purchased inheritance should live and die in their sins. Why, then, are so few reached and saved? It is because so many of those who profess to be Christians are working in the same lines as the great apostate. Thousands who know not God might today be rejoicing in His love if those who claim to serve Him would work as Christ worked.—*Testimonies for the Church*, vol. 6, 273.

I urge, then, first of all, that petitions, prayers, intercession and thanksgiving
be made for all people. . . . This is good, and pleases God our Savior,
who wants all people to be saved and to come to a knowledge of the truth.

—1 Timothy 2:1, 3, 4, NIV

Serving Is the Source of Our Greatest Joy

"Behold, My servants shall sing for joy of heart,
But you shall cry for sorrow of heart,
And wail for grief of spirit."

—Isaiah 65:14, NKJV

IN OUR LIFE HERE, earthly, sin-restricted though it is, the greatest joy and the highest education are in service. And in the future state, untrammeled by the limitations of sinful humanity, it is in service that our greatest joy and our highest education will be found—witnessing, and ever as we witness learning anew "the riches of the glory of this mystery;" "which is Christ in you, the hope of glory." Colossians 1:27.—*Education*, 309.

We do not, as followers of Christ, realize our true position. We do not have correct views of our responsibilities as hired servants of Christ. He has advanced us the wages in His suffering life and spilled blood, to bind us in willing servitude to Himself. All the good things we have are a loan from our Saviour. He has made us stewards. Our smallest offerings, our humblest services, presented in faith and love, may be consecrated gifts to win souls to the service of the Master and to promote His glory. The interest and prosperity of Christ's kingdom should be paramount to every other consideration. Those who make their pleasure and selfish interest the chief objects of their lives are not faithful stewards.

Those who deny self to do others good, and who devote themselves and all they have to Christ's service, will realize the happiness which the selfish man seeks for in vain.—*Testimonies for the Church*, vol. 3, 397.

And whatever you do, do it heartily, as to the Lord and not to men.

—Colossians 3:23, NKJV

Filled With the Holy Ghost

And the disciples were filled with joy
and with the Holy Spirit.

—Acts 13:52, NKJV

THE HOLY SPIRIT is the breath of spiritual life in the soul. The impartation of the Spirit is the impartation of the life of Christ.—*The Desire of Ages*, 805.

No sooner does one come to Christ than there is born in his heart a desire to make known to others what a precious friend he has found in Jesus; the saving and sanctifying truth cannot be shut up in his heart. If we are clothed with the righteousness of Christ and are filled with the joy of His indwelling Spirit, we shall not be able to hold our peace. If we have tasted and seen that the Lord is good we shall have something to tell. Like Philip when he found the Saviour, we shall invite others into His presence. We shall seek to present to them the attractions of Christ and the unseen realities of the world to come. There will be an intensity of desire to follow in the path that Jesus trod. There will be an earnest longing that those around us may "behold the Lamb of God, which taketh away the sin of the world." John 1:29.

And the effort to bless others will react in blessings upon ourselves. This was the purpose of God in giving us a part to act in the plan of redemption. He has granted men the privilege of becoming partakers of the divine nature and, in their turn, of diffusing blessings to their fellow men.—*Steps to Christ*, 78, 79.

And because of his glory and excellence, he has given us great and precious promises.
These are the promises that enable you to share his divine nature
and escape the world's corruption caused by human desires.

—2 Peter 1:4, NLT

The Revelation of the Lord's Joy in Our Lives

Then he said unto them, "Go your way, eat the fat, drink the sweet, and send portions to those for whom nothing is prepared; for this day is holy to our Lord. Do not sorrow, for the joy of the LORD *is your strength."*

—Nehemiah 8:10, NKJV

GOD IN HIS PROVIDENCE has willed that no one can secure happiness by living for himself alone. The joy of our Lord consisted in enduring toil and shame for others, that they might be benefited thereby. We are capable of being happy in following His example and living to bless our fellow men.

We are invited by our Lord to take His yoke and bear His burden. In doing this we may be happy. In bearing our own self-imposed yoke and carrying our own burdens, we find no rest; but in bearing the yoke of Christ there is rest to the soul. Those who want some great work to do for the Master can find it just where they are, in doing good and in being self-forgetful and self-sacrificing, remembering others and carrying sunshine wherever they go.—*Testimonies for the Church*, vol. 4, 224.

All heaven is waiting for channels through which can be poured the holy oil to be a joy and blessing to human hearts.

Christ has made every provision that His church shall be a transformed body, illumined with the Light of the world, possessing the glory of Emmanuel. It is His purpose that every Christian shall be surrounded with a spiritual atmosphere of light and peace. He desires that we shall reveal His own joy in our lives.—*Christ's Object Lessons*, 419.

"Don't be dejected and sad, for the joy of the LORD *is your strength!"*

—Nehemiah 8:10, NLT

The Joy Found in Saving the Lost

*"And he said to him, 'Son, you are always with me,
and all that I have is yours. It was right that we should make merry and be glad, for your brother was dead and is alive again,
and was lost and is found.' "*

—Luke 15:31, 32, NKJV

You claim to be a child of God; but if this claim be true, it is "thy brother" that was "dead, and is alive again; and was lost, and is found." He is bound to you by the closest ties; for God recognizes him as a son. Deny your relationship to him, and you show that you are but a hireling in the household, not a child in the family.—*Christ's Object Lessons*, 211.

When you see yourselves as sinners saved only by the love of your heavenly Father, you will have tender pity for others who are suffering in sin. You will no longer meet misery and repentance with jealousy and censure. When the ice of selfishness is melted from your hearts, you will be in sympathy with God, and will share His joy in the saving of the lost.—*Christ's Object Lessons*, 210.

God has qualified His people to enlighten the world. He has entrusted them with faculties by which they are to extend His work until it shall encircle the globe. . . .

. . . In far-off countries, from those whose hearts are by these agencies turned from the service of sin unto righteousness, will be heard thanksgiving and the voice of melody. By their songs of grateful praise a testimony will be borne that will win others to allegiance to and fellowship with Christ.

The conversion of souls to God is the greatest, the noblest work in which human beings can have a part. In this work are revealed God's power, His holiness, His forbearance, and His unbounded love. Every true conversion glorifies Him and causes the angels to break forth into singing.—*Testimonies for the Church*, vol. 7, 51, 52.

The Joy of Christ

"Now I am coming to you.
I told them many things while I was with them
in this world so they would be filled with my joy."

—John 17:13, NLT

THE JOY SET BEFORE CHRIST, the joy that sustained Him through sacrifice and suffering, was the joy of seeing sinners saved. This should be the joy of every follower of His, the spur to his ambition.—*Prophets and Kings*, 172.

God has given to every man his work, and no one else can do that work for him. Oh, that you individually would apply the eyesalve, that you might see your defects of character and realize how God regards your love of the world, which is crowding out the love of God. Nothing can give you such power, such true self-reliance and nobility of soul, as a sense of the dignity of your work, an assurance that you are co-laborers with God in doing good and saving souls.

The Son of God came to this world to leave an example of a perfect life. He sacrificed Himself for the joy that was set before Him, the joy of seeing souls rescued from Satan's grasp and saved in the kingdom of God. "Follow Me" was Christ's command. Those who follow His example will share in the divine work of doing good and will finally enter into the joy of their Lord.—*Testimonies for the Church*, vol. 4, 615.

That joy, to which Christ Himself looks forward with eager desire, is presented in His request to His Father, "I will that they also, whom Thou hast given Me, be with Me where I am." [John 17:24].—*Gospel Workers*, 516.

"Father, I desire that they also whom You gave Me may be with Me where I am,
that they may behold My glory which You have given Me;
for You loved Me before the foundation of the world."

—John 17:24, NKJV

The Angels Rejoice When Sinners Repent

"I say to you that likewise there will be more joy in heaven over one sinner who repents than over ninety-nine just persons who need no repentance. . . .
. . . Likewise, I say to you, there is joy in the presence of the angels of God over one sinner who repents."
—Luke 15:7, 10, NKJV

THERE IS MORE JOY in the presence of the angels in heaven over one sinner that repents than over ninety and nine just persons who need no repentance. There is joy with the Father and with Christ. All heaven is interested in the salvation of man. He who is instrumental in saving a soul is at liberty to rejoice; for angels of God have witnessed his efforts with the most intense interest, and rejoice with him in his success.—*Testimonies for the Church*, vol. 4, 263.

Humanity is still as much the object of heaven's solicitude as when common men of common occupations met angels at noonday, and talked with the heavenly messengers in the vineyards and the fields. To us in the common walks of life, heaven may be very near. Angels from the courts above will attend the steps of those who come and go at God's command.—*The Desire of Ages*, 48.

All the resources of heaven are at the command of those who are seeking to save the lost. Angels will help you to reach the most careless and the most hardened. And when one is brought back to God, all heaven is made glad; seraphs and cherubs touch their golden harps, and sing praises to God and the Lamb for their mercy and loving-kindness to the children of men.—*Christ's Object Lessons*, 197.

For God saved us and called us to live a holy life.
He did this, not because we deserved it, but because that was his plan from before the beginning of time—to show us his grace through Christ Jesus.
—2 Timothy 1:9, NLT

The Angels Labor With Us

Bless the LORD, you His angels,
Who excel in strength, who do His word,
Heeding the voice of His word.

—Psalm 103:20, NKJV

IN THE PRESENCE CHAMBER of the King of kings they wait—"angels, that excel in strength," "ministers of His, that do His pleasure," "hearkening unto the voice of His word." Psalm 103:19–21; Revelation 5:11. Ten thousand times ten thousand and thousands of thousands, were the heavenly messengers beheld by the prophet Daniel. The apostle Paul declared them "an innumerable company." Daniel 7:10; Hebrews 12:22. As God's messengers they go forth, like "the appearance of a flash of lightning" (Ezekiel 1:14), so dazzling their glory, and so swift their flight. . . .

Angels are sent on missions of mercy to the children of God. To Abraham, with promises of blessing; to the gates of Sodom, to rescue righteous Lot from its fiery doom; to Elijah, as he was about to perish from weariness and hunger in the desert; to Elisha, with chariots and horses of fire surrounding the little town where he was shut in by his foes; to Daniel, while seeking divine wisdom in the court of a heathen king, or abandoned to become the lions' prey; to Peter, doomed to death in Herod's dungeon; to the prisoners at Philippi; to Paul and his companions in the night of tempest on the sea; to open the mind of Cornelius to receive the gospel; to dispatch Peter with the message of salvation to the Gentile stranger—thus holy angels have, in all ages, ministered to God's people.—*The Great Controversy*, 511, 512.

And the angel answered and said to him, "I am Gabriel, who stands
in the presence of God, and was sent to speak to you
and bring you these glad tidings."

—Luke 1:19, NKJV

United With the Angels

Bless the L*ORD*, *all you His hosts,*
You ministers of His, who do His pleasure.

—Psalm 103:21, NKJV

ANGELS OF GLORY that do always behold the face of the Father in heaven, joy in ministering to His little ones. Angels are ever present where they are most needed, with those who have the hardest battles with self to fight, and whose surroundings are the most discouraging. Weak and trembling souls who have many objectionable traits of character are their special charge. That which selfish hearts would regard as humiliating service, ministering to those who are wretched and in every way inferior in character, is the work of the pure, sinless beings from the courts above.—*The Ministry of Healing*, 105.

We are to be laborers together with the heavenly angels in presenting Jesus to the world. With almost impatient eagerness the angels wait for our co-operation; for man must be the channel to communicate with man. And when we give ourselves to Christ in wholehearted devotion, angels rejoice that they may speak through our voices to reveal God's love.—*The Desire of Ages*, 297.

Is there not something stimulating and inspiring in this thought, that the human agent stands as the visible instrument to confer the blessings of angelic agencies? As we are thus laborers together with God, the work bears the inscription of the divine. The knowledge and activity of the heavenly workers, united with the knowledge and power that are imparted to human agencies, bring relief to the oppressed and distressed. Our acts of unselfish ministry make us partakers in the success that results from the relief offered.

With what joy heaven looks upon these blended influences!—*Testimonies for the Church*, vol. 6, 457.

Angels Minister to Our Needs

Are they not all ministering spirits sent forth to minister for those who will inherit salvation?

—Hebrews 1:14, NKJV

TODAY, AS VERILY AS IN THE DAYS of the apostles, heavenly messengers are passing through the length and breadth of the land, seeking to comfort the sorrowing, to protect the impenitent, to win the hearts of men to Christ. We cannot see them personally; nevertheless they are with us, guiding, directing, protecting.

Heaven is brought near to earth by that mystic ladder, the base of which is firmly planted on the earth, while the topmost round reaches the throne of the Infinite. Angels are constantly ascending and descending this ladder of shining brightness, bearing the prayers of the needy and distressed to the Father above, and bringing blessing and hope, courage and help, to the children of men. These angels of light create a heavenly atmosphere about the soul, lifting us toward the unseen and the eternal. We cannot behold their forms with our natural sight; only by spiritual vision can we discern heavenly things. The spiritual ear alone can hear the harmony of heavenly voices. . . .

We need to understand better than we do the mission of the angels. It would be well to remember that every true child of God has the co-operation of heavenly beings. Invisible armies of light and power attend the meek and lowly ones who believe and claim the promises of God. Cherubim and seraphim, and angels that excel in strength, stand at God's right hand, "all ministering spirits, sent forth to minister for them who shall be heirs of salvation." Hebrews 1:14.—*The Acts of the Apostles*, 152–154.

Guardian Angels

He shall give His angels charge over you,
To keep you in all your ways.
In their hands they shall bear you up,
Lest you dash your foot against a stone.
—Psalm 91:11, 12, NKJV

THE ANGEL OF THE LORD encampeth round about them that fear Him, and delivereth them." Psalm 34:7. God commissions His angels to save His chosen ones from calamity, to guard them from "the pestilence that walketh in darkness" and "the destruction that wasteth at noonday." Psalm 91:6. Again and again have angels talked with men as a man speaketh with a friend, and led them to places of security. Again and again have the encouraging words of angels renewed the drooping spirits of the faithful and, carrying their minds above the things of earth, caused them to behold by faith the white robes, the crowns, the palm branches of victory, which overcomers will receive when they surround the great white throne.—*The Acts of the Apostles*, 153.

Oh, that we could all realize the nearness of heaven to earth! When the earthborn children know it not, they have angels of light as their companions. A silent witness guards every soul that lives, seeking to draw that soul to Christ. As long as there is hope, until men resist the Holy Spirit to their eternal ruin, they are guarded by heavenly intelligences.—*Testimonies for the Church*, vol. 6, 366.

In all ages, angels have been near to Christ's faithful followers. The vast confederacy of evil is arrayed against all who would overcome; but Christ would have us look to the things which are not seen, to the armies of heaven encamped about all who love God, to deliver them. From what dangers, seen and unseen, we have been preserved through the interposition of the angels, we shall never know, until in the light of eternity we see the providences of God. Then we shall know that the whole family of heaven was interested in the family here below, and that messengers from the throne of God attended our steps from day to day.—*The Desire of Ages*, 240.

AUGUST 1
Delight and Goodwill

God Finds Pleasure in Rectitude

"I know, my God, that you examine our hearts and rejoice when you find integrity there. You know I have done all this with good motives, and I have watched your people offer their gifts willingly and joyously."

—1 Chronicles 29:17, NLT

CHRIST IS PLEASED with His followers when they show that, though human, they are partakers of the divine nature.—*The Desire of Ages*, 153.

Not by their wealth, their education, or their position does God estimate men. He estimates them by their purity of motive and their beauty of character.—*The Ministry of Healing*, 477.

Moral perfection is required of all. Never should we lower the standard of righteousness in order to accommodate inherited or cultivated tendencies to wrong-doing. We need to understand that imperfection of character is sin. All righteous attributes of character dwell in God as a perfect, harmonious whole, and everyone who receives Christ as a personal Saviour is privileged to possess these attributes.—*Christ's Object Lessons*, 330.

Be ambitious, for the Master's glory, to cultivate every grace of character. In every phase of your character building you are to please God. This you may do; for Enoch pleased Him though living in a degenerate age. And there are Enochs in this our day.—*Christ's Object Lessons*, 332.

By faith Enoch was taken away so that he did not see death, "and was not found, because God had taken him"; for before he was taken he had this testimony, that he pleased God.

—Hebrews 11:5, NKJV

The Road to Perdition Is Wide, Not Easy

*"Do I have any pleasure at all that the wicked should die?"
says the* L*ORD* *God, "and not that he should turn from his ways,
and live?"*

–Ezekiel 18:23, NKJV

SATAN WILL PRESENT the path of holiness as difficult while the paths of worldly pleasure are strewed with flowers. In false and flattering colors will the tempter array the world with its pleasures before you.–*Testimonies for the Church*, vol. 1, 502.

Yet do not therefore conclude that the upward path is the hard and the downward road the easy way. All along the road that leads to death there are pains and penalties, there are sorrows and disappointments, there are warnings not to go on. God's love has made it hard for the heedless and headstrong to destroy themselves. It is true that Satan's path is made to appear attractive, but it is all a deception; in the way of evil there are bitter remorse and cankering care. We may think it pleasant to follow pride and worldly ambition, but the end is pain and sorrow. Selfish plans may present flattering promises and hold out the hope of enjoyment, but we shall find that our happiness is poisoned and our life embittered by hopes that center in self. In the downward road the gateway may be bright with flowers, but thorns are in the path. The light of hope which shines from its entrance fades into the darkness of despair, and the soul who follows that path descends into the shadows of unending night.–*Thoughts From the Mount of Blessing*, 139.

"Thus says the L*ORD* *of hosts:
'If you will walk in My ways,
And if you will keep My command,
Then you shall also judge My house,
And likewise have charge of My courts;
I will give you places to walk
Among these who stand here.' "*

–Zechariah 3:7, NKJV

Finding Delight in God's Word

"If they obey and serve Him,
They shall spend their days in prosperity,
And their years in pleasures."

—Job 36:11, NKJV

THE CHRISTIAN HAS A SOURCE of strength and happiness to which the lovers of pleasure are strangers.—*Testimonies for the Church*, vol. 1, 616.

Conversion is a work that most do not appreciate. It is not a small matter to transform an earthly, sin-loving mind and bring it to understand the unspeakable love of Christ, the charms of His grace, and the excellency of God, so that the soul shall be imbued with divine love and captivated with the heavenly mysteries. When he understands these things, his former life appears disgusting and hateful. He hates sin, and, breaking his heart before God, he embraces Christ as the life and joy of the soul. He renounces his former pleasures. He has a new mind, new affections, new interest, new will; his sorrows, and desires, and love are all new. The lust of the flesh, the lust of the eye, and the pride of life, which have heretofore been preferred before Christ, are now turned from, and Christ is the charm of his life, the crown of his rejoicing. Heaven, which once possessed no charms, is now viewed in its riches and glory; and he contemplates it as his future home, where he shall see, love, and praise the One who hath redeemed him by His precious blood.

The works of holiness, which appeared wearisome, are now his delight. The word of God, which was dull and uninteresting, is now chosen as his study, the man of his counsel. It is as a letter written to him from God, bearing the inscription of the Eternal.—*Testimonies for the Church*, vol. 2, 294.

If your instructions hadn't sustained me with joy,
I would have died in my misery.
I will never forget your commandments,
for by them you give me life.

—Psalm 119:92, 93, NLT

Joyfully Ministering to Others

I know that nothing is better for them than to rejoice,
and to do good in their lives.

—Ecclesiastes 3:12, NKJV

GOD CALLS UPON MEN to minister gladly to their fellow men.—*The Ministry of Healing*, 103.

Every effort we make for Christ will be rewarded by Him, and every duty we perform in His name will minister to our own happiness.—*Testimonies for the Church*, vol. 4, 19.

Life is too valuable, too full of solemn, sacred responsibilities, to be wasted in pleasing self. . . .

Men and women have hardly begun to understand the true object of life. They are attracted by glitter and show. They are ambitious for worldly pre-eminence. To this the true aims of life are sacrificed. Life's best things—simplicity, honesty, truthfulness, purity, integrity—cannot be bought or sold. They are as free to the ignorant as to the educated, to the humble laborer as to the honored statesman. For everyone God has provided pleasure that may be enjoyed by rich and poor alike—the pleasure found in cultivating pureness of thought and unselfishness of action, the pleasure that comes from speaking sympathizing words and doing kindly deeds. From those who perform such service the light of Christ shines to brighten lives darkened by many shadows.—*The Ministry of Healing*, 98.

I pray that your hearts will be flooded with light
so that you can understand the confident hope
he has given to those he called—his holy people
who are his rich and glorious inheritance.

—Ephesians 1:18, NLT

The Christian's Many Sources of Happiness

Do you have faith? Have it to yourself before God.
Happy is he who does not condemn himself in what he approves.
—Romans 14:22, NKJV

THOSE WHO FIND true happiness must have the blessing of Heaven upon all that they possess and all that they do.—*The Adventist Home*, 67.

Let us never lose sight of the fact that Jesus is a wellspring of joy. He does not delight in the misery of human beings, but loves to see them happy.

Christians have many sources of happiness at their command, and they may tell with unerring accuracy what pleasures are lawful and right. They may enjoy such recreations as will not dissipate the mind or debase the soul, such as will not disappoint and leave a sad after-influence to destroy self-respect or bar the way to usefulness. If they can take Jesus with them and maintain a prayerful spirit, they are perfectly safe.

Any amusement in which you can engage asking the blessing of God upon it in faith will not be dangerous. But any amusement which disqualifies you for secret prayer, for devotion at the altar of prayer, or for taking part in the prayer meeting is not safe, but dangerous.—*The Adventist Home*, 513.

O LORD, *You are my God.*
I will exalt You,
I will praise Your name,
For You have done wonderful things;
Your counsels of old are faithfulness and truth.
—Isaiah 25:1, NKJV

To Do Justice

It is a joy for the just to do justice,
but destruction will come to the workers of iniquity.
—Proverbs 21:15, NKJV

He who is fully content to receive his commission from above will be cheered by the promises of God, as he seeks to do justice and judgment. To have unwavering trust in God, to be a doer of His word, is to pursue a safe course. The counsel of God simplifies the perplexities of business transactions and domestic duties. The followers of Christ who work with an eye single to the glory of God will have heavenly wisdom.—*Testimonies for the Church*, vol. 8, 141.

The words and law of God, written in the soul, and exhibited in a consecrated, holy life, have a powerful influence to convict the world. Covetousness, which is idolatry, and envy, and love of the world, will be rooted from the hearts of those who are obedient to Christ, and it will be their pleasure to deal justly, to love mercy, and to walk humbly before God.—*Testimonies for the Church*, vol. 3, 201.

Therefore we also, since we are surrounded by so great a cloud of witnesses,
let us lay aside every weight, and the sin which so easily ensnares us,
and let us run with endurance the race that is set before us,
looking unto Jesus, the author and finisher of our faith,
who for the joy that was set before Him endured the cross,
despising the shame, and has sat down
at the right hand of the throne of God.
—Hebrews 12:1, 2, NKJV

The Best Life Has to Offer

Nothing is better for a man than that he should eat and drink,
and that his soul should enjoy good in his labor.
This also, I saw, was from the hand of God.
—Ecclesiastes 2:24, NKJV

At the creation, labor was appointed as a blessing. It meant development, power, happiness. The changed condition of the earth through the curse of sin has brought a change in the conditions of labor; yet though now attended with anxiety, weariness, and pain, it is still a source of happiness and development. And it is a safeguard against temptation. Its discipline places a check on self-indulgence, and promotes industry, purity, and firmness. Thus it becomes a part of God's great plan for our recovery from the Fall. . . .

. . . While God has created and constantly controls all things, He has endowed us with a power not wholly unlike His. To us has been given a degree of control over the forces of nature. As God called forth the earth in its beauty out of chaos, so we can bring order and beauty out of confusion. And though all things are now marred with evil, yet in our completed work we feel a joy akin to His, when, looking on the fair earth, He pronounced it "very good."—*Education*, 214.

Whatever you do, do it heartily,
as to the Lord and not to men,
knowing that from the Lord you will receive
the reward of the inheritance; for you serve the Lord Christ.
—Colossians 3:23, 24, NKJV

Enjoyment of Nature

The works of the L*ORD* *are great,*
Studied by all who have pleasure in them.

—Psalm 111:2, NKJV

ALTHOUGH SIN HAS cast its shadow over the earth, God desires His children to find delight in the works of His hands.—*The Ministry of Healing*, 261.

Men, in their pride, delight in magnificent and costly edifices and glory in the works of their own hands; but God placed Adam in a garden. This was his dwelling. The blue heavens were its dome; the earth, with its delicate flowers and carpet of living green, was its floor; and the leafy branches of the goodly trees were its canopy. Its walls were hung with the most magnificent adornings—the handiwork of the great Master Artist. In the surroundings of the holy pair was a lesson for all time—that true happiness is found, not in the indulgence of pride and luxury, but in communion with God through His created works. If men would give less attention to the artificial, and would cultivate greater simplicity, they would come far nearer to answering the purpose of God in their creation. Pride and ambition are never satisfied, but those who are truly wise will find substantial and elevating pleasure in the sources of enjoyment that God has placed within the reach of all.—*Patriarchs and Prophets*, 49.

"You alone are the L*ORD;*
You have made heaven,
The heaven of heavens, with all their host,
The earth and everything on it,
The seas and all that is in them,
And You preserve them all.
The host of heaven worships You."

—Nehemiah 9:6, NKJV

The Only Source of True Happiness

I will sing to the LORD as long as I live;
I will sing praise to my God while I have my being.
May my meditation be sweet to Him;
I will be glad in the LORD.
May sinners be consumed from the earth,
And the wicked be no more.
Bless the LORD, O my soul!
Praise the LORD!

—Psalm 104:33–35, NKJV

YOU HAVE NOT EXPERIENCED the saving power of God as it is your privilege, because you have not made it the great aim of your life to glorify Christ. Let every purpose you form, every work in which you engage, and every pleasure you enjoy, be to the glory of God. Let this be the language of your heart: I am thine, O God, to live for Thee, to work for Thee, and to suffer for Thee.

Many profess to be on the Lord's side, but they are not; the weight of all their actions is on Satan's side. By what means shall we determine whose side we are on? Who has the heart? With whom are our thoughts? Upon whom do we love to converse? Who has our warmest affections and our best energies? If we are on the Lord's side, our thoughts are with Him, and our sweetest thoughts are of Him. We have no friendship with the world; we have consecrated all that we have and are to Him. We long to bear His image, breathe His Spirit, do His will, and please Him in all things.—*Testimonies for the Church*, vol. 2, 262.

To be brought into favor with God—what a privilege! To commune with Him—what can more elevate, refine, and exalt us above the frivolous pleasures of earth? To have our corrupt natures renovated by grace, our lustful appetites and animal propensities in subjection, to stand forth with noble, moral independence, achieving victories every day, will give peace of conscience which can arise alone from rightdoing.

Young friends, I saw that with such employment and diversion as this you might be happy. But the reason why you are restless is, you do not seek to the only true source for happiness. You are ever trying to find *out* of Christ that enjoyment which is found only *in* Him.—*Testimonies for the Church*, vol. 1, 503, 504.

AUGUST 10
Delight and Goodwill

Choosing Suffering Over Corruption

By faith Moses, when he became of age,
refused to be called the son of Pharaoh's daughter,
choosing rather to suffer affliction with the people of God
than to enjoy the passing pleasures of sin.
—Hebrews 11:24, 25, NKJV

MOSES WAS OFFERED the palace of the Pharaohs and the monarch's throne; but the sinful pleasures that make men forget God were in those lordly courts, and he chose instead the "durable riches and righteousness." Proverbs 8:18. Instead of linking himself with the greatness of Egypt, he chose to bind up his life with God's purpose. Instead of giving laws to Egypt, he by divine direction enacted laws for the world. He became God's instrument in giving to men those principles that are the safeguard alike of the home and of society, that are the cornerstone of the prosperity of nations—principles recognized today by the world's greatest men as the foundation of all that is best in human governments.

The greatness of Egypt is in the dust. Its power and civilization have passed away. But the work of Moses can never perish. The great principles of righteousness which he lived to establish are eternal.—*Education*, 68, 69.

All who will turn from the pleasures of earth, and with Moses choose rather to suffer affliction with the people of God than to enjoy the pleasures of sin for a season, esteeming the reproach of Christ greater riches than the treasures of the world, will, with faithful Moses, receive the unfading crown of immortality and the far more exceeding and eternal weight of glory.—*Testimonies for the Church*, vol. 2, 100.

Love in Disguise

"[They said] to Aaron, 'Make us gods to go before us;
as for this Moses who brought us out of the land of Egypt,
we do not know what has become of him.'
And they made a calf in those days, offered sacrifices to the idol,
and rejoiced in the works of their own hands."
—Acts 7:40, 41, NKJV

THE FELLOW LABORER OF MOSES, who was left with the solemn charge of the people in his absence, heard them uttering complaints that Moses had left them, and expressing a desire to return to Egypt; yet, through fear of offending the people, he was silent. He did not stand up boldly for God, but to please the people he made a golden calf. He seemed to be asleep to the beginning of the evil. When the first rebellious word was spoken, Aaron might have checked it; but so fearful was he of offending the people that he apparently united with them and was finally persuaded to make a golden calf for them to worship.—*Testimonies for the Church*, vol. 4, 514.

"These," said Aaron without hesitation or shame, "be thy gods, O Israel, which brought thee up out of the land of Egypt." Aaron influenced the children of Israel to go to greater lengths in idolatry than had entered their minds. They were no longer troubled lest the burning glory like flaming fire upon the mount had consumed their leader. They thought they had a general who just suited them, and they were ready to do anything that he suggested. They sacrificed to their golden god; they offered peace offerings, and gave themselves up to pleasure, rioting, and drunkenness.—*Testimonies for the Church*, vol. 3, 300.

How often, in our own day, is the love of pleasure disguised by a "form of godliness"! A religion that permits men, while observing the rites of worship, to devote themselves to selfish or sensual gratification, is as pleasing to the multitudes now as in the days of Israel. And there are still pliant Aarons, who, while holding positions of authority in the church, will yield to the desires of the unconsecrated, and thus encourage them in sin.—*Patriarchs and Prophets*, 317.

The Pitfall of Boasting

But now you boast in your arrogance. All such boasting is evil.
—James 4:16, NKJV

IF MEN COULD SEE for a moment beyond the range of finite vision, if they could catch a glimpse of the Eternal, every mouth would be stopped in its boasting.—*Counsels to Parents, Teachers, and Students*, 66.

It is a wicked pride that delights in the vanity of one's own works, that boasts of one's excellent qualities, seeking to make others seem inferior in order to exalt self, claiming more glory than the cold heart is willing to give to God. The disciples of Christ will heed the Master's instruction. He has bidden us love one another even as He has loved us.—*Testimonies for the Church*, vol. 4, 223.

Love rejoices in the truth and institutes no envious comparisons. He who possesses love compares only the loveliness of Christ and his own imperfect character.

. . . There is no religion in the enthronement of self. He who makes self-glorification his aim will find himself destitute of that grace which alone can make him efficient in Christ's service. Whenever pride and self-complacency are indulged, the work is marred.

. . . The smallest duty done in sincerity and self-forgetfulness is more pleasing to God than the greatest work when marred with self-seeking.—*Christ's Object Lessons*, 402.

Every man who praises himself brushes the luster from his best efforts.—*Testimonies for the Church*, vol. 4, 607.

All boasting of merit in ourselves is out of place.—*Christ's Object Lessons*, 401.

Though the LORD is great, he cares for the humble,
but he keeps his distance from the proud.
—Psalm 138:6, NLT

Pride Which Comes From Prosperity

I also gathered for myself silver
and gold and the special treasure of kings
and of the provinces. I acquired male and female singers,
the delights of the sons of men, and musical instruments
of all kinds.

—Ecclesiastes 2:8, NKJV

NOBLE IN YOUTH, noble in manhood, the beloved of his God, Solomon entered on a reign that gave high promise of prosperity and honor. Nations marveled at the knowledge and insight of the man to whom God had given wisdom. But the pride of prosperity brought separation from God. From the joy of divine communion Solomon turned to find satisfaction in the pleasures of sense. Of this experience he says:

"I made me great works; I builded me houses; I planted me vineyards: I made me gardens and orchards: . . . I got me servants and maidens: . . . I gathered me also silver and gold, and the peculiar treasure of kings and of the provinces: I gat me men singers and women singers, and the delights of the sons of men, as musical instruments, and that of all sorts. So I was great, and increased more than all that were before me in Jerusalem. . . . And whatsoever mine eyes desired I kept not from them, I withheld not my heart from any joy; for my heart rejoiced in all my labor. . . . Then I looked on all the works that my hands had wrought, and on the labor that I had labored to do: and, behold, all was vanity and vexation of spirit, and there was no profit under the sun. And I turned myself to behold wisdom, and madness, and folly: for what can the man do that cometh after the king? even that which hath been already done."

"I hated life. . . . Yea, I hated all my labor which I had taken under the sun." Ecclesiastes 2:4–12, 17, 18.

By his own bitter experience, Solomon learned the emptiness of a life that seeks in earthly things its highest good.—*Education*, 152, 153.

AUGUST 14
Delight and Goodwill

Sinful Pleasures Hinder a Fruitful Life

"Now the ones that fell among thorns are those who,
when they have heard, go out and are choked with cares, riches,
and pleasures of life, and bring no fruit to maturity."

—Luke 8:14, NKJV

SATAN PRESENTS THE WORLD with its most alluring, flattering charms to poor mortals, and they gaze upon it, and its glitter and tinsel eclipse the glory of heaven and that life which is as enduring as the throne of God. A life of peace, happiness, joy unspeakable, which shall know nothing of sorrow, sadness, pain, nor death, is sacrificed for a short lifetime of sin.—*Testimonies for the Church*, vol. 2, 100.

Life in the cities is false and artificial. The intense passion for money getting, the whirl of excitement and pleasure seeking, the thirst for display, the luxury and extravagance, all are forces that, with the great masses of mankind, are turning the mind from life's true purpose. They are opening the door to a thousand evils. Upon the youth they have almost irresistible power.

One of the most subtle and dangerous temptations that assail the children and youth in the cities is the love of pleasure. Holidays are numerous; games and horse racing draw thousands, and the whirl of excitement and pleasure attracts them away from the sober duties of life. Money that should have been saved for better uses is frittered away for amusements.—*The Ministry of Healing*, 364.

No testing has overtaken you that is not common to everyone.
God is faithful, and he will not let you be tested beyond your strength,
but with the testing he will also provide the way out
so that you may be able to endure it.

—1 Corinthians 10:13, NRSV

The Pleasures That Separate Us From God

But the widow who lives for pleasure is dead even while she lives.
—1 Timothy 5:6, NIV

THOSE WHO LOVE PLEASURE may keep up a form of godliness, but they have no vital connections with God. Their faith is dead, their zeal has departed.—*Messages to Young People*, 141.

Though church members, they are unconverted. They may take part in the church service, they may chant the psalm, "As the hart panteth after the water brooks, so panteth my soul after Thee, O God" (Psalm 42:1); but they testify to a falsehood. They are no more righteous in God's sight than is the veriest sinner. The soul that longs after the excitement of worldly pleasure, the mind that is full of love for display, cannot serve God. . . . Such a one has no inclination to war against the lust of the flesh. He longs to indulge appetite. He chooses the atmosphere of sin.—*Christ's Object Lessons*, 269.

Professed Christians, worldly Christians, are unacquainted with heavenly things. They will never be brought to the gates of the New Jerusalem to engage in exercises which have not hitherto specially interested them. They have not trained their minds to delight in devotion and in meditation upon things of God and heaven. How, then, can they engage in the services of heaven? how delight in the spiritual, the pure, the holy in heaven, when it was not a special delight to them upon earth?—*Testimonies for the Church*, vol. 2, 265.

Why, my soul, are you downcast?
Why so disturbed within me?
Put your hope in God,
for I will yet praise him,
my Savior and my God.

—Psalm 42:11, NIV

AUGUST 16

Delight and Goodwill

Stay Far Away From Them

Treacherous, reckless, swollen with conceit, lovers of pleasure rather than lovers of God, having the appearance of godliness, but denying its power. Avoid such people.

—2 Timothy 3:4, 5, ESV

THERE IS A FORM OF RELIGION which is nothing more than selfishness. It takes pleasure in worldly enjoyment. It is satisfied with contemplating the religion of Christ, and knows nothing of its saving power.—*Messages to Young People*, 106.

One of the sins that constitute one of the signs of the last days, is that professed Christians are lovers of pleasure more than lovers of God. Deal truly with your own souls. Search carefully. How few, after a faithful examination, can look up to Heaven and say, "I am not one of those thus described. I am not a lover of pleasure more than a lover of God."—*Messages to Young People*, 84.

God does not own the pleasure-seeker as His follower. Those only who are self-denying, and who live lives of sobriety, humility, and holiness, are true followers of Jesus. And such cannot enjoy the frivolous, empty conversation of the lover of the world. . . .

The true followers of Christ will have sacrifices to make. They will shun places of worldly amusement because they find no Jesus there—no influence which will make them heavenly minded and increase their growth in grace. Obedience to the Word of God will lead them to come out from all these things, and be separate.—*Messages to Young People*, 376.

Brethren, if a man is overtaken in any trespass,
you who are spiritual restore such a one in a spirit of gentleness,
considering yourself lest you also be tempted.
Bear one another's burdens, and so fulfill the law of Christ.

—Galatians 6:1, 2, NKJV

Counterfeit Pleasures: The Knowledge of Evil

So when the woman saw that the tree was good for food, that it was pleasant to the eyes, and a tree desirable to make one wise, she took of its fruit and ate. She also gave to her husband with her, and he ate.

—Genesis 3:6, NKJV

It was the will of God that Adam and Eve should not know evil. The knowledge of good had been freely given them; but the knowledge of evil,—of sin and its results, of wearing toil, of anxious care, of disappointment and grief, of pain and death,—this was in love withheld.

While God was seeking man's good, Satan was seeking his ruin. . . .

Satan desired to make it appear that this knowledge of good mingled with evil would be a blessing, and that in forbidding them to take of the fruit of the tree, God was withholding great good. He urged that it was because of its wonderful properties for imparting wisdom and power that God had forbidden them to taste it, that He was thus seeking to prevent them from reaching a nobler development and finding greater happiness. . . .

When Eve saw "that the tree was good for food, and that it was pleasant to the eyes, and a tree to be desired to make one wise, she took of the fruit thereof, and did eat." It was grateful to the taste, and, as she ate, she seemed to feel a vivifying power, and imagined herself entering upon a higher state of existence. Having herself transgressed, she became a tempter to her husband, "and he did eat." Genesis 3:6.

"Your eyes shall be opened," the enemy had said; "ye shall be as gods, knowing good and evil." Genesis 3:5. Their eyes were indeed opened; but how sad the opening!—*Education*, 23–25.

If Adam and Eve had never touched the forbidden tree, the Lord would have imparted to them knowledge, knowledge upon which rested no curse of sin, knowledge that would have brought them everlasting joy.—*Testimonies for the Church*, vol. 8, 290.

Unsound Doctrine

*So God will cause them to be greatly deceived,
and they will believe these lies. Then they will be condemned
for enjoying evil rather than believing the truth.*
—2 Thessalonians 2:11, 12, NLT

THOSE WHO ARE UNWILLING to accept the plain, cutting truths of the Bible are continually seeking for pleasing fables that will quiet the conscience. The less spiritual, self-denying, and humiliating the doctrines presented, the greater the favor with which they are received. These persons degrade the intellectual powers to serve their carnal desires. Too wise in their own conceit to search the Scriptures with contrition of soul and earnest prayer for divine guidance, they have no shield from delusion. Satan is ready to supply the heart's desire, and he palms off his deceptions in the place of truth. . . . All who neglect the word of God to study convenience and policy, that they may not be at variance with the world, will be left to receive damnable heresy for religious truth. Every conceivable form of error will be accepted by those who willfully reject the truth. He who looks with horror upon one deception will readily receive another. The apostle Paul, speaking of a class who "received not the love of the truth, that they might be saved," declares: "For this cause God shall send them strong delusion, that they should believe a lie: that they all might be damned who believed not the truth, but had pleasure in unrighteousness." 2 Thessalonians 2:10–12. With such a warning before us it behooves us to be on our guard as to what doctrines we receive.—*The Great Controversy*, 523.

Draw Me From the Path of Uprightness

To deliver you from the way of evil,
From the man who speaks perverse things,
From those who leave the paths of uprightness
To walk in the ways of darkness;
Who rejoice in doing evil,
And delight in the perversity of the wicked.
—Proverbs 2:12–14, NKJV

SINCE THE FALL OF ADAM it has been the fashion of the world to sin.—*Testimonies for the Church*, vol. 6, 129.

In the unregenerate heart there is love of sin and a disposition to cherish and excuse it.—*The Great Controversy*, 508.

The prevalence of a sinful desire shows the delusion of the soul. Every indulgence of that desire strengthens the soul's aversion to God. The pains of duty and the pleasures of sin are the cords with which Satan binds men in his snares.—*Testimonies for the Church*, vol. 5, 53.

By beholding we become changed. Though formed in the image of his Maker, man can so educate his mind that sin which he once loathed will become pleasant to him. As he ceases to watch and pray, he ceases to guard the citadel, the heart, and engages in sin and crime. The mind is debased, and it is impossible to elevate it from corruption while it is being educated to enslave the moral and intellectual powers, and bring them in subjection to grosser passions. Constant war against the carnal mind must be maintained; and we must be aided by the refining influence of the grace of God, which will attract the mind upward and habituate it to meditate upon pure and holy things.—*Testimonies for the Church*, vol. 2, 478.

The Spirit of God is continually impressing the minds of men to seek for those things which alone will give peace and rest—the higher, holier joys of heaven. Christ, the Lord of life and glory, gave His life to redeem man from Satan's power. Our Saviour is constantly at work, through influences seen and unseen, to attract the minds of men from the unsatisfying pleasures of this life to the priceless treasure which may be theirs in the immortal future.—*Testimonies for the Church*, vol. 4, 580.

Self-Destructive Feelings of Bitterness

"If I have rejoiced at my enemy's misfortune
or gloated over the trouble that came to him . . .
. . . then let briers come up instead of wheat
and stinkweed instead of barley."

–Job 31:29, 40, NIV

BITTER FEELINGS . . . are foreign to the spirit of Christ.—*Testimonies for the Church*, vol. 2, 51.

Jesus, when reviled, abused, and insulted, did not retaliate. "Who, when He was reviled, reviled not again." When the cruelty of man caused Him to suffer painful stripes and wounds, He threatened not, but committed Himself to Him who judgeth righteously. . . . Is the servant greater than his master? Christ has given us His life as a pattern, and we dishonor Him when we become jealous of every slight, and are ready to resent every injury, supposed or real. It is not an evidence of a noble mind to be prepared to defend self, to preserve our own dignity. We would better suffer wrongfully a hundred times than wound the soul by a spirit of retaliation, or by giving vent to wrath.—*Testimonies for the Church*, vol. 2, 426.

No resentment must come into our hearts. When reviled, we must not revile again. O jealousy and evil surmising, what mischief have ye wrought! how have ye turned friendship and love into bitterness and hatred! We must be less proud, less sensitive, have less self-love, and be dead to self-interest.—*Testimonies for the Church*, vol. 2, 566.

Do not rejoice when your enemy falls,
And do not let your heart be glad when he stumbles;
lest the LORD *see it, and it displease Him,*
And He turn away His wrath from him.

–Proverbs 24:17, 18, NKJV

Foolish Wickedness

To do evil is like sport to a fool,
But a man of understanding has wisdom.
—Proverbs 10:23, NKJV

IN THE OLD TESTAMENT the word "fool" is used to designate an apostate, or one who has abandoned himself to wickedness.—*Thoughts From the Mount of Blessing*, 57.

There were many giants [in Noah's day], men of great stature and strength, renowned for wisdom, skillful in devising the most cunning and wonderful works; but their guilt in giving loose rein to iniquity was in proportion to their skill and mental ability.

God bestowed upon these antediluvians many and rich gifts; but they used His bounties to glorify themselves, and turned them into a curse by fixing their affections upon the gifts instead of the Giver. They employed the gold and silver, the precious stones and the choice wood, in the construction of habitations for themselves, and endeavored to excel one another in beautifying their dwellings with the most skillful workmanship. They sought only to gratify the desires of their own proud hearts, and reveled in scenes of pleasure and wickedness. . . .

. . . "God saw that the wickedness of man was great in the earth, and that every imagination of the thoughts of his heart was only evil continually. . . . The earth also was corrupt before God; and the earth was filled with violence." God had given men His commandments as a rule of life, but His law was transgressed, and every conceivable sin was the result. The wickedness of men was open and daring, justice was trampled in the dust, and the cries of the oppressed reached unto heaven.—*Patriarchs and Prophets*, 90, 91.

The sins that called for vengeance upon the antediluvian world exist today. The fear of God is banished from the hearts of men, and His law is treated with indifference and contempt. The intense worldliness of that generation is equaled by that of the generation now living.—*Patriarchs and Prophers*, 101.

AUGUST 22
Delight and Goodwill

Folly, Foolishness, Nonsense

Folly is joy to him who is destitute of discernment,
But a man of understanding walks uprightly.

—Proverbs 15:21, NKJV

OUR RECREATIONS should not be scenes of senseless mirth, taking the form of the nonsensical. We can conduct them in such a manner as will benefit and elevate those with whom we associate, and better qualify us and them to more successfully attend to the duties devolving upon us as Christians.

We cannot be excusable in the sight of God if we engage in amusements which have a tendency to unfit us for the faithful performance of the ordinary duties of life, and thus lessen our relish for the contemplation of God and heavenly things. The religion of Christ is cheering and elevating in its influence. It is above everything like foolish jesting and joking, vain and frivolous chit-chat.—*Messages to Young People*, 364.

It is by leading the followers of Christ to associate with the ungodly and unite in their amusements that Satan is most successful in alluring them into sin. . . .

. . . Through the drama he has worked for ages to excite passion and glorify vice. The opera, with its fascinating display and bewildering music, the masquerade, the dance, the card table, Satan employs to break down the barriers of principle and open the door to sensual indulgence. In every gathering for pleasure where pride is fostered or appetite indulged, where one is led to forget God and lose sight of eternal interests, there Satan is binding his chains about the soul.—*Patriarchs and Prophets*, 458, 459.

Flee also youthful lusts; but pursue righteousness, faith,
love, peace with those who call on the Lord out of a pure heart.

—2 Timothy 2:22, NKJV

Distasteful Jests and Jokes

It is better to hear the rebuke of the wise,
Than for a man to hear the song of fools.
For like the crackling of thorns under a pot,
So is the laughter of the fool.
This also is vanity.

—Ecclesiastes 7:5, 6, NKJV

JESTING, JOKING, AND WORLDLY CONVERSATION belong to the world. Christians who have the peace of God in their hearts will be cheerful and happy without indulging in lightness or frivolity. While watching unto prayer they will have a serenity and peace which will elevate them above all superfluities.—*Testimonies for the Church*, vol. 3, 241.

The giddy laugh, the jesting, the joking, sickens the soul that is feeding on Christ. Cheap, foolish talk is painful to Him.—*Fundamentals of Christian Education*, 457.

Lightness, jesting, and joking will result in barrenness of soul and the loss of the favor of God.—*Testimonies for the Church*, vol. 2, 236.

A mind that is intent upon having the prize, upon securing heaven, will reject with firm, determined purpose every attempt at wit and jest concerning religious things.—*Messages to Young People*, 266.

Let no low witticism escape your lips.—*The Ministry of Healing*, 491.

All frivolous words, all lightness and trifling, are enticements of the enemy to deprive you of spiritual strength. Brace yourselves against this evil, in the name of the God of Israel. . . . Trim your lamps, and keep them burning, that wherever you may go you may reveal in speech and action precious rays of light.—*Testimonies for the Church*, vol. 9, 133.

Obscene stories, foolish talk, and coarse jokes—these are not for you.
Instead, let there be thankfulness to God.

—Ephesians 5:4, NLT

The Triumph of the Wicked Is Temporary

"Don't you realize that from the beginning of time,
ever since people were first placed on the earth,
the triumph of the wicked has been short lived
and the joy of the godless has been only temporary?"

–Job 20:4, 5, NLT

THINK, OH, THINK, in your pleasure-seeking hours, that all these things have an end. Did you have correct views of life, endless life with God, how quickly would you turn from a life of pleasure and sin. How quickly would you change your mind, your course, and your company, and turn the strength of your affection to God and heavenly things. How resolutely would you scorn to yield to temptations which have deceived and captivated you. How zealous would be your efforts for the blessed life; how earnest and persevering your prayers to God for His grace to abide upon you, for His power to sustain you and help you resist the devil. How diligent would you be to improve every religious privilege to learn the ways and will of God. How careful would you be in meditating upon the law of God, and in comparing your life with its claims. How fearful would you be lest you sin in word or deed, and how earnest to grow in grace and true holiness. Your conversation would not be on trifling things, but in heaven. Then glorious and eternal things would open before you, and you would not rest until you should increase more and more in spirituality. But earthly things claim your attention, and God is forgotten. I implore you to face rightabout, and to seek the Lord, that He may be found of you; call upon Him while He is near.–*Testimonies for the Church*, vol. 2, 290.

Seek the LORD while He may be found,
Call upon Him while He is near.
Let the wicked forsake his way,
And the unrighteous man his thoughts;
Let him return to the LORD,
And He will have mercy on him;
And to our God,
For He will abundantly pardon.
—Isaiah 55:6, 7, NKJV

Worldly Pleasure Will Pass Away

Do not love the world or anything in the world.
If anyone loves the world, love for the Father is not in them. . . .
The world and its desires pass away,
but whoever does the will of God lives forever.

—1 John 2:15, 17, NIV

THERE ARE LOVERS of the world even among those who profess to be waiting for the Lord. There is ambition for riches and honor. Christ describes this class when He declares that the day of God is to come as a snare upon all that dwell upon the earth. This world is their home. They make it their business to secure earthly treasures. They erect costly dwellings and furnish them with every good thing; they find pleasure in dress and the indulgence of appetite. The things of the world are their idols. These interpose between the soul and Christ, and the solemn and awful realities that are crowding upon us are but dimly seen and faintly realized.—*Testimonies for the Church*, vol. 5, 456.

If we would permit our minds to dwell more upon Christ and the heavenly world, we should find a powerful stimulus and support in fighting the battles of the Lord. Pride and love of the world will lose their power as we contemplate the glories of that better land so soon to be our home. Beside the loveliness of Christ, all earthly attractions will seem of little worth.—*Messages to Young People*, 113.

Better than all the friendship of the world is the friendship of Christ's redeemed. Better than a title to the noblest palace on earth is a title to the mansions our Lord has gone to prepare. And better than all the words of earthly praise will be the Saviour's words to His faithful servants, "Come, ye blessed of My Father, inherit the kingdom prepared for you from the foundation of the world." Matthew 25:34.—*Christ's Object Lessons*, 374.

And this world is fading away, along with everything that people crave.
But anyone who does what pleases God will live forever.

—1 John 2:17, NLT

Treasures That Will Be Lost

" 'And I will say to my soul,
"Soul, you have many goods laid up for many years;
take your ease; eat, drink, and be merry." But God said to him,
'Fool! This night your soul will be required of you;
then whose will those things be which you have provided?' "
—Luke 12:19, 20, NKJV

THE LENGTH AND HAPPINESS OF LIFE does not consist in the amount of our earthly possessions. This foolish rich man in his supreme selfishness had laid up for himself treasures that he could not use. He had lived only for himself. He had over-reached in trade, had made sharp bargains, and had not exercised mercy or the love of God. He had robbed the fatherless and widow, and defrauded his fellow men, to add to his increasing stock of worldly possessions. He might have laid up his treasure in heaven in bags that wax not old; but through his covetousness he lost both worlds.—*Testimonies for the Church*, vol. 3, 402.

The man who finds pleasure at the gaming table, the man who loves to indulge perverted appetite, the amusement lover, the frequenters of the theater and the ball-room, put eternity out of their reckoning. The whole burden of their life is: What shall we eat? what shall we drink? and wherewithal shall we be clothed? They are not in the procession that is moving heavenward. They are led by the great apostate, and with him will be destroyed.—*Testimonies for the Church*, vol. 6, 406.

"That is why I tell you not to worry about everyday life—
whether you have enough food and drink, or enough clothes to wear.
Isn't life more than food, and your body more than clothing?"
—Matthew 6:25, NLT

Only Bitter Regrets Remain

The joy of our heart has ceased;
Our dance has turned into mourning.
The crown has fallen from our head.
Woe to us, for we have sinned!
—Lamentations 5:15, 16, NKJV

MULTITUDES ARE ATTRACTED by a life of selfish and sensual pleasure. They cannot discern the hidden dangers or the fearful ending of the path that seems to them the way of happiness. Through the indulgence of appetite and passion, their energies are wasted, and millions are ruined for this world and for the world to come.—*The Ministry of Healing*, 371.

The true Christian will not desire to enter any place of amusement or engage in any diversion upon which he cannot ask the blessing of God. He will not be found at the theater, the billiard hall, or the bowling saloon. He will not unite with the gay waltzers, or indulge in any other bewitching pleasure that will banish Christ from the mind. . . .

When we come to the final hour, and stand face to face with the record of our lives, shall we regret that we have attended so few parties of pleasure? that we have participated in so few scenes of thoughtless mirth? Shall we not, rather, bitterly regret that so many precious hours have been wasted in self-gratification—so many opportunities neglected, which, rightly improved, would have secured for us immortal treasures?—*Messages to Young People*, 398.

See then that you walk circumspectly, not as fools but as wise,
redeeming the time, because the days are evil.
Therefore do not be unwise, but understand what the will of the Lord is.
—Ephesians 5:15–17, NKJV

Short-Lived Laughter and Mirth

Even in laughter the heart may ache,
and rejoicing may end in grief.

—Proverbs 14:13, NIV

NO REAL JOY can be found in the path forbidden by Him who knows what is best, and who plans for the good of His creatures. The path of transgression leads to misery and destruction.—*Patriarchs and Prophets*, 600.

Happiness that is sought from selfish motives, outside of the path of duty, is ill-balanced, fitful, and transitory; it passes away, and the soul is filled with loneliness and sorrow.—*Steps to Christ*, 124.

The continual craving for pleasurable amusements reveals the deep longings of the soul. But those who drink at this fountain of worldly pleasure will find their soul-thirst still unsatisfied. They are deceived; they mistake mirth for happiness; and when the excitement ceases many sink down into the depths of despondency and despair. O what madness, what folly, to forsake the "Fountain of living waters" for the "broken cisterns" of worldly pleasure!—*Messages to Young People*, 370.

For my people have committed two evils:
they have forsaken me,
the fountain of living water,
and dug out cisterns for themselves,
cracked cisterns
that can hold no water.

—Jeremiah 2:13, NRSV

The "Gifts" of the World

Remember your creator in the days of your youth,
before the days of trouble come, and the years draw near
when you will say, "I have no pleasure in them."

—Ecclesiastes 12:1, NRSV

HAVE YOU SOUGHT to feast upon the fruits of transgression, only to find them turn to ashes upon your lips? And now, your substance spent, your life-plans thwarted, and your hopes dead, do you sit alone and desolate? Now that voice which has long been speaking to your heart but to which you would not listen comes to you distinct and clear, "Arise ye, and depart; for this is not your rest; because it is polluted, it shall destroy you, even with a sore destruction." Micah 2:10. Return to your Father's house. He invites you, saying, "Return unto Me; for I have redeemed thee." Isaiah 44:22.—*Christ's Object Lessons*, 205.

As men set forth the best wine first, then afterward that which is worse, so does the world with its gifts. That which it offers may please the eye and fascinate the senses, but it proves to be unsatisfying. The wine turns to bitterness, the gaiety to gloom. That which was begun with songs and mirth ends in weariness and disgust. But the gifts of Jesus are ever fresh and new. The feast that He provides for the soul never fails to give satisfaction and joy. Each new gift increases the capacity of the receiver to appreciate and enjoy the blessings of the Lord. He gives grace for grace. There can be no failure of supply. If you abide in Him, the fact that you receive a rich gift today insures the reception of a richer gift tomorrow.—*The Desire of Ages*, 148.

I have swept away your transgressions like a cloud,
and your sins like mist;
return to me, for I have redeemed you.

—Isaiah 44:22, NRSV

AUGUST 30
Delight and Goodwill

The Sinner Is Not Happy in God's Presence

"For what is the hope of the hypocrite,
Though he may gain much,
If God takes away his life? . . .
Will he delight himself in the Almighty?
Will he always call upon God?"

—Job 27:8, 10, NKJV

IN HIS SINLESS STATE, man held joyful communion with Him "in whom are hid all the treasures of wisdom and knowledge." Colossians 2:3. But after his sin, he could no longer find joy in holiness, and he sought to hide from the presence of God. Such is still the condition of the unrenewed heart. It is not in harmony with God, and finds no joy in communion with Him. The sinner could not be happy in God's presence; he would shrink from the companionship of holy beings. Could he be permitted to enter heaven, it would have no joy for him. The spirit of unselfish love that reigns there—every heart responding to the heart of Infinite Love—would touch no answering chord in his soul. His thoughts, his interests, his motives, would be alien to those that actuate the sinless dwellers there. He would be a discordant note in the melody of heaven. Heaven would be to him a place of torture; he would long to be hidden from Him who is its light, and the center of its joy. It is no arbitrary decree on the part of God that excludes the wicked from heaven; they are shut out by their own unfitness for its companionship. The glory of God would be to them a consuming fire. They would welcome destruction, that they might be hidden from the face of Him who died to redeem them.—*Steps to Christ*, 17.

A New Heart and a New Spirit

"Cast away from you all the transgressions
which you have committed, and get yourselves a new heart
and a new spirit. For why should you die, O house of Israel?
For I have no pleasure in the death of one who dies,"
says the Lord God. *"Therefore turn and live!"*
—Ezekiel 18:31, 32, NKJV

EVERY TRUE TURNING to the Lord brings abiding joy into the life.—*Prophets and Kings*, 668.

Many have a twilight perception of Christ's excellence, and their hearts thrill with joy. They long for a fuller, deeper sense of the Saviour's love. Let these cherish every desire of the soul after God. The Holy Spirit works with those who will be worked, molds those who will be molded, fashions those who will be fashioned. Give yourselves the culture of spiritual thoughts and holy communings. You have seen but the first rays of the early dawn of His glory. As you follow on to know the Lord, you will know that "the path of the righteous is as the light of dawn, that shineth more and more unto the perfect day." Proverbs 4:18, R.V., margin.—*The Ministry of Healing*, 503.

In Christ is fullness of joy forevermore.—*Testimonies to Ministers and Gospel Workers*, 390.

If we know God, and Jesus Christ whom He has sent, unspeakable gladness will come to the soul.—*Testimonies to Ministers and Gospel Workers*, 169.

Yet in all these things we are more than conquerors through Him who loved us.
For I am persuaded that neither death nor life, nor angels nor principalities nor powers,
nor things present nor things to come, nor height nor depth, nor any other created thing,
shall be able to separate us from the love of God which is in Christ Jesus our Lord.
—Romans 8:37–39, NKJV

"And this is eternal life, that they may know You,
the only true God, and Jesus Christ whom You have sent."
—John 17:3, NKJV

SEPTEMBER 1
Make a Joyful Noise

We All Ought to Praise Him

Make a joyful shout to God, all the earth!
Sing out the honor of His name;
Make His praise glorious.

—Psalm 66:1, 2, NKJV

TO PRAISE GOD in fullness and sincerity of heart is as much a duty as is prayer. We are to show to the world and to all the heavenly intelligences that we appreciate the wonderful love of God for fallen humanity and that we are expecting larger and yet larger blessings from His infinite fullness. Far more than we do, we need to speak of the precious chapters in our experience. After a special outpouring of the Holy Spirit, our joy in the Lord and our efficiency in His service would be greatly increased by recounting His goodness and His wonderful works in behalf of His children.—*Christ's Object Lessons*, 299.

Let praise and thanksgiving be expressed in song. When tempted, instead of giving utterance to our feelings, let us by faith lift up a song of thanksgiving to God. . . .

Song is a weapon that we can always use against discouragement.—*The Ministry of Healing*, 254.

"Rejoice in the Lord alway," the apostle Paul exhorts, "and again I say, Rejoice." Philippians 4:4. Whatever your disposition may be, God is able so to mold it that it will be sweet and Christlike. By the exercise of living faith you can separate from everything that is not in accordance with the mind of God, and thus bring heaven into your life here below. Doing this, you will have sunshine at every step. When the enemy seeks to enshroud the soul with darkness, sing faith and talk faith, and you will find that you have sung and talked yourself into the light.—*Counsels to Parents, Teachers, and Students*, 233.

Always be full of joy in the Lord. I say it again—rejoice!

—Philippians 4:4, NLT

Praising With Voices and Instruments

Sing aloud to God our strength;
shout for joy to the God of Jacob.
Raise a song, sound the tambourine,
the sweet lyre with the harp.

—Psalm 81:1, 2, NRSV

GOD IS GLORIFIED by songs of praise from a pure heart filled with love and devotion to Him. . . . Those who adhere strictly to the admonitions and instructions of God's word, prayerfully seeking to know and do His righteous will, feel not the petty grievances daily occurring. The gratitude which they feel, and the peace of God ruling within, cause them to make melody in their hearts unto the Lord and by words to make mention of the debt of love and thankfulness due the dear Saviour, who so loved them as to die that they might have life.—*Testimonies for the Church*, vol. 1, 509.

God's children are not to be subject to feelings and emotions. When they fluctuate between hope and fear, the heart of Christ is hurt; for He has given them unmistakable evidence of His love. He wants them to be established, strengthened, and settled in the most holy faith. He wants them to do the work He has given them; then their hearts will become in His hands as sacred harps, every chord of which will send forth praise and thanksgiving to the One sent by God to take away the sins of the world.—*Testimonies to Ministers and Gospel Workers*, 518.

Therefore, let us offer through Jesus a continual sacrifice of praise to God,
proclaiming our allegiance to his name.

—Hebrews 13:15, NLT

Make a Joyful Noise in His Sanctuary

Come, let us sing to the L*ORD*!
Let us shout joyfully to the Rock of our salvation.
Let us come to him with thanksgiving.
Let us sing psalms of praise to him.

—Psalm 95:1, 2, NLT

TO THE HUMBLE, believing soul, the house of God on earth is the gate of heaven. The song of praise, the prayer, the words spoken by Christ's representatives, are God's appointed agencies to prepare a people for the church above, for that loftier worship into which there can enter nothing that defileth. . . .

. . . Happy are those who have a sanctuary, be it high or low, in the city or among the rugged mountain caves, in the lowly cabin or in the wilderness. If it is the best they can secure for the Master, He will hallow the place with His presence.—*Testimonies for the Church*, vol. 5, 491.

The melody of song, poured forth from many hearts in clear, distinct utterance, is one of God's instrumentalities in the work of saving souls. All the service should be conducted with solemnity and awe, as if in the visible presence of the Master of assemblies.—*Testimonies for the Church*, vol. 5, 492.

The voice of thanksgiving, praise, and rejoicing is heard in heaven. The voices of the angels in heaven unite with the voices of the children of God on earth as they ascribe honor and glory and praise to God and to the Lamb for the great salvation provided.—*Counsels to Parents, Teachers, and Students*, 246.

I will praise you, L*ORD*, *with all my heart;*
I will tell of all the marvelous things you have done.
I will be filled with joy because of you.
I will sing praises to your name, O Most High.

—Psalm 9:1, 2, NLT

Shout for Joy

Songs of joy and victory are sung in the camp of the godly.
The strong right arm of the LORD has done glorious things!
The strong right arm of the LORD is raised in triumph.
The strong right arm of the LORD has done glorious things!
—Psalm 118:15, 16, NLT

WE OPEN TO OURSELVES the floodgates of woe or joy. If we permit our thoughts to be engrossed with the troubles and trifles of earth, our hearts will be filled with unbelief, gloom, and foreboding. If we set our affections on things above, the voice of Jesus will speak to our hearts, murmuring will cease, and vexing thoughts will be lost in praise to our Redeemer. Those who dwell upon God's great mercies and are not unmindful of His lesser gifts, will put on the girdle of gladness and make melody in their hearts to the Lord.—*Counsels to Parents, Teachers, and Students*, 234.

Let there be singing in the home, of songs that are sweet and pure, and there will be fewer words of censure and more of cheerfulness and hope and joy.—*Education*, 168.

In a sense the father is the priest of the household, laying upon the family altar the morning and evening sacrifice. But the wife and children should unite in prayer and join in the song of praise. In the morning before he leaves home for his daily labor, let the father gather his children about him and, bowing before God, commit them to the care of the Father in heaven. When the cares of the day are past, let the family unite in offering grateful prayer and raising the song of praise, in acknowledgment of divine care during the day.—*The Ministry of Healing*, 392.

"Keep these words that I am commanding you today in your heart.
Recite them to your children and talk about them when you are at home
and when you are away, when you lie down and when you rise."
—Deuteronomy 6:6, 7, NRSV

SEPTEMBER 5
Make a Joyful Noise

Singing With the Angels

My soul is satisfied as with a rich feast,
and my mouth praises you with joyful lips.

—Psalm 63:5, NRSV

THOSE WHO ABIDE IN JESUS will be happy, cheerful, and joyful in God. A subdued gentleness will mark the voice, reverence for spiritual and eternal things will be expressed in the actions, and music, joyful music, will echo from the lips; for it is wafted from the throne of God. This is the mystery of godliness, not easily explained, but nonetheless felt and enjoyed. A stubborn and rebellious heart can close its doors to all the sweet influences of the grace of God and all the joy in the Holy Ghost; but the ways of wisdom are ways of pleasantness, and all her paths are peace.—*Testimonies for the Church*, vol. 4, 625.

Those who walk in wisdom's ways are, even in tribulation, exceeding joyful; for He whom their soul loveth, walks, invisible, beside them. At each upward step they discern more distinctly the touch of His hand; at every step brighter gleamings of glory from the Unseen fall upon their path; and their songs of praise, reaching ever a higher note, ascend to join the songs of angels before the throne.—*Thoughts From the Mount of Blessing*, 140.

You will show me the path of life;
In Your presence is fullness of joy;
At Your right hand are pleasures forevermore.

—Psalm 16:11, NKJV

Praise Promotes Health of Body and Soul

Blessed are the people who know the joyful sound!
They walk, O LORD, in the light of Your countenance.
—Psalm 89:15, NKJV

NOTHING TENDS MORE to promote health of body and of soul than does a spirit of gratitude and praise. It is a positive duty to resist melancholy, discontented thoughts and feelings—as much a duty as it is to pray. If we are heaven-bound, how can we go as a band of mourners, groaning and complaining all along the way to our Father's house?

Those professed Christians who are constantly complaining, and who seem to think cheerfulness and happiness a sin, have not genuine religion. Those who take a mournful pleasure in all that is melancholy in the natural world, who choose to look upon dead leaves rather than to gather the beautiful living flowers, who see no beauty in grand mountain heights and in valleys clothed with living green, who close their senses to the joyful voice which speaks to them in nature, and which is sweet and musical to the listening ear—these are not in Christ. They are gathering to themselves gloom and darkness, when they might have brightness, even the Sun of Righteousness arising in their hearts with healing in His beams.—*The Ministry of Healing*, 251.

Rejoice always, pray without ceasing,
in everything give thanks;
for this is the will of God in Christ Jesus for you.
—1 Thessalonians 5:16–18, NKJV

Sing With Gladness, for It Is Good and Pleasant

Praise the L*ORD*!
For it is good to sing praises to our God. . . .
. . . He heals the brokenhearted
And binds up their wounds.

—Psalm 147:1, 3, NKJV

THE SOUL MAY ASCEND nearer heaven on the wings of praise. God is worshiped with song and music in the courts above, and as we express our gratitude we are approximating to the worship of the heavenly hosts. "Whoso offereth praise glorifieth" God. Psalm 50:23. Let us with reverent joy come before our Creator, with "thanksgiving, and the voice of melody." Isaiah 51:3.—*Steps to Christ*, 104.

When human beings sing with the spirit and the understanding, heavenly musicians take up the strain and join in the song of thanksgiving. He who has bestowed upon us all the gifts that enable us to be workers together with God, expects His servants to cultivate their voices so that they can speak and sing in a way that all can understand. It is not loud singing that is needed, but clear intonation, correct pronunciation, and distinct utterance. Let all take time to cultivate the voice so that God's praise can be sung in clear, soft tones, not with harshness and shrillness that offend the ear. The ability to sing is the gift of God; let it be used to His glory.—*Testimonies for the Church*, vol. 9, 143.

Make a joyful shout to the L*ORD*, *all you lands!*
Serve the L*ORD* *with gladness;*
Come before His presence with singing. . . .
. . . Be thankful to Him, and bless His name.
For the L*ORD* *is good;*
His mercy is everlasting,
And His truth endures to all generations.

—Psalm 100:1, 2, 4, 5, NKJV

A Weapon Against Discouragement

Sing, O daughter of Zion!
Shout, O Israel!
Be glad and rejoice with all your heart,
O daughter of Jerusalem!

—Zephaniah 3:14, NKJV

THE MELODY OF PRAISE is the atmosphere of heaven; and when heaven comes in touch with the earth, there is music and song—"thanksgiving, and the voice of melody." Isaiah 51:3.

Above the new-created earth, as it lay, fair and unblemished, under the smile of God, "the morning stars sang together, and all the sons of God shouted for joy." Job 38:7. So human hearts, in sympathy with heaven, have responded to God's goodness in notes of praise.—*Education*, 161.

With a song, Jesus in His earthly life met temptation. Often when sharp, stinging words were spoken, often when the atmosphere about Him was heavy with gloom, with dissatisfaction, distrust, or oppressive fear, was heard His song of faith and holy cheer.

On that last sad night of the Passover supper, as He was about to go forth to betrayal and to death, His voice was lifted in the psalm:

"Blessed be the name of the Lord
From this time forth and for evermore.
From the rising of the sun until the going down of the same
The Lord's name is to be praised." . . . Psalm 113:2, 3.—*Education*, 166.

As our Redeemer leads us to the threshold of the Infinite, flushed with the glory of God, we may catch the themes of praise and thanksgiving from the heavenly choir round about the throne; and as the echo of the angels' song is awakened in our earthly homes, hearts will be drawn closer to the heavenly singers. Heaven's communion begins on earth. We learn here the keynote of its praise.—*Education*, 168.

Singing Chases Away Sadness

Let the saints be joyful in glory;
Let them sing aloud on their beds.

—Psalm 149:5, NKJV

When we have a sense of Christ's sacrifice in our behalf, our lips are tuned to the highest, loftiest themes of praise.—*Counsels to Parents, Teachers, and Students*, 369.

Music is often perverted to serve purposes of evil, and it thus becomes one of the most alluring agencies of temptation. But, rightly employed, it is a precious gift of God, designed to uplift the thoughts to high and noble themes, to inspire and elevate the soul.

As the children of Israel, journeying through the wilderness, cheered their way by the music of sacred song, so God bids His children today gladden their pilgrim life. There are few means more effective for fixing His words in the memory than repeating them in song. And such song has wonderful power. It has power to subdue rude and uncultivated natures; power to quicken thought and to awaken sympathy, to promote harmony of action, and to banish the gloom and foreboding that destroy courage and weaken effort.—*Education*, 167.

Amidst the deepening shadows of earth's last great crisis, God's light will shine brightest, and the song of hope and trust will be heard in clearest and loftiest strains.—*Education*, 166.

My heart is steadfast, O God!
I will sing and make melody with all my being!
Awake, O harp and lyre!
I will awake the dawn!
I will give thanks to you, O Lord, among the peoples;
I will sing praises to you among the nations.

—Psalm 108:1–3, ESV

Singing Is an Act of Worship

Moreover King Hezekiah and the leaders commanded
the Levites to sing praise to the LORD *with the words of David*
and of Asaph the seer. So they sang praises with gladness,
and they bowed their heads and worshiped.
—2 Chronicles 29:30, NKJV

SINGING, AS A PART OF RELIGIOUS SERVICE, is as much an act of worship as is prayer. —*Patriarchs and Prophets*, 594.

A congregation may be the poorest in the land. It may be without the attraction of any outward show; but if the members possess the principles of the character of Christ, they will have His joy in their souls. Angels will unite with them in their worship. The praise and thanksgiving from grateful hearts will ascend to God as a sweet oblation. . . .

. . . The people of Israel, as they journeyed through the wilderness, praised God in sacred song. The commandments and promises of the Lord were set to music, and all along the journey these were sung by the pilgrim travelers. And in Canaan as they met at their sacred feasts God's wonderful works were to be recounted, and grateful thanksgiving was to be offered to His name. God desired that the whole life of His people should be a life of praise. Thus His way was to be made "known upon earth," His "saving health among all nations." Psalm 67:2.

So it should be now.—*Christ's Object Lessons*, 298, 299.

God be merciful to us and bless us,
And cause His face to shine upon us, . . .
That Your way may be known on earth,
Your salvation among all nations.
Let the peoples praise You, O God;
Let all the peoples praise You.
—Psalm 67:1–3, NKJV

Singing Brings Joy and Cheer

My lips shall greatly rejoice when I sing to You,
And my soul, which You have redeemed.

—Psalm 71:23, NKJV

THE HISTORY OF THE SONGS of the Bible is full of suggestion as to the uses and benefits of music and song.—*Education*, 167.

It was with songs of praise that the armies of Israel went forth to the great deliverance under Jehoshaphat. . . .

. . . Before the army went singers, lifting their voices in praise to God—praising Him for the victory promised.

On the fourth day thereafter, the army returned to Jerusalem, laden with the spoil of their enemies, singing praise for the victory won.—*Education*, 163.

With a song, Jesus in His earthly life met temptation. Often when sharp, stinging words were spoken, often when the atmosphere about Him was heavy with gloom, with dissatisfaction, distrust, or oppressive fear, was heard His song of faith and holy cheer.—*Education*, 166.

Then let us educate our hearts and lips to speak the praise of God for His matchless love. Let us educate our souls to be hopeful and to abide in the light shining from the cross of Calvary. Never should we forget that we are children of the heavenly King, sons and daughters of the Lord of hosts.—*The Ministry of Healing*, 253.

Blessed are the people who know the joyful sound!
They walk, O LORD, *in the light of Your countenance.*
In Your name they rejoice all day long,
And in Your righteousness they are exalted.
For You are the glory of their strength,
And in Your favor our horn is exalted.

—Psalm 89:15–17, NKJV

Nature Sings His Praise

Break forth into joy, sing together,
You waste places of Jerusalem!
For the LORD *has comforted His people,*
He has redeemed Jerusalem.

—Isaiah 52:9, NKJV

IT WAS CHRIST THAT SPREAD the heavens, and laid the foundations of the earth. It was His hand that hung the worlds in space, and fashioned the flowers of the field. "His strength setteth fast the mountains." "The sea is His, and He made it." Psalm 65:6; 95:5. It was He that filled the earth with beauty, and the air with song.—*The Desire of Ages*, 20.

From the solemn roll of the deep-toned thunder and old ocean's ceaseless roar, to the glad songs that make the forests vocal with melody, nature's ten thousand voices speak His praise.—*The Ministry of Healing*, 411.

The birds are teachers of the sweet lesson of trust. Our heavenly Father provides for them; but they must gather the food, they must build their nests and rear their young. Every moment they are exposed to enemies that seek to destroy them. Yet how cheerily they go about their work! how full of joy are their little songs!—*Education*, 117.

They also who dwell in the farthest parts are afraid of Your signs;
You make the outgoings of the morning and evening rejoice. . . .
. . . They drop on the pastures of the wilderness,
And the little hills rejoice on every side.

—Psalm 65:8, 12, NKJV

SEPTEMBER 13

Make a Joyful Noise

Singing Brings Joy, Faith, and Hope

Is anyone among you suffering?
Let him pray. Is anyone cheerful? Let him sing psalms.
—James 5:13, NKJV

GREAT HAVE BEEN the blessings received by men in response to songs of praise. . . .

How often in spiritual experience is this history repeated! how often by words of holy song are unsealed in the soul the springs of penitence and faith, of hope and love and joy!—*Education*, 162.

Jesus is our example. . . .

. . . He was never so full of worldly care as to have no time or thought for heavenly things. Often He expressed the gladness of His heart by singing psalms and heavenly songs. Often the dwellers in Nazareth heard His voice raised in praise and thanksgiving to God. He held communion with heaven in song; and as His companions complained of weariness from labor, they were cheered by the sweet melody from His lips. His praise seemed to banish the evil angels, and, like incense, fill the place with fragrance. The minds of His hearers were carried away from their earthly exile, to the heavenly home.—*The Desire of Ages*, 74, 73.

Shout joyfully to the LORD, all the earth;
Break forth in song, rejoice, and sing praises.
Sing to the LORD with the harp,
With the harp and the sound of a psalm,
With trumpets and the sound of a horn;
Shout joyfully before the LORD, the King.
—Psalm 98:4–6, NKJV

The Heavens Marveled and Rejoiced at God's Creation

"To what were its foundations fastened?
Or who laid its cornerstone,
When the morning stars sang together,
And all the sons of God shouted for joy?"

—Job 38:6, 7, NKJV

When "the heavens and the earth were finished, and all the host of them" (Genesis 2:1), the Creator and all heavenly beings rejoiced in contemplation of the glorious scene. "The morning stars sang together, and all the sons of God shouted for joy." Job 38:7.—*The Desire of Ages*, 769.

As the earth came forth from the hand of its Maker, it was exceedingly beautiful. Its surface was diversified with mountains, hills, and plains, interspersed with noble rivers and lovely lakes; but the hills and mountains were not abrupt and rugged, abounding in terrific steeps and frightful chasms, as they now do; the sharp, ragged edges of earth's rocky framework were buried beneath the fruitful soil, which everywhere produced a luxuriant growth of verdure. There were no loathsome swamps or barren deserts. Graceful shrubs and delicate flowers greeted the eye at every turn. The heights were crowned with trees more majestic than any that now exist. The air, untainted by foul miasma, was clear and healthful. The entire landscape outvied in beauty the decorated grounds of the proudest palace. The angelic host viewed the scene with delight, and rejoiced at the wonderful works of God.—*Patriarchs and Prophets*, 44.

Before the mountains were born,
before you gave birth to the earth and the world,
from beginning to end, you are God.

—Psalm 90:2, NLT

Songs of Celebration

You crown the year with Your goodness,
And Your paths drip with abundance.
They drop on the pastures of the wilderness,
And the little hills rejoice on every side.
The pastures are clothed with flocks;
The valleys also are covered over with grain;
They shout for joy, they also sing.

—Psalm 65:11–13, NKJV

Under the rulership of King David, Israel had joyfully united in chanting hymns of praise to the Most High, in recognition of their entire dependence on Him for daily mercies. Listen to their words of adoration as then they sang:

"O God of our salvation, . . .
Thou makest the outgoings of the morning
and evening to rejoice.
Thou visitest the earth, and waterest it:
Thou greatly enrichest it with the river
of God, which is full of water:
Thou preparest them corn,
when Thou hast so provided for it. . . .
The little hills rejoice on every side.
The pastures are clothed with flocks;
The valleys also are covered over with corn;
They shout for joy, they also sing"
(Psalm 65:5, 8, 9, 12, 13).—*Prophets and Kings*, 133.

Blessed is the man You choose,
And cause to approach You,
That he may dwell in Your courts.
We shall be satisfied with the goodness of Your house,
Of Your holy temple.

—Psalm 65:4, NKJV

We Are God's Special Treasure

Sing to the LORD,
For He has done excellent things;
This is known in all the earth.
Cry out and shout, O inhabitant of Zion,
For great is the Holy One of Israel in your midst!
—Isaiah 12:5, 6, NKJV

WHEN THE LIGHT OF CHRIST is shining in the soul, the lips will be filled with praise and thanksgiving to God.—*Thoughts From the Mount of Blessing*, 80.

The gifts which the gospel offers are not to be secured by stealth or enjoyed in secret.

"Ye are My witnesses, saith the Lord,
That I am God." Isaiah 43:12.

Our confession of His faithfulness is Heaven's chosen agency for revealing Christ to the world.—*The Ministry of Healing*, 100.

The daily blessings that we receive from the hand of God, and above all else the death of Jesus to bring happiness and heaven within our reach, should be a theme for constant gratitude. What compassion, what matchless love, has God shown to us, lost sinners, in connecting us with Himself, to be to Him a peculiar treasure! What a sacrifice has been made by our Redeemer, that we may be called children of God! We should praise God for the blessed hope held out before us in the great plan of redemption, we should praise Him for the heavenly inheritance and for His rich promises; praise Him that Jesus lives to intercede for us.—*Patriarchs and Prophets*, 289.

With such a . . . glorious hope, such a redemption that Christ has purchased for us by His own blood, shall we hold our peace? Shall we not praise God even with a loud voice, as did the disciples when Jesus rode into Jerusalem? Is not our prospect far more glorious than was theirs? Who dare then forbid us glorifying God, even with a loud voice, when we have such a hope, big with immortality, and full of glory?—*Early Writings*, 110.

"Now therefore, if you will indeed obey My voice and keep My covenant,
then you shall be a special treasure to Me above all people; for all the earth is Mine."
—Exodus 19:5, NKJV

"They will be my people," says the LORD of Heaven's Armies.
"On the day when I act in judgment, they will be my own special treasure.
I will spare them as a father spares an obedient child."
—Malachi 3:17, NLT

SEPTEMBER 17

Make a Joyful Noise

His Mercy Endures Forever

Many of the priests and Levites and heads of the fathers' houses,
old men who had seen the first temple, wept with a loud voice
when the foundation of this temple was laid before their eyes.
Yet many shouted aloud for joy.

—Ezra 3:12, NKJV

THE SETTING UP OF THE ALTAR of daily burnt offerings greatly cheered the faithful remnant. Heartily they entered into the preparations necessary for the rebuilding of the temple, gathering courage as these preparations advanced from month to month. . . . With joyous anticipation they looked forward to the time when, with temple rebuilt, they might behold the shining forth of His glory from within. . . .

. . . Soon the work was advanced to the point where the foundation stone must be laid. This was done in the presence of many thousands who had assembled to witness the progress of the work and to give expression to their joy in having a part in it. While the cornerstone was being set in position, the people, accompanied by the trumpets of the priests and the cymbals of the sons of Asaph, "sang together by course in praising and giving thanks unto the Lord; because He is good, for His mercy endureth forever toward Israel" [Ezra 3:11].—*Prophets and Kings*, 560, 563.

All of us used to live that way, following the passionate desires and inclinations
of our sinful nature. By our very nature we were subject to God's anger,
just like everyone else.
But God is so rich in mercy, and he loved us so much,
that even though we were dead because of our sins,
he gave us life when he raised Christ from the dead.
(It is only by God's grace that you have been saved!)

—Ephesians 2:3–5, NLT

Christ, Our Leader

And they sang responsively, praising and giving thanks to the LORD:
"For He is good,
For His mercy endures forever toward Israel."
Then all the people shouted with a great shout, when they praised the LORD,
because the foundation of the house of the LORD was laid. . . .
. . . The people could not discern the noise of the shout of joy
from the noise of the weeping of the people, for the people shouted
with a loud shout, and the soun was heard afar off.

—Ezra 3:11, 13, NKJV

MINGLED WITH THE MUSIC and the shouts of praise that were heard on that glad day, was a discordant note. "Many of the priests and Levites and chief of the fathers, who were ancient men, that had seen the first house, when the foundation of this house was laid before their eyes, wept with a loud voice" [Ezra 3:12]. . . .

. . . But some failed of discerning God's opening providences. Instead of rejoicing, they cherished thoughts of discontent and discouragement. They had seen the glory of Solomon's temple, and they lamented because of the inferiority of the building now to be erected. . . .

Could those who failed to rejoice at the laying of the foundation stone of the temple have foreseen the results of their lack of faith on that day, they would have been appalled. Little did they realize the weight of their words of disapproval and disappointment; little did they know how much their expressed dissatisfaction would delay the completion of the Lord's house.

There were many in the congregation, however, whose larger faith and broader vision did not lead them to view this lesser glory with such dissatisfaction. "Many shouted aloud for joy: so that the people could not discern the noise of the shout of joy from the noise of the weeping of the people: for the people shouted with a loud shout, and the noise was heard afar off" [Ezra 3:12, 13].—*Prophets and Kings*, 563, 565, 564.

Rejoicing for the King's Arrival

Rejoice, O people of Zion!
Shout in triumph, O people of Jerusalem!
Look, your King is coming to you.
He is righteous and victorious,
yet he is humble, riding on a donkey–
riding on a donkey's colt.

–Zechariah 9:9, NLT

When Jesus rode triumphantly into Jerusalem, His followers believed that He was about to ascend the throne of David and deliver Israel from her oppressors. With high hopes and joyful anticipations they vied with one another in showing honor to their King. Many spread their outer garments as a carpet in His path, or strewed before Him the leafy branches of the palm. In their enthusiastic joy they united in the glad acclaim: "Hosanna to the Son of David!"–*The Great Controversy*, 404.

As they proceeded, the multitude was continually increased by those who had heard of the coming of Jesus and hastened to join the procession. Spectators were constantly mingling with the throng, and asking, Who is this? What does all this commotion signify? . . .

Their questionings are silenced by a shout of triumph. Again and again it is repeated by the eager throng; it is taken up by the people afar off, and echoed from the surrounding hills and valleys. And now the procession is joined by crowds from Jerusalem. From the multitudes gathered to attend the Passover, thousands go forth to welcome Jesus. They greet Him with the waving of palm branches and a burst of sacred song.–*The Desire of Ages*, 570, 571.

"Hosanna to the Son of David!
'Blessed is He who comes in the name of the Lord!
Hosanna in the highest!' "

–Matthew 21:9, NKJV

The Battle for Victory

Thus says the L*ORD*:
"Sing with gladness for Jacob,
And shout among the chief of the nations;
Proclaim, give praise, and say,
'O L*ORD*, *save Your people, the remnant of Israel' "*
—Jeremiah 31:7, NKJV

IN VISION I SAW TWO ARMIES in terrible conflict. One army was led by banners bearing the world's insignia; the other was led by the bloodstained banner of Prince Immanuel. Standard after standard was left to trail in the dust as company after company from the Lord's army joined the foe and tribe after tribe from the ranks of the enemy united with the commandment-keeping people of God. . . .

The battle raged. Victory alternated from side to side. Now the soldiers of the cross gave way, "as when a standardbearer fainteth." Isaiah 10:18. But their apparent retreat was but to gain a more advantageous position. Shouts of joy were heard. A song of praise to God went up, and angel voices united in the song, as Christ's soldiers planted His banner on the walls of fortresses till then held by the enemy. The Captain of our salvation was ordering the battle and sending support to His soldiers. His power was mightily displayed, encouraging them to press the battle to the gates. He taught them terrible things in righteousness as He led them on step by step, conquering and to conquer.—*Testimonies for the Church*, vol. 8, 41.

"You must not fear them, for the L*ORD your God Himself fights for you."*
—Deuteronomy 3:22, NKJV

Praising Night and Day

At the dedication of the wall of Jerusalem
they sought out the Levites in all their places,
to bring them to Jerusalem to celebrate the dedication with gladness,
both with thanksgivings and with singing,
with cymbals and string instruments and harps.

—Nehemiah 12:27, NKJV

LESSONS OF GREAT PROFIT, even in this age of educational progress, may be found in the history of God's ancient people.—*Fundamentals of Christian Education*, 95.

The art of sacred melody was diligently cultivated. No frivolous waltz was heard, nor flippant song that should extol man and divert the attention from God; but sacred, solemn psalms of praise to the Creator, exalting His name and recounting His wondrous works. Thus music was made to serve a holy purpose, to lift the thoughts to that which was pure and noble and elevating, and to awaken in the soul devotion and gratitude to God.—*Fundamentals of Christian Education*, 97.

Music should have beauty, pathos, and power. Let the voices be lifted in songs of praise and devotion. Call to your aid, if practicable, instrumental music, and let the glorious harmony ascend to God, an acceptable offering.—*Testimonies for the Church*, vol. 4, 71.

It is good to proclaim your unfailing love in the morning,
your faithfulness in the evening,
accompanied by a ten-stringed instrument, a harp,
and the melody of a lyre.

—Psalm 92:2, 3, NLT

Sound of the Trumpets

"Also in the day of your gladness, in your appointed feasts,
and at the beginning of your months, you shall blow the trumpets
over your burnt offerings and over the sacrifices
of your peace offerings; and they shall be a memorial for you
before your God: I am the LORD *your God."*

—Numbers 10:10, NKJV

THE FEAST OF TABERNACLES was the closing gathering of the year. It was God's design that at this time the people should reflect on His goodness and mercy. . . .

. . . From far and near the people came, bringing in their hands a token of rejoicing. Old and young, rich and poor, all brought some gift as a tribute of thanksgiving to Him who had crowned the year with His goodness, and made His paths drop fatness. Everything that could please the eye, and give expression to the universal joy, was brought from the woods; the city bore the appearance of a beautiful forest.

At the first dawn of day, the priests sounded a long, shrill blast upon their silver trumpets, and the answering trumpets, and the glad shouts of the people from their booths, echoing over hill and valley, welcomed the festal day.—*The Desire of Ages*, 447, 448.

The temple was the center of the universal joy. Here was the pomp of the sacrificial ceremonies. Here, ranged on either side of the white marble steps of the sacred building, the choir of Levites led the service of song. The multitude of worshipers, waving their branches of palm and myrtle, took up the strain, and echoed the chorus; and again the melody was caught up by voices near and afar off, till the encircling hills were vocal with praise.—*The Desire of Ages*, 448.

All inhabitants of the world and dwellers on the earth:
When he lifts up a banner on the mountains, you see it;
And when he blows a trumpet, you hear it.

—Isaiah 18:3, NKJV

In Tune With Heaven

Then I will go to the altar of God,
To God my exceeding joy;
And on the harp I will praise You,
O God, my God.

—Psalm 43:4, NKJV

THROUGH SONG, DAVID, amidst the vicissitudes of his changeful life, held communion with heaven.—*Education*, 164.

The simple shepherd boy sang the songs of his own composing, and the music of his harp made a sweet accompaniment to the melody of his fresh young voice.—*Patriarchs and Prophets*, 637.

Daily revelations of the character and majesty of his Creator filled the young poet's heart with adoration and rejoicing. In contemplation of God and His works the faculties of David's mind and heart were developing and strengthening for the work of his afterlife. He was daily coming into a more intimate communion with God. His mind was constantly penetrating into new depths for fresh themes to inspire his song and to wake the music of his harp. The rich melody of his voice poured out upon the air, echoed from the hills as if responsive to the rejoicing of the angels' songs in heaven. . . .

. . . His talents, as precious gifts from God, were employed to extol the glory of the divine Giver. His opportunities of contemplation and meditation served to enrich him with that wisdom and piety that made him beloved of God and angels. . . . Each ray of new light called forth fresh bursts of rapture, and sweeter anthems of devotion, to the glory of God and the Redeemer. The love that moved him, the sorrows that beset him, the triumphs that attended him, were all themes for his active thought; and as he beheld the love of God in all the providences of his life, his heart throbbed with more fervent adoration and gratitude, his voice rang out in a richer melody, his harp was swept with more exultant joy.—*Patriarchs and Prophets*, 641, 642.

Rejoice in the Strength of the Lord

Then they returned, every man of Judah and Jerusalem,
with Jehoshaphat in front of them, to go back to Jerusalem with joy,
for the LORD *had made them rejoice over their enemies.*
So they came to Jerusalem, with stringed instruments
and harps and trumpets, to the house of the LORD.
—2 Chronicles 20:27, 28, NKJV

TOWARD THE CLOSE of Jehoshaphat's reign the kingdom of Judah was invaded by an army before whose approach the inhabitants of the land had reason to tremble. "The children of Moab, and the children of Ammon, and with them other beside the Ammonites, came against Jehoshaphat to battle." . . . 2 Chronicles 20:1.—*Prophets and Kings*, 198.

As they advanced to the battle, Jehoshaphat said, "Hear me, O Judah, and ye inhabitants of Jerusalem; Believe in the Lord your God, so shall ye be established: believe His prophets, so shall ye prosper." "And when he had consulted with the people, he appointed singers unto the Lord, and that should praise the beauty of holiness." 2 Chronicles 20:14–21. These singers went before the army, lifting their voices in praise to God for the promise of victory. . . .

God was the strength of Judah in this crisis, and He is the strength of His people today. . . .

Laden with spoil, the armies of Judah returned "with joy; for the Lord had made them to rejoice over their enemies. And they came to Jerusalem with psalteries and harps and trumpets unto the house of the Lord." 2 Chronicles 20:27, 28. Great was their cause for rejoicing. In obedience to the command, "Stand ye still, and see the salvation of the Lord: . . . fear not, nor be dismayed," they had put their trust wholly in God, and He had proved to be their fortress and their deliverer. Verse 17.—*Prophets and Kings*, 201–203.

At the Sound of the Trumpets

Indeed it came to pass,
when the trumpeters and singers were as one,
to make one sound to be heard in praising and thanking the LORD,
and when they lifted up their voice with the trumpets and cymbals
and instruments of music, and praised the LORD, *saying,*
"For he is good,
For His mercy endures forever,"
that the house, the house of the LORD, *was filled with a cloud.*
—2 Chronicles 5:13, NKJV

AT LAST THE TEMPLE planned by King David, and built by Solomon his son, was completed. "All that came into Solomon's heart to make in the house of the Lord," he had "prosperously effected." 2 Chronicles 7:11. And now, in order that the palace crowning the heights of Mount Moriah might indeed be, as David had so much desired, a dwelling place "not for man, but for the Lord God" (1 Chronicles 29:1), there remained the solemn ceremony of formally dedicating it to Jehovah and His worship. . . .

At the appointed time the hosts of Israel, with richly clad representatives from many foreign nations, assembled in the temple courts. The scene was one of unusual splendor. Solomon, with the elders of Israel and the most influential men among the people, had returned from another part of the city, whence they had brought the ark of the testament. . . .

. . . With singing and with music and with great ceremony, "the priests brought in the ark of the covenant of the Lord unto his place, to the oracle of the house, into the most holy place" [2 Chronicles 5:7]. As they came out of the inner sanctuary, they took the positions assigned them. The singers—Levites arrayed in white linen, having cymbals and psalteries and harps—stood at the east end of the altar, and with them a hundred and twenty priests sounding with trumpets.—*Prophets and Kings*, 37, 38.

The Song of Victory

Then Miriam the prophetess,
the sister of Aaron, took a timbrel in her hand;
and all the women went out after her with timbrels and with dances.
And Miriam answered them,
"Sing to the Lord,
For he has triumphed gloriously!
The horse and its rider
He has thrown into the sea!"

—Exodus 15:20, 21, NKJV

FROM THE MOST TERRIBLE PERIL, one night had brought complete deliverance. That vast, helpless throng—bondmen unused to battle, women, children, and cattle, with the sea before them, and the mighty armies of Egypt pressing behind—had seen their path opened through the waters and their enemies overwhelmed in the moment of expected triumph. Jehovah alone had brought them deliverance, and to Him their hearts were turned in gratitude and faith. Their emotion found utterance in songs of praise. The Spirit of God rested upon Moses, and he led the people in a triumphant anthem of thanksgiving, the earliest and one of the most sublime that are known to man. . . .

Like the voice of the great deep, rose from the vast hosts of Israel that sublime ascription. It was taken up by the women of Israel, Miriam, the sister of Moses, leading the way, as they went forth with timbrel and dance. Far over desert and sea rang the joyous refrain, and the mountains re-echoed the words of their praise—"Sing ye to Jehovah, for He hath triumphed gloriously."

. . . That song does not belong to the Jewish people alone. It points forward to the destruction of all the foes of righteousness and the final victory of the Israel of God.—*Patriarchs and Prophets*, 287–289.

The Joy of the Victors

And I saw something like a sea of glass mingled with fire,
and those who have the victory over the beast, over his image
and over his mark and over the number of his name,
standing on the sea of glass, having the harps of God.
They sing the song of Moses,
the servant of God, and the song of the Lamb, saying:
"Great and marvelous are Your works,
Lord God Almighty!
Just and true are Your ways,
O King of the saints!"

—Revelation 15:2, 3, NKJV

BEFORE ENTERING THE CITY OF GOD, the Saviour bestows upon His followers the emblems of victory and invests them with the insignia of their royal state. The glittering ranks are drawn up in the form of a hollow square about their King, whose form rises in majesty high above saint and angel, whose countenance beams upon them full of benignant love. Throughout the unnumbered host of the redeemed every glance is fixed upon Him, every eye beholds His glory whose "visage was so marred more than any man, and His form more than the sons of men." Upon the heads of the overcomers, Jesus with His own right hand places the crown of glory. For each there is a crown, bearing his own "new name" (Revelation 2:17), and the inscription, "Holiness to the Lord." In every hand are placed the victor's palm and the shining harp. Then, as the commanding angels strike the note, every hand sweeps the harp strings with skillful touch, awaking sweet music in rich, melodious strains. Rapture unutterable thrills every heart, and each voice is raised in grateful praise: "Unto Him that loved us, and washed us from our sins in His own blood, and hath made us kings and priests unto God and His Father; to Him be glory and dominion for ever and ever." Revelation 1:5, 6.—*The Great Controversy*, 645.

Beware the Tongue

The thoughts of the wicked are an abomination to the LORD,
But the words of the pure are pleasant.

—Proverbs 15:26, NKJV

WHEN CHRIST ABIDES in the heart, there will be purity and refinement of thought and manner.—*Thoughts From the Mount of Blessing*, 24.

There will be manifest a growing distaste for careless manners, unseemly language, and coarse thought.—*Thoughts From the Mount of Blessing*, 24.

We should accustom ourselves to speak in pleasant tones, to use pure and correct language, and words that are kind and courteous. Sweet, kind words are as dew and gentle showers to the soul. The Scripture says of Christ that grace was poured into His lips that He might "know how to speak a word in season to him that is weary." Psalm 45:2; Isaiah 50:4. And the Lord bids us, "Let your speech be alway with grace" (Colossians 4:6) "that it may minister grace unto the hearers" (Ephesians 4:29).—*Christ's Object Lessons*, 336.

Kind, cheerful, and encouraging words will prove more effective than the most healing medicines. These will bring courage to the heart of the desponding and discouraged, and the happiness and sunshine brought . . . by kind acts and encouraging words will repay the effort tenfold.—*Testimonies for the Church*, vol. 1, 306.

Never allow censure to escape your lips, for it is like desolating hail to those around you. Let cheerful, happy, loving words fall from your lips.—*Testimonies for the Church*, vol. 1, 704.

Even so the tongue is a little member and boasts great things.
See how great a forest a little fire kindles!

—James 3:5, NKJV

Be Careful What You Say and How You Say It

The wise are known for their understanding,
and pleasant words are persuasive. . . .
From a wise mind comes wise speech;
the words of the wise are persuasive.
Kind words are like honey–
sweet to the soul and healthy for the body.

—Proverbs 16:21, 23, 24, NLT

WORDS OF CHEER and encouragement spoken when the soul is sick and the pulse of courage is low—these are regarded by the Saviour as if spoken to Himself. As hearts are cheered, the heavenly angels look on in pleased recognition.—*The Ministry of Healing*, 159.

The grace of Christ is to control the temper and the voice. Its working will be seen in politeness and tender regard shown by brother for brother, in kind, encouraging words.—*Christ's Object Lessons*, 102.

The influence of the mind on the body, as well as of the body on the mind, should be emphasized. . . . The depressing and even ruinous effect of anger, discontent, selfishness, or impurity, and, on the other hand, the marvelous life-giving power to be found in cheerfulness, unselfishness, gratitude, should also be shown. . . .

. . . "Pleasant words" the Scriptures declare to be not only "sweet to the soul," but "health to the bones." Proverbs 16:24.—*Education*, 197.

"And I tell you this, you must give an account
on judgment day for every idle word you speak.
The words you say will either acquit you or condemn you."

—Matthew 12:36, 37, NLT

Words of Help and Encouragement

Plans go wrong for lack of advice;
many advisers bring success.
Everyone enjoys a fitting reply;
it is wonderful to say the right thing at the right time!
—Proverbs 15:22, 23, NLT

THE POWER OF SPEECH is of great value, and the voice should be cultivated for the blessing of those with whom we come in contact.—*Counsels to Parents, Teachers, and Students*, 240.

As followers of Christ we should make our words such as to be a help and an encouragement to one another in the Christian life. Far more than we do, we need to speak of the precious chapters in our experience. We should speak of the mercy and loving-kindness of God, of the matchless depths of the Saviour's love. Our words should be words of praise and thanksgiving. If the mind and heart are full of the love of God, this will be revealed in the conversation.—*Christ's Object Lessons*, 338.

Precious indeed in this world of sin and ignorance is the gift of speech, the melody of the human voice, when devoted to the praise of Him who hath loved us and given Himself for us.—*Counsels to Parents, Teachers, and Students*, 245.

The love of Christ in the soul is as "a well of water, springing up into everlasting life." . . . Those who posses this love will delight to talk of the things that God has prepared for them that love Him.—*Messages to Young People*, 390.

The wise at heart have a reputation for understanding;
pleasant words make the lips more persuasive.
—Proverbs 16:21, VOICE

OCTOBER 1

Happy People

The Joy of Seeing Christ

"Your father Abraham rejoiced to see My day, and he saw it and was glad."

—John 8:56, NKJV

ABRAHAM HAD GREATLY DESIRED to see the promised Saviour. He offered up the most earnest prayer that before his death he might behold the Messiah. And he saw Christ. A supernatural light was given him, and he acknowledged Christ's divine character. He saw His day, and was glad. He was given a view of the divine sacrifice for sin. Of this sacrifice he had an illustration in his own experience. The command came to him, "Take now thy son, thine only son Isaac, whom thou lovest, . . . and offer him . . . for a burnt offering." Genesis 22:2. Upon the altar of sacrifice he laid the son of promise, the son in whom his hopes were centered. Then as he waited beside the altar with knife upraised to obey God, he heard a voice from heaven saying, "Lay not thine hand upon the lad, neither do thou anything unto him: for now I know that thou fearest God, seeing thou hast not withheld thy son, thine only son from Me." Genesis 22:12. This terrible ordeal was imposed upon Abraham that he might see the day of Christ, and realize the great love of God for the world, so great that to raise it from its degradation, He gave His only-begotten Son to a most shameful death.

Abraham learned of God the greatest lesson ever given to mortal. His prayer that he might see Christ before he should die was answered. He saw Christ; he saw all that mortal can see, and live. By making an entire surrender, he was able to understand the vision of Christ, which had been given him. He was shown that in giving His only-begotten Son to save sinners from eternal ruin, God was making a greater and more wonderful sacrifice than ever man could make.—*The Desire of Ages*, 468, 469.

The Joy at the Birth of a Child

And Sarah said, "God has made me laugh,
and all who hear will laugh with me."
—Genesis 21:6, NKJV

There was given to Abraham the promise, especially dear to the people of that age, of a numerous posterity and of national greatness: "I will make of thee a great nation, and I will bless thee, and make thy name great; and thou shalt be a blessing." And to this was added the assurance, precious above every other to the inheritor of faith, that of his line the Redeemer of the world should come: "In thee shall all families of the earth be blessed."—*Patriarchs and Prophets*, 125.

When Abraham was nearly one hundred years old, the promise of a son was repeated to him, with the assurance that the future heir should be the child of Sarah. But Abraham did not yet understand the promise. His mind at once turned to Ishmael, clinging to the belief that through him God's gracious purposes were to be accomplished. . . . Again the promise was given, in words that could not be mistaken: "Sarah thy wife shall bear thee a son indeed; and thou shalt call his name Isaac: and I will establish My covenant with him." . . .

The birth of Isaac, bringing, after a lifelong waiting, the fulfillment of their dearest hopes, filled the tents of Abraham and Sarah with gladness.—*Patriarchs and Prophets*, 146.

Isaac was her joy and pride; her life was bound up in him.—*Patriarchs and Prophets*, 148.

And Sarah said, "God has made me to laugh, and all who hear will laugh with me."
She also said, "Who would have said to Abraham that Sarah
would nurse children? For I have borne him a son in his old age."
—Genesis 21:6, 7, NKJV

OCTOBER 3

Happy People

The Joy of an Answered Prayer

Hannah prayed and said:
"My heart rejoices in the LORD;
My horn is exalted in the LORD.
I smile at my enemies,
Because I rejoice in Your salvation."

—1 Samuel 2:1, NKJV

HANNAH'S PRAYER WAS GRANTED; she received the gift for which she had so earnestly entreated. As she looked upon the child, she called him Samuel—"asked of God." As soon as the little one was old enough to be separated from his mother, she fulfilled her vow. She loved her child with all the devotion of a mother's heart; day by day, as she watched his expanding powers and listened to his childish prattle, her affections entwined about him more closely. He was her only son, the special gift of Heaven; but she had received him as a treasure consecrated to God, and she would not withhold from the Giver His own.

Once more Hannah journeyed with her husband to Shiloh and presented to the priest, in the name of God, her precious gift, saying, "For this child I prayed; and the Lord hath given me my petition which I asked of Him: therefore also I have lent him to the Lord; as long as he liveth he shall be lent to the Lord." . . .

The mother's heart was filled with joy and praise, and she longed to pour forth her gratitude to God. The Spirit of Inspiration came upon her; "and Hannah prayed, and said:

'My heart rejoiceth in the Lord;
Mine horn is exalted in the Lord.' "

—*Patriarchs and Prophets*, 570, 571.

"O LORD of Heaven's Armies, if you will look upon my sorrow
and answer my prayer and give me a son, then I will give him back to you.
He will be yours for his entire lifetime, and as a sign
that he has been dedicated to the LORD, his hair will never be cut."

—1 Samuel 1:11, NLT

The Joy Found in Deliverance

And Moses told his father-in-law all that the LORD had done
to Pharaoh and to the Egyptians for Israel's sake,
and all the hardship that had come upon them on the way,
and how the LORD had delivered them.
Then Jethro rejoiced for all the good
which the LORD had done for Israel, whom He had delivered
out of the hand of the Egyptians.

—Exodus 18:8, 9, NKJV

NOT FAR DISTANT from where the Israelites were now encamped was the home of Jethro, the father-in-law of Moses. Jethro had heard of the deliverance of the Hebrews, and he now set out to visit them, and restore to Moses his wife and two sons. The great leader was informed by messengers of their approach, and he went out with joy to meet them, and, the first greetings over, conducted them to his tent. He had sent back his family when on his way to the perils of leading Israel from Egypt, but now he could again enjoy the relief and comfort of their society. To Jethro he recounted the wonderful dealings of God with Israel, and the patriarch rejoiced and blessed the Lord, and with Moses and the elders he united in offering sacrifice and holding a solemn feast in commemoration of God's mercy.—*Patriarchs and Prophets*, 300.

Jethro said, "Blessed be the LORD, who has delivered you
from the Egyptians and from Pharaoh. Now I know that the LORD
is greater than all gods, because he delivered the people from the Egyptians,
when they dealt arrogantly with them."

—Exodus 18:10, 11, NRSV

The Joy of Giving to Build God's Temple

Then the people rejoiced because these had given willingly,
for with single mind they had offered freely to the LORD;
King David also rejoiced greatly.
—1 Chronicles 29:9, NRSV

WITH DEEPEST INTEREST the king had gathered the rich material for building and beautifying the temple. He had composed the glorious anthems that in afteryears should echo through its courts. Now his heart was made glad in God, as the chief of the fathers and the princes of Israel so nobly responded to his appeal, and offered themselves to the important work before them. And as they gave their service, they were disposed to do more. They swelled the offerings, giving of their own possessions into the treasury. David had felt deeply his own unworthiness in gathering the material for the house of God, and the expression of loyalty in the ready response of the nobles of his kingdom, as with willing hearts they dedicated their treasures to Jehovah and devoted themselves to His service, filled him with joy. But it was God alone who had imparted this disposition to His people. He, not man, must be glorified. It was He who had provided the people with the riches of earth, and His Spirit had made them willing to bring their precious things for the temple. It was all of the Lord; if His love had not moved upon the hearts of the people, the king's efforts would have been vain, and the temple would never have been erected.

All that man receives of God's bounty still belongs to God. Whatever God has bestowed in the valuable and beautiful things of earth is placed in the hands of men to test them—to sound the depths of their love for Him and their appreciation of His favors. Whether it be the treasures of wealth or of intellect, they are to be laid, a willing offering, at the feet of Jesus; the giver saying, meanwhile, with David, "All things come of Thee, and of Thine own have we given Thee."—*Patriarchs and Prophets*, 752, 753.

Rejoicing in God's Goodness

Solomon held a feast,
and all Israel with him, a great assembly from the entrance
of Hamath to the Brook of Egypt, before the LORD our God,
seven days and seven more days–fourteen days.
On the eighth day he sent the people away;
and they blessed the king, and went to their tents joyful
and glad of heart for all the good that the LORD had done
for His servant David, and for Israel His people.
—1 Kings 8:65, 66, NKJV

OF SURPASSING BEAUTY and unrivaled splendor was the palatial building which Solomon and his associates erected for God and His worship. Garnished with precious stones, surrounded by spacious courts with magnificent approaches, and lined with carved cedar and burnished gold, the temple structure, with its broidered hangings and rich furnishings, was a fit emblem of the living church of God on earth, which through the ages has been building in accordance with the divine pattern, with materials that have been likened to "gold, silver, precious stones," "polished after the similitude of a palace." 1 Corinthians 3:12; Psalm 144:12.—*Prophets and Kings*, 36.

"So the king and all the people dedicated the house of God." 2 Chronicles 7:1–5. For seven days the multitudes from every part of the kingdom, from the borders "of Hamath unto the river of Egypt," "a very great congregation," kept a joyous feast. The week following was spent by the happy throng in observing the Feast of Tabernacles. At the close of the season of reconsecration and rejoicing the people returned to their homes, "glad and merry in heart for the goodness that the Lord had showed unto David, and to Solomon, and to Israel His people." Verses 8, 10.—*Prophets and Kings*, 45.

When all the children of Israel saw how the fire came down,
and the glory of the LORD on the temple,
they bowed their faces to the ground on the pavement,
and worshiped and praised the LORD, saying:
"For He is good,
For His mercy endures forever."
—2 Chronicles 7:3, NKJV

OCTOBER 7
Happy People

Rejoicing at the Restoration of the Temple Services

"Then Hezekiah and all the people rejoiced that God had prepared the people, since the events took place so suddenly."

—2 Chronicles 29:36, NKJV

HEZEKIAH CAME TO THE THRONE determined to do all in his power to save Judah from the fate that was overtaking the northern kingdom. . . .

. . . No sooner had he ascended the throne than he began to plan and to execute. He first turned his attention to the restoration of the temple services, so long neglected; and in this work he earnestly solicited the co-operation of a band of priests and Levites who had remained true to their sacred calling. . . .

It was a time for quick action. The priests began at once. . . . They engaged heartily in the work of cleansing and sanctifying the temple. Because of the years of desecration and neglect, this was attended with many difficulties; but the priests and the Levites labored untiringly, and within a remarkably short time they were able to report their task completed. The temple doors had been repaired and thrown open; the sacred vessels had been assembled and put into place; and all was in readiness for the re-establishment of the sanctuary services.

In the first service held, the rulers of the city united with King Hezekiah and with the priests and Levites in seeking forgiveness for the sins of the nation. Upon the altar were placed sin offerings "to make an atonement for all Israel." "And when they had made an end of offering, the king and all that were present with him bowed themselves, and worshiped." Once more the temple courts resounded with words of praise and adoration. The songs of David and of Asaph were sung with joy, as the worshipers realized that they were being delivered from the bondage of sin and apostasy. "Hezekiah rejoiced, and all the people, that God had prepared the people: for the thing was done suddenly" [2 Chronicles 29:24, 29, 36].—*Prophets and Kings*, 331–333.

Joy at the Passover Feast

So the children of Israel who were present at Jerusalem
kept the Feast of Unleavened Bread seven days with great gladness;
and the Levites and the priests praised the L*ORD day by day,*
singing to the L*ORD, accompanied by loud instruments. . . .*
Then the whole assembly agreed to keep the feast another
seven days, and they kept it another seven days with gladness.
—2 Chronicles 30:21, 23, NKJV

IN HIS ZEAL to make the temple services a real blessing to the people, Hezekiah determined to revive the ancient custom of gathering the Israelites together for the celebration of the Passover feast.—*Prophets and Kings*, 335.

On the appointed day the Passover was observed, and the week was spent by the people in offering peace offerings and in learning what God would have them do. Daily the Levites "taught the good knowledge of the Lord;" and those who had prepared their hearts to seek God, found pardon. A great gladness took possession of the worshiping multitude; "the Levites and the priests praised the Lord day by day, singing with loud instruments;" all were united in their desire to praise Him who had proved so gracious and merciful.

The seven days usually allotted to the Passover feast passed all too quickly, and the worshipers determined to spend another seven days in learning more fully the way of the Lord. The teaching priests continued their work of instruction from the book of the law; daily the people assembled at the temple to offer their tribute of praise and thanksgiving; and as the great meeting drew to a close, it was evident that God had wrought marvelously in the conversion of backsliding Judah and in stemming the tide of idolatry which threatened to sweep all before it. The solemn warnings of the prophets had not been uttered in vain. "There was great joy in Jerusalem: for since the time of Solomon the son of David king of Israel there was not the like in Jerusalem" [2 Chronicles 30:26].—*Prophets and Kings*, 337.

OCTOBER 9
Happy People

Rejoicing at the Dedication of the Temple

Now the temple was finished on the third day of the month of Adar,
which was in the sixth year of the reign of King Darius.
Then the children of Israel, the priests and the Levites
and the rest of the descendants of the captivity, celebrated
the dedication of this house of God with joy.

—Ezra 6:15, 16, NKJV

IN REBUILDING THE HOUSE of the Lord, Zerubbabel had labored in the face of manifold difficulties. From the beginning, adversaries had "weakened the hands of the people of Judah, and troubled them in building," "and made them to cease by force and power." Ezra 4:4, 23. But the Lord had interposed in behalf of the builders.—*Prophets and Kings*, 594.

The promise, "The hands of Zerubbabel have laid the foundation of this house; his hands shall also finish it," was literally fulfilled [Zechariah 4:9]. "The elders of the Jews builded, and they prospered through the prophesying of Haggai the prophet and Zechariah the son of Iddo. And they builded, and finished it, according to the commandment of the God of Israel, and according to the commandment of Cyrus, and Darius, and Artaxerxes king of Persia. And this house was finished on the third day of the month Adar [the twelfth month], which was in the sixth year of the reign of Darius the king." Ezra 6:14, 15.

Shortly afterward the restored temple was dedicated. "The children of Israel, the priests, and the Levites, and the rest of the children of the captivity, kept the dedication of this house of God with joy;"—*Prophets and Kings*, 596.

And they kept the Feast of Unleavened Bread seven days with joy;
for the LORD made them joyful, and turned the heart
of the king of Assyria toward them, to strengthen their hands
in the work of the house of God, the God of Israel.

—Ezra 6:22, NKJV

The Joy of Returning to God

So the Levites quieted all the people, saying,
"Be still, for the day is holy; do not be grieved."
And all the people went their way to eat
and drink, to send portions and rejoice greatly,
because they understood
the words that were declared to them.
—Nehemiah 8:11, 12, NKJV

IT WAS THE TIME OF THE FEAST OF TRUMPETS. Many were gathered at Jerusalem. The scene was one of mournful interest. The wall of Jerusalem had been rebuilt and the gates set up, but a large part of the city was still in ruins.

On a platform of wood, erected in one of the broadest streets, and surrounded on every hand by the sad reminders of Judah's departed glory, stood Ezra, now an aged man. . . .

. . . Certain of the priests and Levites united with Ezra in explaining the principles of the law. . . .

"And the ears of all the people were attentive unto the book of the law." They listened, intent and reverent, to the words of the Most High. As the law was explained, they were convinced of their guilt, and they mourned because of their transgressions. But this day was a festival, a day of rejoicing, a holy convocation, a day which the Lord had commanded the people to keep with joy and gladness; and in view of this they were bidden to restrain their grief and to rejoice because of God's great mercy toward them. . . .

The earlier part of the day was devoted to religious exercises, and the people spent the remainder of the time in gratefully recounting the blessings of God and in enjoying the bounties that He had provided. Portions were also sent to the poor, who had nothing to prepare. There was great rejoicing because the words of the law had been read and understood.—*Prophets and Kings*, 661, 662.

And Ezra blessed the L*ORD, the great God.*
Then all the people answered, "Amen, Amen!"
—Nehemiah 8:6, NKJV

OCTOBER 11
Happy People

The Joy of Being Accepted Again

So everyone who had returned from captivity lived in these shelters
during the festival, and they were all filled with great joy!
The Israelites had not celebrated like this
since the days of Joshua son of Nun.

—Nehemiah 8:17, NLT

AND AT THE TIME APPOINTED—on the tenth day of the seventh month—the solemn services of the Day of Atonement were performed according to the command of God.

From the fifteenth to the twenty-second of the same month the people and their rulers kept once more the Feast of Tabernacles. It was proclaimed "in all their cities, and in Jerusalem, saying, Go forth unto the mount, and fetch olive branches, and pine branches, and myrtle branches, and palm branches, and branches of thick trees, to make booths, as it is written. So the people went forth, and brought them, and made themselves booths, everyone upon the roof of his house, and in their courts, and in the courts of the house of God. . . . And there was very great gladness."—*Prophets and Kings*, 665.

Israel had returned to God with deep sorrow for backsliding. They had made confession with mourning and lamentation. They had acknowledged the righteousness of God's dealings with them, and had covenanted to obey His law. Now they must manifest faith in His promises. God had accepted their repentance; they were now to rejoice in the assurance of sins forgiven and their restoration to divine favor.—*Prophets and Kings*, 667.

"Go and celebrate with a feast of rich foods and sweet drinks,
and share gifts of food with people who have nothing prepared.
This is a sacred day before our Lord. Don't be dejected and sad,
for the joy of the LORD *is your strength!"*

—Nehemiah 8:10, NLT

The Joy of Having a King

So all the people went to Gilgal, and there they made Saul king before the LORD *in Gilgal. There they made sacrifices of peace offerings before the* LORD, *and there Saul and all the men of Israel rejoiced greatly.*
—1 Samuel 11:15, NKJV

SAMUEL CONVOKED THE PEOPLE AT MIZPEH. Prayer was offered for divine guidance; then followed the solemn ceremony of casting the lot. In silence the assembled multitude awaited the issue. The tribe, the family, and the household were successively designated, and then Saul, the son of Kish, was pointed out as the individual chosen. But Saul was not in the assembly. Burdened with a sense of the great responsibility about to fall upon him, he had secretly withdrawn. He was brought back to the congregation, who observed with pride and satisfaction that he was of kingly bearing and noble form, being "higher than any of the people from his shoulders and upward." Even Samuel, when presenting him to the assembly, exclaimed, "See ye him whom the Lord hath chosen, that there is none like him among all the people?" And in response arose from the vast throng one long, loud shout of joy, "God save the king!"—*Patriarchs and Prophets*, 611.

While the people in general were ready to acknowledge Saul as their king, there was a large party in opposition. . . .

In this condition of affairs Saul did not see fit to assume the royal dignity. Leaving Samuel to administer the government as formerly, he returned to Gibeah. . . . In his home among the uplands of Benjamin he quietly occupied himself in the duties of a husbandman, leaving the establishment of his authority entirely to God.—*Patriarchs and Prophets*, 611, 612.

Samuel now proposed that a national assembly should be convoked at Gilgal, that the kingdom might there be publicly confirmed to Saul. It was done; "and there they sacrificed sacrifices of peace offerings before the Lord; and there Saul and all the men of Israel rejoiced greatly."—*Patriarchs and Prophets*, 613.

Rejoicing for Wisdom and Prosperity

*"Happy are your men and happy are these your servants,
who stand continually before you and hear your wisdom!
Blessed be the LORD your God, who delighted in you,
setting you on the throne of Israel! Because the LORD
has loved Israel forever, therefore He made you king,
to do justice and righteousness."*

—1 Kings 10:8, 9, NKJV

THE QUEEN OF SHEBA came to visit Solomon. Hearing of his wisdom and of the magnificent temple he had built, she determined "to prove him with hard questions" and to see for herself his famous works. Attended by a retinue of servants, and with camels bearing "spices, and gold in abundance, and precious stones," she made the long journey to Jerusalem. "And when she was come to Solomon, she communed with him of all that was in her heart." She talked with him of the mysteries of nature; and Solomon taught her of the God of nature, the great Creator, who dwells in the highest heaven and rules over all. "Solomon told her all her questions: there was not anything hid from the king, which he told her not," 1 Kings 10:1–3; 2 Chronicles 9:1, 2. . . .

By the time of the close of her visit the queen had been so fully taught by Solomon as to the source of his wisdom and prosperity that she was constrained, not to extol the human agent, but to exclaim, "Blessed be the Lord thy God, which delighted in thee, to set thee on the throne of Israel: because the Lord loved Israel forever, therefore made He thee king, to do judgment and justice." 1 Kings 10:9.—*Prophets and Kings*, 66, 67.

*So King Solomon surpassed all the kings of the earth in riches and wisdom.
Now all the earth sought the presence of Solomon to hear his wisdom,
which God had put in his heart.*

—1 Kings 10:23, 24, NKJV

The Joy Found in Reformation

And he brought out the king's son, put the crown on him,
and gave him the Testimony; they made him king and anointed him,
and they clapped their hands and said, "Long live the king!" . . .
. . . So all the people of the land rejoiced; and the city was quiet,
for they had slain Athaliah with the sword in the king's house.
—2 Kings 11:12, 20, NKJV

"The Levites and all Judah" (2 Chronicles 23:8) united with Jehoiada the high priest in crowning and anointing the child Joash and acclaiming him their king. "And they clapped their hands, and said, God save the king." 2 Kings 11:12.

"Now when Athaliah heard the noise of the people running and praising the king, she came to the people into the house of the Lord." 2 Chronicles 23:12. "And when she looked, behold, the king stood by a pillar, as the manner was, and the princes and the trumpeters by the king, and all the people of the land rejoiced, and blew with trumpets."

"Athaliah rent her clothes, and cried, Treason, Treason." 2 Kings 11:14. But Jehoiada commanded the officers to lay hold of Athaliah and all her followers and lead them out of the temple to a place of execution, where they were to be slain.

. . . Immediately after the execution of the impenitent queen "all the people of the land went into the house of Baal, and brake it down; his altars and his images brake they in pieces thoroughly, and slew Mattan the priest of Baal before the altars." Verse 18.

A reformation followed. Those who took part in acclaiming Joash king, had solemnly covenanted "that they should be the Lord's people." And now that the evil influence of the daughter of Jezebel had been removed from the kingdom of Judah, and the priests of Baal had been slain and their temple destroyed, "all the people of the land rejoiced: and the city was quiet." 2 Chronicles 23:16, 21.—*Prophets and Kings*, 215, 216.

OCTOBER 15
Happy People

Joy in Deliverance From Death

The Jews had light and gladness, joy and honor.
And in every province and city, wherever the king's command
and his decree came, the Jews had joy and gladness, a feast
and a holiday. Then many of the people of the land became
Jews, because fear of the Jews fell upon them.

—Esther 8:16, 17, NKJV

Darius Hystaspes, under whose reign the Jews had been shown marked favor, was succeeded by Xerxes the Great. It was during his reign that those of the Jews who had failed of heeding the message to flee were called upon to face a terrible crisis. Having refused to take advantage of the way of escape God had provided, now they were brought face to face with death. . . .

. . . In the providence of God, Esther, a Jewess who feared the Most High, had been made queen of the Medo-Persian kingdom. Mordecai was a near relative of hers. In their extremity they decided to appeal to Xerxes in behalf of their people. . . .

The events that followed in rapid succession,—the appearance of Esther before the king, the marked favor shown her, the banquets of the king and queen with Haman as the only guest, the troubled sleep of the king, the public honor shown Mordecai, and the humiliation and fall of Haman upon the discovery of his wicked plot,—all these are parts of a familiar story. God wrought marvelously for His penitent people; and a counter decree issued by the king, allowing them to fight for their lives, was rapidly communicated to every part of the realm by mounted couriers, who were "hastened and pressed on by the king's commandment." "And in every province, and in every city, whithersoever the king's commandment and his decree came, the Jews had joy and gladness, a feast and a good day. And many of the people of the land became Jews; for the fear of the Jews fell upon them." Esther 8:14, 17.—*Prophets and Kings*, 600–602.

The King Was Exceedingly Glad That Daniel's God Was Able

Now the king was exceedingly glad for him,
and commanded that they should take Daniel up out of the den.
So Daniel was taken up out of the den, and no injury whatever
was found on him, because he believed in his God.
—Daniel 6:23, NKJV

"It pleased Darius to set over the kingdom an hundred and twenty princes, which should be over the whole kingdom; and over these three presidents; of whom Daniel was first" (Daniel 6:1, 2).

The honors bestowed upon Daniel excited the jealousy of the leading men of the kingdom, and they sought for occasion of complaint against him. But they could find none, "forasmuch as he was faithful, neither was there any error or fault found in him." . . .

Thereupon the presidents and princes, counseling together, devised a scheme whereby they hoped to accomplish the prophet's destruction.—*Prophets and Kings*, 539, 540.

"The king . . . was sore displeased . . ., and set his heart on Daniel to deliver him: and he laboured till the going down of the sun to deliver him. . . . Then the king went to his palace, and passed the night fasting: neither were instruments of musick brought before him: and his sleep went from him" (Daniel 6:14, 18).

God did not prevent Daniel's enemies from casting him into the lions' den; He permitted evil angels and wicked men thus far to accomplish their purpose; but it was that He might make the deliverance of His servant more marked, and the defeat of the enemies of truth and righteousness more complete. . . .

Early the next morning King Darius hastened to the den and "cried with a lamentable voice," "O Daniel, servant of the living God, is thy God, whom thou servest continually, able to deliver thee from the lions?"

The voice of the prophet replied: "O king, live forever. My God hath sent His angel, and hath shut the lions' mouths, that they have not hurt me." . . .

"Then was the king exceeding glad for him, and commanded that they should take Daniel up out of the den."—*Prophets and Kings*, 543, 544.

OCTOBER 17

Happy People

The Wise Men Rejoice for the Lord's Guidance

When they heard the king, they departed; and behold,
the star which they had seen in the East went before them,
till it came and stood over where the young Child was.
When they saw the star, they rejoiced with exceedingly great joy.
—Matthew 2:9, 10, NKJV

THE WISE MEN FROM THE EAST were philosophers. They belonged to a large and influential class that included men of noble birth, and comprised much of the wealth and learning of their nation. . . .

. . . As these magi studied the starry heavens, and sought to fathom the mystery hidden in their bright paths, they beheld the glory of the Creator. Seeking clearer knowledge, they turned to the Hebrew Scriptures. In their own land were treasured prophetic writings that predicted the coming of a divine teacher. . . . But in the Old Testament the Saviour's advent was more clearly revealed. The magi learned with joy that His coming was near, and that the whole world was to be filled with a knowledge of the glory of the Lord.

The wise men had seen a mysterious light in the heavens upon that night when the glory of God flooded the hills of Bethlehem. As the light faded, a luminous star appeared, and lingered in the sky. . . . Could this strange star have been sent as a harbinger of the Promised One? . . . Through dreams they were instructed to go in search of the newborn Prince. . . .

. . . The journey, though long, was a happy one to them.

They have reached the land of Israel, and are descending the Mount of Olives, with Jerusalem in sight, when, lo, the star that has guided them all the weary way rests above the temple, and after a season fades from their view. With eager steps they press onward, confidently expecting the Messiah's birth to be the joyful burden of every tongue. But their inquiries are in vain. Entering the holy city, they repair to the temple. To their amazement they find none who seem to have a knowledge of the newborn king. . . .

The wise men departed alone from Jerusalem. The shadows of night were falling as they left the gates, but to their great joy they again saw the star, and were directed to Bethlehem.—*The Desire of Ages*, 59, 60, 63.

Rejoicing at Christ's Royal Entry

When he reached the placed where the road started down
the Mount of Olives, all of his followers began to shout and sing
as they walked along, praising God for all the wonderful miracles they had seen.
"Blessings on the King who comes in the name of the LORD!
Peace in heaven, and glory in highest heaven!"

—Luke 19:37, 38, NLT

CHRIST WAS FOLLOWING THE JEWISH custom for a royal entry. The animal on which He rode was that ridden by the kings of Israel, and prophecy had foretold that thus the Messiah should come to His kingdom. No sooner was He seated upon the colt than a loud shout of triumph rent the air. The multitude hailed Him as Messiah, their King. Jesus now accepted the homage which He had never before permitted, and the disciples received this as proof that their glad hopes were to be realized by seeing Him established on the throne. The multitude were convinced that the hour of their emancipation was at hand. In imagination they saw the Roman armies driven from Jerusalem, and Israel once more an independent nation.

All were happy and excited; the people vied with one another in paying Him homage. They could not display outward pomp and splendor, but they gave Him the worship of happy hearts. They were unable to present Him with costly gifts, but they spread their outer garments as a carpet in His path, and they also strewed the leafy branches of the olive and the palm in the way. They could lead the triumphal procession with no royal standards, but they cut down the spreading palm boughs, Nature's emblem of victory, and waved them aloft with loud acclamations and hosannas.—*The Desire of Ages*, 570.

" 'Blessed is the King who comes in the name of the LORD!'
Peace in heaven and glory in the highest!"

—Luke 19:38, NKJV

The Joy of Having a Unique Son

But the angel said to him,
"Do not be afraid, Zacharias,
for your prayer is heard; and your wife Elizabeth
will bear you a son, and you shall call his name John.
And you will have joy and gladness, and many will rejoice at his birth."
—Luke 1:13, 14, NKJV

FROM AMONG THE FAITHFUL IN ISRAEL, who had long waited for the coming of the Messiah, the forerunner of Christ arose. The aged priest Zacharias and his wife Elisabeth were "both righteous before God;" and in their quiet and holy lives the light of faith shone out like a star amid the darkness of those evil days. To this godly pair was given the promise of a son, who should "go before the face of the Lord to prepare His ways."

Zacharias dwelt in "the hill country of Judea," but he had gone up to Jerusalem to minister for one week in the temple, a service required twice a year from the priests of each course. . . .

He was standing before the golden altar in the holy place of the sanctuary. The cloud of incense with the prayers of Israel was ascending before God. Suddenly he became conscious of a divine presence. An angel of the Lord was "standing on the right side of the altar." The position of the angel was an indication of favor, but Zacharias took no note of this. For many years he had prayed for the coming of the Redeemer; now heaven had sent its messenger to announce that these prayers were about to be answered; but the mercy of God seemed too great for him to credit. He was filled with fear and self-condemnation.

But he was greeted with the joyful assurance: "Fear not, Zacharias: for thy prayer is heard; and thy wife Elisabeth shall bear thee a son, and thou shalt call his name John. And thou shalt have joy and gladness; and many shall rejoice at his birth. For he shall be great in the sight of the Lord, . . . and he shall be filled with the Holy Ghost."—*The Desire of Ages*, 97, 98.

The Joy Found in Preparing the Savior's way

"He who has the bride is the bridegroom;
but the friend of the bridegroom,
who stands and hears him, rejoices greatly because
of the bridegroom's voice. Therefore this joy of mine is fulfilled."
—John 3:29, NKJV

JOHN HAD BY NATURE the faults and weaknesses common to humanity, but the touch of divine love had transformed him. He dwelt in an atmosphere uncontaminated with selfishness and ambition, and far above the miasma of jealousy. He . . . showed how clearly he understood his relation to the Messiah, and how gladly he welcomed the One for whom he had prepared the way.

. . . John represented himself as the friend who acted as a messenger between the betrothed parties, preparing the way for the marriage. When the bridegroom had received his bride, the mission of the friend was fulfilled. He rejoiced in the happiness of those whose union he had promoted. So John had been called to direct the people to Jesus, and it was his joy to witness the success of the Saviour's work. He said, "This my joy therefore is fulfilled. He must increase, but I must decrease."

Looking in faith to the Redeemer, John had risen to the height of self-abnegation. He sought not to attract men to himself, but to lift their thoughts higher and still higher, until they should rest upon the Lamb of God. He himself had been only a voice, a cry in the wilderness. Now with joy he accepted silence and obscurity, that the eyes of all might be turned to the Light of life.—*The Desire of Ages*, 179.

John bore witness of Him and cried out, saying,
"This was He of whom I said, 'He who comes after me
is preferred before me, for He was before me.' "
—John 1:15, NKJV

The Joy Found in Repentance

And when Jesus came to the place,
He looked up and saw him, and said to him,
"Zacchaeus, make haste and come down,
for today I must stay at your house."
So he made haste and came down, and received Him joyfully.
—Luke 19:5, 6, NKJV

MANY CARAVANS ON THEIR WAY to the feast passed through Jericho. Their arrival was always a festive season, but now a deeper interest stirred the people. It was known that the Galilean Rabbi who had so lately brought Lazarus to life was in the throng; and though whispers were rife as to the plottings of the priests, the multitudes were eager to do Him homage. . . .

. . . Zacchaeus had heard of Jesus. The report of One who had borne Himself with kindness and courtesy toward the proscribed classes had spread far and wide. In this chief of the publicans was awakened a longing for a better life. . . .

. . . The news sounded through Jericho that Jesus was entering the town. Zacchaeus determined to see Him. . . .

The streets were crowded, and Zacchaeus, who was small of stature, could see nothing over the heads of the people. None would give way for him; so, running a little in advance of the multitude, to where a wide-branching fig tree hung over the way, the rich tax collector climbed to a seat among the boughs, whence he could survey the procession as it passed below. The crowd comes near, it is going by, and Zacchaeus scans with eager eyes to discern the one figure he longs to see.

. . . Suddenly, just beneath the fig tree, a group halts, the company before and behind come to a standstill, and One looks upward whose glance seems to read the soul. Almost doubting his senses, the man in the tree hears the words, "Zacchaeus, make haste, and come down; for today I must abide at thy house."

The multitude give way, and Zacchaeus, walking as in a dream, leads the way toward his own home. . . .

. . . Christ went to his home to give him lessons of truth, and to instruct his household in the things of the kingdom. They had been shut out from the synagogues by the contempt of rabbis and worshipers; but now, the most favored household in all Jericho, they gathered in their own home about the divine Teacher, and heard for themselves the words of life.—*The Desire of Ages*, 552–554, 556.

The Seventy Disciples Rejoiced in His Power

Then the seventy returned with joy, saying,
"Lord, even the demons are subject to us in Your name."
—Luke 10:17, NKJV

LIKE THE TWELVE APOSTLES, the seventy disciples whom Christ sent forth later received supernatural endowments as a seal of their mission. When their work was completed, they returned with joy, saying, "Lord, even the devils are subject unto us through Thy name." Jesus answered, "I beheld Satan as lightning fall from heaven." Luke 10:17, 18.

Henceforth Christ's followers are to look upon Satan as a conquered foe. Upon the cross, Jesus was to gain the victory for them; that victory He desired them to accept as their own. "Behold," He said, "I give unto you power to tread on serpents and scorpions, and over all the power of the enemy: and nothing shall by any means hurt you." Verse 19.

. . . It is true that Satan is a powerful being; but, thank God, we have a mighty Saviour, who cast out the evil one from heaven. Satan is pleased when we magnify his power. Why not talk of Jesus? Why not magnify His power and His love?—*The Ministry of Healing*, 94.

In that hour Jesus rejoiced in the Spirit and said,
"I thank You, Father, Lord of heaven and earth,
that You have hidden these things from the wise and prudent
and revealed them to babes. Even so, Father, for so it seemed good in Your sight."
—Luke 10:21, NKJV

Great Joy at the News of the Resurrection

The women ran quickly from the tomb.
They were very frightened but also filled with great joy,
and they rushed to give the disciples the angel's message.
—Matthew 28:8, NLT

THE WOMEN WHO HAD STOOD by the cross of Christ waited and watched for the hours of the Sabbath to pass. On the first day of the week, very early, they made their way to the tomb, taking with them precious spices to anoint the Saviour's body. . . .

The women had not all come to the tomb from the same direction. Mary Magdalene was the first to reach the place; and upon seeing that the stone was removed, she hurried away to tell the disciples. Meanwhile the other women came up. A light was shining about the tomb, but the body of Jesus was not there. As they lingered about the place, suddenly they saw that they were not alone. A young man clothed in shining garments was sitting by the tomb. It was the angel who had rolled away the stone. . . . "Fear not ye," he said; "for I know that ye seek Jesus, which was crucified. He is not here: for He is risen, as He said. Come, see the place where the Lord lay. And go quickly, and tell His disciples that He is risen from the dead." . . .

He is risen, He is risen! The women repeat the words again and again. No need now for the anointing spices. The Saviour is living, and not dead. They remember now that when speaking of His death He said that He would rise again. What a day is this to the world! Quickly the women departed from the sepulcher "with fear and great joy; and did run to bring His disciples word."—*The Desire of Ages*, 788, 789.

The Joy of the Disciples When They Saw the Risen Lord

When He had said this, He showed them His hands and His side.
Then the disciples were glad when they saw the Lord.
—John 20:20, NKJV

ON REACHING JERUSALEM the two disciples enter [returning from Emmaus] at the eastern gate, which is open at night on festal occasions. The houses are dark and silent, but the travelers make their way through the narrow streets by the light of the rising moon. They go to the upper chamber where Jesus spent the hours of the last evening before His death. Here they know that their brethren are to be found. Late as it is, they know that the disciples will not sleep till they learn for a certainty what has become of the body of their Lord. They find the door of the chamber securely barred. They knock for admission, but no answer comes. All is still. Then they give their names. The door is carefully unbarred, they enter, and Another, unseen, enters with them. Then the door is again fastened, to keep out spies.

The travelers find all in surprised excitement. The voices of those in the room break out into thanksgiving and praise, saying, "The Lord is risen indeed, and hath appeared to Simon." Then the two travelers, panting with the haste with which they have made their journey, tell the wondrous story of how Jesus has appeared to them. They have just ended, and some are saying that they cannot believe it, for it is too good to be true, when behold, another Person stands before them. Every eye is fastened upon the Stranger. No one has knocked for entrance. No footstep has been heard. The disciples are startled, and wonder what it means. Then they hear a voice which is no other than the voice of their Master. Clear and distinct the words fall from His lips, "Peace be unto you." . . .

They beheld the hands and feet marred by the cruel nails. They recognized His voice, like no other they had ever heard. . . . "Then were the disciples glad, when they saw the Lord." Faith and joy took the place of unbelief, and with feelings which no words could express they acknowledged their risen Saviour.—*The Desire of Ages*, 802, 803.

Great Joy After the Ascension

Now it came to pass, while He blessed them,
that He was parted from them and carried up into heaven.
And they worshiped Him, and returned to Jerusalem
with great joy.

—Luke 24:51, 52, NKJV

CHRIST HAD ASCENDED TO HEAVEN in the form of humanity. The disciples had beheld the cloud receive Him. The same Jesus who had walked and talked and prayed with them; who had broken bread with them; who had been with them in their boats on the lake; and who had that very day toiled with them up the ascent of Olivet,—the same Jesus had now gone to share His Father's throne. And the angels had assured them that the very One whom they had seen go up into heaven, would come again even as He had ascended. . . .

When the disciples went back to Jerusalem, the people looked upon them with amazement. After the trial and crucifixion of Christ, it had been thought that they would appear downcast and ashamed. Their enemies expected to see upon their faces an expression of sorrow and defeat. Instead of this there was only gladness and triumph. Their faces were aglow with a happiness not born of earth. They did not mourn over disappointed hopes, but were full of praise and thanksgiving to God. With rejoicing they told the wonderful story of Christ's resurrection and His ascension to heaven, and their testimony was received by many.—*The Desire of Ages*, 832.

Joy Comes to Samaria

Philip went down to a city in Samaria
and proclaimed the Messiah there.
When the crowds heard Philip and saw the signs he performed,
they all paid close attention to what he said.
For with shrieks, impure spirits came out of many,
and many who were paralyzed or lame were healed.
So there was great joy in that city.

—Acts 8:5, 8, NIV

AMONG THOSE TO WHOM THE SAVIOUR had given the commission, "Go ye therefore, and teach all nations" (Matthew 28:19), were many from the humbler walks of life—men and women who had learned to love their Lord and who had determined to follow His example of unselfish service. To these lowly ones, as well as to the disciples who had been with the Saviour during His earthly ministry, had been given a precious trust. They were to carry to the world the glad tidings of salvation through Christ.

When they were scattered by persecution they went forth filled with missionary zeal. . . . The Lord wrought through them. Wherever they went, the sick were healed and the poor had the gospel preached unto them.

Philip, one of the seven deacons, was among those driven from Jerusalem. He "went down to the city of Samaria, and preached Christ unto them. And the people with one accord gave heed unto those things which Philip spake, hearing and seeing the miracles which he did. For unclean spirits . . . came out of many that were possessed with them: and many taken with palsies, and that were lame, were healed. And there was great joy in that city."—*The Acts of the Apostles*, 105, 106.

The Joy Found in Conversion

When they came up out of the water,
the Spirit of the Lord snatched Philip away.
The eunuch never saw him again but went on his way rejoicing.
—Acts 8:39, NLT

AND, BEHOLD, A MAN OF ETHIOPIA, a eunuch of great authority under Candace queen of the Ethiopians, who had the charge of all her treasure, and had come to Jerusalem for to worship, was returning, and sitting in his chariot read Esaias the prophet." This Ethiopian was a man of good standing and of wide influence. God saw that when converted he would give others the light he had received and would exert a strong influence in favor of the gospel. . . . By the ministration of the Holy Spirit the Lord brought him into touch with one who could lead him to the light.

Philip was directed to go to the Ethiopian and explain to him the prophecy that he was reading. . . .

The man's heart thrilled with interest as the Scriptures were explained to him; and when the disciple had finished, he was ready to accept the light given. He did not make his high worldly position an excuse for refusing the gospel. "As they went on their way, they came unto a certain water: and the eunuch said, See, here is water; what doth hinder me to be baptized? And Philip said, If thou believest with all thine heart, thou mayest. And he answered and said, I believe that Jesus Christ is the Son of God. And he commanded the chariot to stand still: and they went down both into the water, both Philip and the eunuch; and he baptized him."

"And when they were come up out of the water, the Spirit of the Lord caught away Philip, that the eunuch saw him no more: and he went on his way rejoicing."—*The Acts of the Apostles*, 107, 108.

The passage of Scripture he had been reading was this:
"He was led like a sheep to the slaughter.
And as a lamb is silent before the shearers,
he did not open his mouth."
—Acts 8:32, NLT

Gladness for New Believers

Then news of these things came
to the ears of the church in Jerusalem,
and they sent out Barnabas to go as far as Antioch.
When he came and had seen the grace of God, he was glad,
and encouraged them all that with purpose of heart
they should continue with the Lord.

—Acts 11:22, 23, NKJV

AFTER THE DISCIPLES had been driven from Jerusalem by persecution, the gospel message spread rapidly through the regions lying beyond the limits of Palestine; and many small companies of believers were formed in important centers. . . .

Among the places mentioned where the gospel was gladly received is Antioch, at that time the metropolis of Syria. The extensive commerce carried on from that populous center brought to the city many people of various nationalities. Besides, Antioch was favorably known as a resort for lovers of ease and pleasure, because of its healthful situation, its beautiful surroundings, and the wealth, culture, and refinement to be found there. In the days of the apostles it had become a city of luxury and vice.

The gospel was publicly taught in Antioch by certain disciples from Cyprus and Cyrene, who came "preaching the Lord Jesus." "The hand of the Lord was with them," and their earnest labors were productive of fruit. "A great number believed, and turned unto the Lord."

"Tidings of these things came unto the ears of the church which was in Jerusalem: and they sent forth Barnabas, that he should go as far as Antioch." Upon arrival in his new field of labor, Barnabas saw the work that had already been accomplished by divine grace, and he "was glad, and exhorted them all, that with purpose of heart they would cleave unto the Lord."—*The Acts of the Apostles*, 155, 156.

OCTOBER 29
Happy People

Gladness at Peter's Liberation

And as Peter knocked at the door of the gate,
a girl named Rhoda came to answer.
When she recognized Peter's voice, because of her gladness
she did not open the gate, but ran in and announced
that Peter stood before the gate.

—Acts 12:13, 14, NKJV

To Peter, in prison and condemned to death, God's angel appeared; . . . past the armed guards, the massive doors and great iron gateway with their bolts and bars, the angel led God's servant forth in safety.—*Education*, 255.

The apostle made his way at once to the house where his brethren were assembled and where they were at that moment engaged in earnest prayer for him. "As Peter knocked at the door of the gate, a damsel came to hearken, named Rhoda. And when she knew Peter's voice, she opened not the gate for gladness, but ran in, and told how Peter stood before the gate. And they said unto her, Thou art mad. But she constantly affirmed that it was even so. Then said they, It is his angel.

"But Peter continued knocking: and when they had opened the door, and saw him, they were astonished. But he, beckoning unto them with the hand to hold their peace, declared unto them how the Lord had brought him out of the prison." And Peter "departed, and went into another place." Joy and praise filled the hearts of the believers, because God had heard and answered their prayers and had delivered Peter from the hands of Herod.—*The Acts of the Apostles*, 148.

And when Peter had come to himself, he said,
"Now I know for certain that the Lord has sent His angel,
and has delivered me from the hand of Herod
and from all the expectation of the Jewish people."

—Acts 12:11, NKJV

The Gentiles Believed and Were Glad

For so the Lord has commanded us:
"I have set you as a light to the Gentiles,
That you should be for salvation to the ends of the earth."
Now when the Gentiles heard this, they were glad
and glorified the word of the Lord.
And as many as had been appointed to eternal life believed.
—Acts 13:47, 48, NKJV

PAUL AND BARNABAS visited Antioch in Pisidia and on the Sabbath day went into the Jewish synagogue and sat down. . . . Being . . . invited to speak, "Paul stood up, and beckoning with his hand said, Men of Israel, and ye that fear God, give audience." Then followed a wonderful discourse. . . .

The Spirit of God accompanied the words that were spoken, and hearts were touched. The apostle's appeal to Old Testament prophecies, and his declaration that these had been fulfilled in the ministry of Jesus of Nazareth, carried conviction to many a soul longing for the advent of the promised Messiah. And the speaker's words of assurance that the "glad tidings" of salvation were for Jew and Gentile alike, brought hope and joy to those who had not been numbered among the children of Abraham according to the flesh. . . .

The interest aroused in Antioch of Pisidia by Paul's discourse brought together on the next Sabbath day, "almost the whole city . . . to hear the word of God. But when the Jews saw the multitudes, they were filled with envy, and spake against those things which were spoken by Paul, contradicting and blaspheming.

"Then Paul and Barnabas waxed bold, and said, It was necessary that the word of God should first have been spoken to you: but seeing ye put it from you, and judge yourselves unworthy of everlasting life, lo, we turn to the Gentiles. For so hath the Lord commanded us, saying, I have set thee to be a light of the Gentiles, that thou shouldest be for salvation unto the ends of the earth."

"When the Gentiles heard this, they were glad, and glorified the word of the Lord: and as many as were ordained to eternal life believed." They rejoiced exceedingly that Christ recognized them as the children of God, and with grateful hearts they listened to the word preached.—*The Acts of the Apostles*, 170, 172, 173.

OCTOBER 31

Happy People

The Joy of Providing for Those in Need

Moreover, brethren, we make known to you
the grace of God bestowed on the churches of Macedonia:
that in a great trial of affliction the abundance of their joy
and their deep poverty abounded in the riches of their liberality.
For I bear witness that according to their ability,
yes, and beyond their ability, they were freely willing,
imploring us with much urgency that we would receive
the gift and the fellowship of the ministering to the saints.

—2 Corinthians 8:1–4, NKJV

Nearly all the Macedonian believers were poor in this world's goods, but their hearts were overflowing with love for God and His truth, and they gladly gave for the support of the gospel. When general collections were taken up in the Gentile churches for the relief of the Jewish believers, the liberality of the converts in Macedonia was held up as an example to other churches . . . .

The willingness to sacrifice on the part of the Macedonian believers came as a result of wholehearted consecration. Moved by the Spirit of God, they "first gave their own selves to the Lord" (2 Corinthians 8:5), then they were willing to give freely of their means for the support of the gospel. It was not necessary to urge them to give; rather, they rejoiced in the privilege of denying themselves even of necessary things in order to supply the needs of others. When the apostle would have restrained them, they importuned him to accept their offering. In their simplicity and integrity, and in their love for the brethren, they gladly denied self, and thus abounded in the fruit of benevolence.—*The Acts of the Apostles*, 343.

For you know the grace of our Lord Jesus Christ,
that though He was rich, yet for your sakes He became poor,
that you through His poverty might become rich.

—2 Corinthians 8:9, NKJV

NOVEMBER 1

Glad Tidings

The Good News of Salvation

With joy you will draw water from the wells of salvation.

—Isaiah 12:3, NRSV

THE TRUE PRINCIPLES OF CHRISTIANITY open before all a source of happiness, the height and depth, the length and breadth of which are immeasurable. It is Christ in us a well of water springing up into everlasting life. It is a continual wellspring from which the Christian can drink at will and never exhaust the fountain.—*Testimonies for the Church*, vol. 1, 565.

Why do we stay away from the fountain, when we can come and drink? Why do we die for bread, when there is a storehouse full? It is rich and free. O my soul, feast upon it, and daily drink in heavenly joys. I will not hold my peace. The praise of God is in my heart and upon my lips. We can rejoice in the fullness of our Saviour's love. We can feast upon His excellent glory.—*Testimonies for the Church*, vol. 1, 98.

The last words spoken by Christ to John were: "The Spirit and the bride say, Come. And let him that heareth say, Come. And let him that is athirst come. And whosoever will, let him take the water of life freely." Revelation 22:17. When we respond to God and say, "Lord, we come," then with joy shall we draw water out of the wells of salvation.—*Counsels to Parents, Teachers, and Students*, 370.

For God alone my soul waits in silence;
from him comes my salvation.
He alone is my rock and my salvation,
my fortress; I shall never be shaken.

—Psalm 62:1, 2, NRSV

NOVEMBER 2
Glad Tidings

God's Greatest Gift to the World

But the angel said to them, "Do not be afraid;
for see—I am bringing you good news of great joy for all the people:
to you is born this day in the city of David
a Savior, who is the Messiah, the Lord."

—Luke 2:10, 11, NRSV

IN THE FIELDS where the boy David had led his flock, shepherds were still keeping watch by night. Through the silent hours they talked together of the promised Saviour, and prayed for the coming of the King to David's throne. "And, lo, the angel of the Lord came upon them, and the glory of the Lord shone round about them: and they were sore afraid. And the angel said unto them, Fear not: for, behold, I bring you good tidings of great joy, which shall be to all people. For unto you is born this day in the city of David a Saviour, which is Christ the Lord."—*The Desire of Ages*, 47.

The Prince of heaven was among His people. The greatest gift of God had been given to the world. Joy to the poor; for Christ had come to make them heirs of His kingdom. Joy to the rich; for He would teach them how to secure eternal riches. Joy to the ignorant; He would make them wise unto salvation. Joy to the learned; He would open to them deeper mysteries than they had ever fathomed; truths that had been hidden from the foundation of the world would be opened to men by the Saviour's mission.—*The Desire of Ages*, 277.

For unto us a Child is born,
Unto us a Son is given;
And the government will be upon His shoulder.
And His name will be called
Wonderful, Counselor, Mighty God,
Everlasting Father, Prince of Peace.

—Isaiah 9:6, NKJV

Teaching, Preaching, and Healing

It came to pass, afterward,
that He went through every city and village,
preaching and bringing the glad tidings of the kingdom of God.
And the twelve were with Him.

—Luke 8:1, NKJV

CHRIST MIGHT HAVE OCCUPIED the highest place among the teachers of the Jewish nation, but He preferred rather to take the gospel to the poor. He went from place to place, that those in the highways and byways might hear the words of truth. By the sea, on the mountainside, in the streets of the city, in the synagogue, His voice was heard explaining the Scriptures. Often He taught in the outer court of the temple, that the Gentiles might hear His words.—*The Ministry of Healing*, 20.

Jesus watched with deep earnestness the changing countenances of His hearers. The faces that expressed interest and pleasure gave Him great satisfaction. As the arrows of truth pierced to the soul, breaking through the barriers of selfishness, and working contrition, and finally gratitude, the Saviour was made glad. When His eye swept over the throng of listeners, and He recognized among them the faces He had before seen, His countenance lighted up with joy. He saw in them hopeful subjects for His kingdom. When the truth, plainly spoken, touched some cherished idol, He marked the change of countenance, the cold, forbidding look, which told that the light was unwelcome. When He saw men refuse the message of peace, His heart was pierced to the very depths.—*The Desire of Ages*, 255.

And Jesus went about all Galilee, teaching in their synagogues,
preaching the gospel of the kingdom, and healing all kinds of sickness
and all kinds of disease among the people.

—Matthew 4:23, NKJV

Paul and Barnabas Brought Them to Antioch

And now we are here to bring you this Good News.
The promise was made to our ancestors, and God has now fulfilled
it for us, their descendants, by raising Jesus.
This is what the second psalm says about Jesus:
"You are my Son.
Today I have become your Father."

—Acts 13:32, 33, NLT

EVERY TRUE DISCIPLE is born into the kingdom of God as a missionary. He who drinks of the living water becomes a fountain of life. The receiver becomes a giver. The grace of Christ in the soul is like a spring in the desert, welling up to refresh all, and making those who are ready to perish eager to drink of the water of life.—*The Desire of Ages*, 195.

During His ministry, Jesus had kept constantly before the disciples the fact that they were to be one with Him in His work for the recovery of the world from the slavery of sin. When He sent forth the Twelve and afterward the Seventy, to proclaim the kingdom of God, He was teaching them their duty to impart to others what He had made known to them. In all His work He was training them for individual labor, to be extended as their numbers increased, and eventually to reach to the uttermost parts of the earth. The last lesson He gave His followers was that they held in trust for the world the glad tidings of salvation.—*The Acts of the Apostles*, 32.

Then Paul and Barnabas spoke out boldly and declared,
"It was necessary that we first preach the word of God to you Jews. . . .
For the Lord gave us this command when he said,
'I have made you a light to the Gentiles,
to bring salvation to the farthest corners of the earth.' "

—Acts 13:46, 47, NLT

A Joyous Work to Bring Glad Tidings to Others

And how will anyone go and tell them without being sent?
That it why the Scriptures say, "How beautiful
are the feet of messengers who bring good news!"

—Romans 10:15, NLT

IT WAS AT THE ORDINATION OF THE TWELVE that the first step was taken in the organization of the church that after Christ's departure was to carry on His work on the earth. . . .

Look upon the touching scene. Behold the Majesty of heaven surrounded by the Twelve whom He has chosen. He is about to set them apart for their work. By these feeble agencies, through His word and Spirit, He designs to place salvation within the reach of all.

With gladness and rejoicing, God and the angels beheld this scene. The Father knew that from these men the light of heaven would shine forth; that the words spoken by them as they witnessed for His Son, would echo from generation to generation till the close of time.—*The Acts of the Apostles*, 18.

Today the Saviour calls us, as He called Matthew and John and Peter, to His work. If our hearts are touched by His love . . . we shall rejoice to be co-workers with Christ. . . . If we make God our strength we shall have clear perceptions of duty, unselfish aspirations; our life will be actuated by a noble purpose.—*The Ministry of Healing*, 480.

All who commune with God will find abundance of work to do for Him. Those who go forth in the spirit of the Master, seeking to reach souls with the truth, will not find the work of drawing souls to Christ a dull, uninteresting drudgery. They are charged with a work as God's husbandmen, and they will become more and more vitalized as they give themselves to the service of God. It is a joyous work to open the Scriptures to others.—*Testimonies for the Church*, vol. 9, 118.

How beautiful on the mountains
are the feet of the messenger who brings good news,
the good news of peace and salvation,
the news that the God of Israel reigns!

—Isaiah 52:7, NLT

The Most Valuable Treasure

"Again, the kingdom of heaven is like treasure hidden in a field,
which a man found and hid; and for joy over it
he goes and sells all that he has and buys that field."

—Matthew 13:44, NKJV

IN THE PARABLE THE FIELD containing the treasure represents the Holy Scriptures. And the gospel is the treasure. The earth itself is not so interlaced with golden veins and filled with precious things as is the word of God.—*Christ's Object Lessons*, 104.

When Christ was on earth, He was brought in contact with some whose imaginations were fevered with the hope of worldly gain. They were never at rest, but were constantly trying something new, and their extravagant expectations were aroused only to be disappointed. Jesus knew the wants of the human heart, which are the same in all ages; and He called their attention to the only permanent riches. "The kingdom of heaven," said He, "is like unto treasure hid in a field; the which when a man hath found, he hideth, and for joy there-of goeth and selleth all that he hath, and buyeth that field." He tells men of treasure beyond estimate, which is within the reach of all. He came to earth to guide their minds in their search for this treasure. The way is marked out; the very poorest who will follow Him will be made richer than the most wealthy upon earth who know not Jesus, and they will be made increasingly rich by sharing their happiness with others.—*Testimonies for the Church*, vol. 5, 261.

Keep your life free from the love of money,
and be content with what you have; for he has said,
"I will never fail you or forsake you."

—Hebrews 13:5, NRSV

Peace and Joy in the Spirit

So do not let your good be spoken of as evil.
For the kingdom of God is not food and drink
but righteousness and peace and joy in the Holy Spirit.
The one who thus serves Christ is acceptable to God
and has human approval.

—Romans 14:16–18, NRSV

It is the privilege of every Christian to enjoy the deep movings of the Spirit of God. A sweet, heavenly peace will pervade the mind, and you will love to meditate upon God and heaven. You will feast upon the glorious promises of His word.—*Testimonies for the Church*, vol. 1, 159.

When the Spirit of God controls mind and heart, the converted soul breaks forth into a new song; for he realizes that in his experience the promise of God has been fulfilled, that his transgression has been forgiven, his sin covered. He has exercised repentance toward God for the violation of the divine law, and faith toward Christ, who died for man's justification. "Being justified by faith," he has "peace with God through our Lord Jesus Christ." Romans 5:1.—*The Acts of the Apostles*, 476.

There is peace in believing, and joy in the Holy Ghost. Believing brings peace, and trusting in God brings joy. Believe, believe! my soul says, believe. Rest in God. He is able to keep that which you have committed to His trust. He will bring you off more than conqueror through Him who hath loved you.—*Testimonies for the Church*, vol. 2, 319.

And hope does not disappoint us, because God's love has been poured
into our hearts through the Holy Spirit that has been given to us.

—Romans 5:5, NRSV

True and Complete Happiness

We proclaim to you what we ourselves have actually seen and heard
so that you may have fellowship with us.
And our fellowship is with the Father and with his Son, Jesus Christ.
We are writing these things so that you may fully share our joy.
—1 John 1:3, 4, NLT

THROUGH THE STUDY of the Scriptures we obtain a correct knowledge of how to live so as to enjoy the greatest amount of unalloyed happiness.—*Testimonies for the Church*, vol. 3, 374.

The teaching of the Bible has a vital bearing upon man's prosperity in all the relations of this life. It unfolds the principles that are the cornerstone of a nation's prosperity—principles with which is bound up the well-being of society, and which are the safeguard of the family—principles without which no man can attain usefulness, happiness, and honor in this life, or can hope to secure the future, immortal life. There is no position in life, no phase of human experience, for which the teaching of the Bible is not an essential preparation. Studied and obeyed, the word of God would give to the world men of stronger and more active intellect than will the closest application to all the subjects that human philosophy embraces. It would give men of strength and solidity of character, of keen perception and sound judgment—men who would be an honor to God and a blessing to the world.—*Patriarchs and Prophets*, 599.

"When I discovered your words, I devoured them.
They are my joy and my heart's delight,
for I bear your name,
O LORD *God of Heaven's Armies.*
I never joined the people in their merry feasts.
I sat alone because your hand was on me.
I was filled with indignation at their sins."
—Jeremiah 15:16, 17, NLT

Receive the Word With Joy and Rejoicing

When your words came, I ate them;
they were my joy and heart's delight,
for I bear your name,
LORD *God Almighty.*

—Jeremiah 15:16, NIV

THE WORD OF GOD in the Old and New Testaments, if faithfully studied and received into the life, will give spiritual wisdom and life. This word is to be sacredly cherished. Faith in the word of God and in the power of Christ to transform the life will enable the believer to work His works and to live a life of rejoicing in the Lord.—*Testimonies for the Church*, vol. 9, 279.

The life in which the fear of the Lord is cherished will not be a life of sadness and gloom. It is the absence of Christ that makes the countenance sad, and the life a pilgrimage of sighs. Those who are filled with self-esteem and self-love do not feel the need of a living, personal union with Christ. The heart that has not fallen on the Rock is proud of its wholeness. Men want a dignified religion. They desire to walk in a path wide enough to take in their own attributes. Their self-love, their love of popularity and love of praise, exclude the Saviour from their hearts, and without Him there is gloom and sadness. But Christ dwelling in the soul is a wellspring of joy. For all who receive Him, the very keynote of the word of God is rejoicing.—*Christ's Object Lessons*, 162.

I will greatly rejoice in the LORD,
My soul shall be joyful in my God;
For He has clothed me with the garments of salvation,
He has covered me with the robe of righteousness.

—Isaiah 61:10, NKJV

The Bible Is God's Message to Us

I rejoice at Your word
As one who finds great treasure.

—Psalm 119:162, NKJV

WE ARE TO REGARD THE BIBLE as God's disclosure to us of eternal things—the things of most consequence for us to know. By the world it is thrown aside as if the perusal of it were finished, but a thousand years of research would not exhaust the hidden treasure it contains. Eternity alone will disclose the wisdom of this Book, for it is the wisdom of an infinite mind.—*Counsels to Parents, Teachers, and Students*, 443.

But there is but little benefit derived from a hasty reading of the Scriptures. One may read the whole Bible through and yet fail to see its beauty or comprehend its deep and hidden meaning. . . .

. . . Some portions of Scripture are indeed too plain to be misunderstood, but there are others whose meaning does not lie on the surface to be seen at a glance. Scripture must be compared with scripture. There must be careful research and prayerful reflection. And such study will be richly repaid. As the miner discovers veins of precious metal concealed beneath the surface of the earth, so will he who perseveringly searches the word of God as for hid treasure find truths of the greatest value, which are concealed from the view of the careless seeker.—*Steps to Christ*, 90.

If the time and effort spent in seeking to grasp the bright ideas of infidels were given to studying the precious things of the word of God, thousands who now sit in darkness and in the shadow of death would be rejoicing in the glory of the Light of life.—*The Ministry of Healing*, 440.

"You search the Scriptures, for in them you think you have eternal life;
and these are they which testify of Me."

—John 5:39, NKJV

A Source of Wisdom and Happiness

When wisdom enters your heart,
And knowledge is pleasant to your soul,
Discretion will preserve you;
Understanding will keep you.

—Proverbs 2:10, 11, NKJV

EVERY MAN HAS THE OPPORTUNITY, to a great extent, of making himself whatever he chooses to be. The blessings of this life, and also of the immortal state, are within his reach. He may build up a character of solid worth, gaining new strength at every step. He may advance daily in knowledge and wisdom, conscious of new delights as he progresses, adding virtue to virtue, grace to grace. His faculties will improve by use; the more wisdom he gains, the greater will be his capacity for acquiring. His intelligence, knowledge, and virtue will thus develop into greater strength and more perfect symmetry. —*Counsels on Diet and Food*, 15.

Christ could have imparted to men knowledge that would have surpassed any previous disclosures, and put in the background every other discovery. He could have unlocked mystery after mystery, and could have concentrated around these wonderful revelations the active, earnest thought of successive generations till the close of time. But He would not spare a moment from teaching the science of salvation. . . .

Our Saviour did not encourage any to attend the rabbinical schools of His day, for the reason that their minds would be corrupted with the continually repeated, "They say," or, "It has been said." Why, then, should we accept the unstable words of men as exalted wisdom, when a greater, a certain, wisdom is at our command?—*The Ministry of Healing*, 448, 449.

For the LORD gives wisdom;
From His mouth come knowledge and understanding. . . .
Then you will understand righteousness and justice,
Equity and every good path.
When wisdom enters your heart,
And knowledge is pleasant to your soul,
Discretion will preserve you;
Understanding will keep you.

—Proverbs 2:6, 9–11, NKJV

Rooted to Overcome Trials and Temptations

"The seed on the rocky soil represents
those who hear the message and immediately receive it with joy.
But since they don't have deep roots, they don't last long.
They fall away as soon as they have problems
or are persecuted for believing God's word."
—Matthew 13:20, 21, NLT

IT IS NOT BECAUSE MEN receive the word immediately, nor because they rejoice in it, that they fall away. As soon as Matthew heard the Saviour's call, immediately he rose up, left all, and followed Him. As soon as the divine word comes to our hearts, God desires us to receive it; and it is right to accept it with joy. "Joy shall be in heaven over one sinner that repenteth." Luke 15:7. And there is joy in the soul that believes on Christ. But those who in the parable are said to receive the word immediately, do not count the cost. They do not consider what the word of God requires of them. They do not bring it face to face with all their habits of life, and yield themselves fully to its control. . . .

. . . Many receive the gospel as a way of escape from suffering, rather than as a deliverance from sin. They rejoice for a season, for they think that religion will free them from difficulty and trial. While life moves smoothly with them, they may appear to be consistent Christians. But they faint beneath the fiery test of temptation. They cannot bear reproach for Christ's sake. When the word of God points out some cherished sin, or requires self-denial or sacrifice, they are offended. . . . They look at the present inconvenience and trial, and forget the eternal realities.—*Christ's Object Lessons*, 46, 47.

For I am not ashamed of this Good News about Christ.
It is the power of God at work, saving everyone who believes.
—Romans 1:16, NLT

Baptism, the Natural Response

But Peter, standing up with the eleven,
raised his voice and said to them, . . .
he testified and exhorted them saying,
. . . "Be saved from this perverse generation."
Then those who gladly received his word were baptized;
and that day about three thousand souls were added to them.
—Acts 2:14, 40, 41, NKJV

THE SCENE IS ONE FULL OF INTEREST. Behold the people coming from all directions to hear the disciples witness to the truth as it is in Jesus. They press in, crowding the temple. Priests and rulers are there, the dark scowl of malignity still on their faces, their hearts still filled with abiding hatred against Christ. . . . They had thought to find the apostles cowed with fear under the strong hand of oppression and murder, but they find them lifted above all fear and filled with the Spirit, proclaiming with power the divinity of Jesus of Nazareth.—*The Acts of the Apostles*, 42.

Under the influence of this heavenly illumination the scriptures that Christ had explained to the disciples stood out before them with the luster of perfect truth. The veil that had prevented them from seeing to the end of that which had been abolished, was now removed, and they comprehended with perfect clearness the object of Christ's mission and the nature of His kingdom. They could speak with power of the Saviour; and as they unfolded to their hearers the plan of salvation, many were convicted and convinced. The traditions and superstitions inculcated by the priests were swept away from their minds, and the teachings of the Saviour were accepted.

"Then they that gladly received his word were baptized."—*The Acts of the Apostles*, 44.

And they continued steadfastly in the apostles' doctrines and fellowship,
in the breaking of bread, and in prayers.
—Acts 2:42, NKJV

God's Word for All

"Since David himself called the Messiah 'my Lord,'
how can the Messiah be his son?"
The large crowd listened to him with delight.

—Mark 12:37, NLT

CHRIST'S MANNER of teaching was beautiful and attractive, and it was ever characterized by simplicity. He unfolded the mysteries of the kingdom of heaven through the use of figures and symbols with which His hearers were familiar; and the common people heard Him gladly, for they could comprehend His words. There were no high-sounding words used, to understand which it was necessary to consult a dictionary.

Jesus illustrated the glories of the kingdom of God by the use of the experiences and occurrences of earth. In compassionate love and tenderness He cheered and comforted and instructed all who heard Him; for grace was poured upon His lips that He might convey to men in the most attractive way the treasures of truth.

The Saviour's voice was as music to the ears of those who had been accustomed to the monotonous, spiritless preaching of the scribes and Pharisees. He spoke slowly and impressively, emphasizing those words to which He wished His hearers to give special heed. Old and young, ignorant and learned, could catch the full meaning of His words. . . . The people were very attentive to Him, and it was said of Him that He spoke not as the scribes and Pharisees, for His word was as of one who had authority.—*Counsels to Parents, Teachers, and Students*, 240.

He entered the synagogue and taught. And they were astonished at His teaching,
for He taught them as one having authority, and not as the scribes.

—Mark 1:21, 22, NKJV

The Word Is the Light Sought by Many

So it was, when Jesus returned, that the multitude welcomed Him,
for they were all waiting for him.
—Luke 8:40, NKJV

THE TRUTH THAT WE HEAR will save us only as we gladly accept it, showing in our lives the result of its working, growing in grace and in a knowledge of God.—*Notebook Leaflets From the Elmshaven Library*, vol. 1, 13.

Christ "came unto His own, and His own received Him not." John 1:11. The light of God shone into the darkness of the world, and "the darkness comprehended it not." John 1:5. But not all were found indifferent to the gift of heaven. . . . In different nations there were earnest and thoughtful men who had sought in literature and science and the religions of the heathen world for that which they could receive as the soul's treasure. Among the Jews there were those who were seeking for that which they had not. Dissatisfied with a formal religion, they longed for that which was spiritual and uplifting. Christ's chosen disciples belonged to the latter class, Cornelius and the Ethiopian eunuch to the former. They had been longing and praying for light from heaven; and when Christ was revealed to them, they received Him with gladness.—*Christ's Object Lessons*, 116.

There was a certain man in Caesarea called Cornelius,
a centurion of what was called the Italian Regiment,
a devout man and one who feared God with all his household,
who gave alms generously to the people, and prayed to God always. . . .
. . . And those of the circumcision who believed were astonished,
as many as came with Peter, because the gift of the Holy Spirit
had been poured out on the Gentiles also.
—Luke 10:1, 2, 45, NKJV

NOVEMBER 16
Glad Tidings

Delighting in the Law

I long for Your salvation, O LORD,
And Your law is my delight.

—Psalm 119:174, NKJV

WHAT A GOD IS OUR GOD! He rules over His kingdom with diligence and care, and He has built a hedge—the Ten Commandments—about His subjects to preserve them from the results of transgression. In requiring obedience to the laws of His kingdom, God gives His people health and happiness, peace and joy. He teaches them that the perfection of character He requires can be attained only by becoming familiar with His word. —*Counsels to Parents, Teachers and Students*, 454.

Where there is not only a belief in God's word, but a submission of the will to Him; where the heart is yielded to Him, the affections fixed upon Him, there is faith—faith that works by love and purifies the soul. Through this faith the heart is renewed in the image of God. And the heart that in its unrenewed state is not subject to the law of God, neither indeed can be, now delights in its holy precepts, exclaiming with the psalmist, "O how love I Thy law! it is my meditation all the day." Psalm 119:97.—*Steps to Christ*, 63.

"And now, Israel, what does the LORD your God require of you,
but to fear the LORD your God, to walk in all His ways and to love Him,
to serve the LORD your God with all your heart and with all your soul,
and to keep the commandments of the LORD and His statutes
which I command you today for your good? Indeed heaven
and the highest heavens belong to the LORD your God,
also the earth with all that is in it.
The LORD delighted only in your fathers, to love them;
and He chose their descendants after them,
you above all peoples, as it is this day."

—Deuteronomy 10:12–15, NKJV

The Expression of the Principle of Love

And I will delight myself in Your commandments,
Which I love.

—Psalm 119:47, NKJV

There is not a commandment of the law that is not for the good and happiness of man, both in this life and in the life to come. In obedience to God's law, man is surrounded as with a hedge and kept from the evil.—*Thoughts From the Mount of Blessing*, 52.

The law given upon Sinai was the enunciation of the principle of love, a revelation to earth of the law of heaven. It was ordained in the hand of a Mediator—spoken by Him through whose power the hearts of men could be brought into harmony with its principles. God had revealed the purpose of the law when He declared to Israel, "Ye shall be holy men unto Me." Exodus 22:31.—*Thoughts From the Mount of Blessing*, 46.

The new-covenant promise is, "I will put My laws into their hearts, and in their minds will I write them." Hebrews 10:16. While the system of types which pointed to Christ as the Lamb of God that should take away the sin of the world was to pass away at His death, the principles of righteousness embodied in the Decalogue are as immutable as the eternal throne. Not one command has been annulled, not a jot or tittle has been changed. Those principles that were made known to man in Paradise as the great law of life will exist unchanged in Paradise restored. When Eden shall bloom on earth again, God's law of love will be obeyed by all beneath the sun.—*Thoughts From the Mount of Blessing*, 50.

This is the covenant that I will make with them after those days, says the Lord:
I will put My laws into their hearts,
and in their minds I will write them.

—Hebrews 10:16, NKJV

The Joy of Doing What Is Right

Where there is no revelation, the people cast off restraint;
But happy is he who keeps the law.

—Proverbs 29:18, NKJV

OBEDIENCE TO GOD is the first duty of the Christian.—*Testimonies for the Church*, vol. 4, 610.

The man who attempts to keep the commandments of God from a sense of obligation merely—because he is required to do so—will never enter into the joy of obedience. He does not obey. When the requirements of God are accounted a burden because they cut across human inclination, we may know that the life is not a Christian life. True obedience is the outworking of a principle within. It springs from the love of righteousness, the love of the law of God. The essence of all righteousness is loyalty to our Redeemer. This will lead us to do right because it is right—because right doing is pleasing to God.—*Christ's Object Lessons*, 97.

Christ lays loving claims on all for whom He has given His life; they are to obey His will if they would share the joys that He has prepared for all who reflect His character here.—*Testimonies for the Church*, vol. 9, 284.

Of Christ it is written: "In Him was life; and the life was the light of men." John 1:4. He is the Fountain of life. Obedience to Him is the life-giving power that gladdens the soul.—*Testimonies for the Church*, vol. 8, 288.

All the nations you made
will come and bow before you, Lord;
they will praise your holy name.
For you are great and perform wonderful deeds.
You alone are God.
Teach me your ways, O LORD,
that I may live according to your truth!
Grant me purity of heart,
so that I may honor you.

—Psalm 86:9–11, NLT

The Character of God

The law of the LORD is perfect, converting the soul;
The testimony of the LORD is sure, making wise the simple;
The statutes of the LORD are right, rejoicing the heart;
The commandment of the LORD is pure, enlightening the eyes.
—Psalm 19:7, 8, NKJV

BECAUSE THE LAW OF THE LORD is perfect, and therefore changeless, it is impossible for sinful men, in themselves, to meet the standard of its requirement. This was why Jesus came as our Redeemer. It was His mission, by making men partakers of the divine nature, to bring them into harmony with the principles of the law of heaven. When we forsake our sins and receive Christ as our Saviour, the law is exalted. The apostle Paul asks, "Do we then make void the law through faith? God forbid: yea, we establish the law." Romans 3:31.—*Thoughts From the Mount of Blessing*, 50.

God demands nothing less of every one of His followers than that they reveal Christ's character to the world in their individual life, and that they bear testimony by precept and example that it is not in vain that Christ has suffered and died, that the image of God might be restored in them through His redeeming grace.—*Testimonies to Ministers and Gospel Workers*, 438.

God calls upon those who claim to be delegated to bear the truth to the world, to show in all places, both high and low, in public life and in the bypaths of private life, that they are in connection with God, that Christianity has done a noble work for them, that they are holier, happier than those who do not acknowledge their allegiance to God's commandments.—*Testimonies to Ministers and Gospel Workers*, 438.

The fear of the LORD is clean, enduring forever;
The judgments of the LORD are true and righteous altogether.
—Psalm 19:9, NKJV

The Law Is a Guarantee of Eternal Life

Your testimonies I have taken as an heritage forever,
For they are the rejoicing of my heart.

—Psalm 119:111, NKJV

HE CAME TO MANIFEST the nature of His law, to reveal in His own character the beauty of holiness.

Christ came to the world with the accumulated love of eternity. Sweeping away the exactions which had encumbered the law of God, He showed that the law is a law of love, an expression of the Divine Goodness. He showed that in obedience to its principles is involved the happiness of mankind, and with it the stability, the very foundation and framework, of human society.

So far from making arbitrary requirements, God's law is given to men as a hedge, a shield. Whoever accepts its principles is preserved from evil. Fidelity to God involves fidelity to man. Thus the law guards the rights, the individuality, of every human being. It restrains the superior from oppression, and the subordinate from disobedience. It ensures man's well-being, both for this world and for the world to come. To the obedient it is the pledge of eternal life, for it expresses the principles that endure forever.—*Education*, 76.

"The grass withers, the flower fades,
Because the breath of the LORD blows upon it;
Surely the people are grass.
The grass withers, the flower fades,
But the word of our God stands forever."

—Isaiah 40:7, 8, NKJV

The Law Leads to Happiness

Your testimonies also are my delight
And my counselors.

—Psalm 119:24, NKJV

THE LAW OF LOVE being the foundation of the government of God, the happiness of all intelligent beings depends upon their perfect accord with its great principles of righteousness. God desires from all His creatures the service of love—service that springs from an appreciation of His character. He takes no pleasure in a forced obedience; and to all He grants freedom of will, that they may render Him voluntary service.—*Patriarchs and Prophets*, 34.

God's great object in the working out of His providences is to try men, to give them opportunity to develop character. Thus He proves whether they are obedient or disobedient to His commands. Good works do not purchase the love of God, but they reveal that we possess that love. If we surrender the will to God, we shall not work in order to earn God's love. His love as a free gift will be received into the soul, and from love to Him we shall delight to obey His commandments.—*Christ's Object Lessons*, 283.

Oh, how I love Your law!
It is my meditation all the day.
You, through Your commandments, make me wiser than my enemies;
For they are ever with me.

—Psalm 119:97, 98, NKJV

NOVEMBER 22
Glad Tidings

Obedience Is a Test of Loyalty to God

"If you know these things, blessed are you if you do them."
—John 13:17, NKJV

THERE ARE ONLY TWO CLASSES in the world today, and only two classes will be recognized in the judgment—those who violate God's law and those who obey it. Christ gives the test by which to prove our loyalty or disloyalty. "If ye love Me," He says, "keep My commandments. . . . He that hath My commandments, and keepeth them, he it is that loveth Me. And he that loveth Me shall be loved of My Father, and I will love him, and will manifest Myself to him. . . . He that loveth Me not keepeth not My sayings; and the word which ye hear is not Mine, but the Father's which sent Me." "If ye keep My commandments, ye shall abide in My love; even as I have kept My Father's commandments, and abide in His love." John 14:15–24; 15:10.—*Christ's Object Lessons*, 283.

The condition of eternal life is now just what it always has been,—just what it was in Paradise before the fall of our first parents,—perfect obedience to the law of God, perfect righteousness. If eternal life were granted on any condition short of this, then the happiness of the whole universe would be imperiled. The way would be open for sin, with all its train of woe and misery, to be immortalized.—*Steps to Christ*, 62.

But be doers of the word, and not hearers only, deceiving yourselves.
—James 1:22, NKJV

Joyful Worship in the House of the Lord

I was glad when they said to me,
"Let us go into the house of the LORD."

—Psalm 122:1, NKJV

OUR GOD IS A TENDER, merciful Father. His service should not be looked upon as a heart-saddening, distressing exercise. It should be a pleasure to worship the Lord and to take part in His work. God would not have His children, for whom so great salvation has been provided, act as if He were a hard, exacting taskmaster. He is their best friend; and when they worship Him, He expects to be with them, to bless and comfort them, filling their hearts with joy and love. The Lord desires His children to take comfort in His service and to find more pleasure than hardship in His work. He desires that those who come to worship Him shall carry away with them precious thoughts of His care and love, that they may be cheered in all the employments of daily life, that they may have grace to deal honestly and faithfully in all things.—*Steps to Christ*, 103.

It is good to give thanks to the LORD,
And to sing praises to Your name, O Most High;
To declare Your lovingkindness in the morning,
And Your faithfulness every night,
On an instrument of ten strings,
On the lute,
And on the harp,
With harmonious sound.
For You, LORD, have made me glad through Your work;
I will triumph in the works of Your hands.
O LORD, how great are Your works!
Your thoughts are very deep.
A senseless man does not know,
Nor does a fool understand this.

—Psalm 92:1–6, NKJV

In the House of Prayer

"Even them I will bring to My holy mountain,
And make them joyful in My house of prayer.
Their burnt offerings and their sacrifices
Will be accepted on My altar;
For My house shall be called a house of prayer for all nations."

—Isaiah 56:7, NKJV

THERE IS NECESSITY for diligence in prayer; let nothing hinder you. Make every effort to keep open the communion between Jesus and your own soul. Seek every opportunity to go where prayer is wont to be made. Those who are really seeking for communion with God will be seen in the prayer meeting, faithful to do their duty and earnest and anxious to reap all the benefits they can gain. They will improve every opportunity of placing themselves where they can receive the rays of light from heaven.—*Steps to Christ*, 98.

The youth who finds joy and happiness in reading the word of God and in the hour of prayer is constantly refreshed by drafts from the Fountain of life. He will attain a height of moral excellence and a breadth of thought of which others cannot conceive. Communion with God encourages good thoughts, noble aspirations, clear perceptions of truth, and lofty purposes of action. Those who thus connect their souls with God are acknowledged by Him as His sons and daughters. They are constantly reaching higher and still higher, obtaining clearer views of God and of eternity, until the Lord makes them channels of light and wisdom to the world.—*Testimonies for the Church*, vol. 4, 624.

For a day in Your courts is better than a thousand.
I would rather be a doorkeeper in the house of my God
Than dwell in the tents of wickedness.

—Psalm 84:10, NKJV

The Best Day of the Week

"Keep the Sabbath day holy.
Don't pursue your own interests on that day,
but enjoy the Sabbath
and speak of it with delight as the LORD*'s holy day.*
Honor the Sabbath in everything you do on that day,
and don't follow your own desires or talk idly.
Then the LORD *will be your delight.*
I will give you great honor
and satisfy you with the inheritance I promised to your ancestor Jacob.
I, the LORD*, have spoken!"*

—Isaiah 58:13, 14, NLT

GREAT BLESSINGS ARE ENFOLDED in the observance of the Sabbath, and God desires that the Sabbath day shall be to us a day of joy. There was joy at the institution of the Sabbath.—*Testimonies for the Church*, vol. 6, 349.

When the foundation of the earth was laid, the foundation of the Sabbath was laid also. "When the morning stars sang together, and all the sons of God shouted for joy," God saw that a Sabbath was essential for man, even in Paradise. In giving the Sabbath, God considered man's spiritual and physical health.—*Testimonies to Ministers and Gospel Workers*, 136.

The Sabbath is not intended to be a period of useless inactivity. The law forbids secular labor on the rest day of the Lord; the toil that gains a livelihood must cease; no labor for worldly pleasure or profit is lawful upon that day; but as God ceased His labor of creating, and rested upon the Sabbath and blessed it, so man is to leave the occupations of his daily life, and devote those sacred hours to healthful rest, to worship, and to holy deeds.—*The Desire of Ages*, 207.

The Lord says, "If thou turn away thy foot from the Sabbath, from doing thy pleasure on My holy day; and call the Sabbath a delight, the holy of the Lord, honorable; . . . then shalt thou delight thyself in the Lord." Isaiah 58:13, 14. To all who receive the Sabbath as a sign of Christ's creative and redeeming power, it will be a delight. Seeing Christ in it, they delight themselves in Him.—*The Desire of Ages*, 289.

NOVEMBER 26
Glad Tidings

Praises That Flow From the Heart

Save me so I can praise you publicly at Jerusalem's gates,
so I can rejoice that you have rescued me.

—Psalm 9:14, NLT

IT IS YOUR PRIVILEGE TO TRUST in the love of Jesus for salvation, in the fullest, surest, noblest manner; to say, He loves me, He receives me; I will trust Him, for He gave His life for me. Nothing so dispels doubt as coming in contact with the character of Christ. He declares, "Him that cometh to Me I will in no wise cast out;" that is, there is no possibility of My casting him out, for I have pledged My word to receive him. Take Christ at His word, and let your lips declare that you have gained the victory.—*Testimonies to Ministers and Gospel Workers*, 517.

You desire to please the Lord, and you can do this by believing His promises. He is waiting to take you into a harbor of gracious experience, and He bids you, "Be still, and know that I am God." You have had a time of unrest; but Jesus says to you, "Come unto Me, . . . and I will give you rest." The joy of Christ in the soul is worth everything. "Then are they glad," because they are privileged to rest in the arms of everlasting love.—*Testimonies to Ministers and Gospel Workers*, 516.

How pleased the Saviour would be to hear His followers talking of His precious lessons of instruction, and to know that they had a relish for holy things! When the truth abides in the heart, there is no place for criticism of God's servants, or for picking flaws with the message He sends. That which is in the heart will flow from the lips. It cannot be repressed. The things that God has prepared for those that love Him will be the theme of conversation. The love of Christ is in the soul as well of water, springing up into everlasting life, sending forth living streams that bring life and gladness wherever they flow.—*Testimonies to Ministers and Gospel Workers*, 88.

Serving and Worshiping in Spirit

For we are the circumcision, who worship God in the Spirit,
rejoice in Christ Jesus, and have no confidence in the flesh.
—Philippians 3:3, NKJV

God is a Spirit: and they that worship Him must worship Him in spirit and in truth." . . .

. . . Religion is not to be confined to external forms and ceremonies. The religion that comes from God is the only religion that will lead to God. In order to serve Him aright, we must be born of the divine Spirit. This will purify the heart and renew the mind, giving us a new capacity for knowing and loving God. It will give us a willing obedience to all His requirements. This is true worship.—*The Desire of Ages*, 189.

The religion of Christ means more than the forgiveness sin; it means taking away our sins, and filling the vacuum with the graces of the Holy Spirit. It means divine illumination, rejoicing in God. It means a heart emptied of self, and blessed with the abiding presence of Christ. When Christ reigns in the soul, there is purity, freedom from sin. The glory, the fullness, the completeness of the gospel plan is fulfilled in the life. The acceptance of the Saviour brings a glow of perfect peace, perfect love, perfect assurance. The beauty and fragrance of the character of Christ revealed in the life testifies that God has indeed sent His Son into the world to be its Saviour.—*Christ's Object Lessons*, 419.

Pure and undefiled religion before God and the Father is this:
to visit orphans and widows in their trouble,
and to keep oneself unspotted from the world.
—James 1:27, NKJV

Contemplating Christ

You love him even though you have never seen him.
Though you do not see him now, you trust him;
and you rejoice with a glorious, inexpressible joy.
The reward for trusting him will be the salvation of your souls.
—1 Peter 1:8, 9, NLT

CHRIST AND HIM CRUCIFIED should be the theme of contemplation, of conversation, and of our most joyful emotion. We should keep in our thoughts every blessing we receive from God, and when we realize His great love we should be willing to trust everything to the hand that was nailed to the cross for us.—*Steps to Christ*, 103.

When His words of instruction have been received, and have taken possession of us, Jesus is to us an abiding presence, controlling our thoughts and ideas and actions. We are imbued with the instruction of the greatest Teacher the world ever knew.—*Testimonies to Ministers and Gospel Workers*, 389.

We have the companionship of the divine presence, and as we realize this presence, our thoughts are brought into captivity to Jesus Christ. Our spiritual exercises are in accordance with the vividness of our sense of this companionship. Enoch walked with God in this way; and Christ is dwelling in our hearts by faith when we will consider what He is to us, and what a work He has wrought out for us in the plan of redemption. We shall be most happy in cultivating a sense of this great gift of God to our world and to us personally.—*Testimonies to Ministers and Gospel Workers*, 388.

"For God so loved the world that He gave His only begotten Son,
that whoever believes in Him should not perish but have everlasting life."
—John 3:16, NKJV

Trusting the Only One Truly Trustworthy

Finally, my brethren, rejoice in the Lord.
For me to write the same things to you
is not tedious, but for you it is safe.
—Philippians 3:1, NKJV

THE CHRISTIAN'S LIFE should be one of faith, of victory, and joy in God. . . . Truly spoke God's servant Nehemiah: "The *joy* of the Lord is your strength." Nehemiah 8:10. And Paul says: . . . "Rejoice evermore. Pray without ceasing. In everything give thanks: for this is the will of God in Christ Jesus concerning you." . . . 1 Thessalonians 5:16–18. —*The Great Controversy*, 477.

Decided perseverance in a course of righteousness, disciplining the mind by religious exercises to love devotion and heavenly things, will bring the greatest amount of happiness.

If we make God our trust, we have it in our power to control the mind in these things. Through continued exercise it will become strong to battle with internal foes and to subdue self, until there is a complete transformation, and the passions, appetites, and will are brought into perfect subjection. Then there will be daily piety at home and abroad, and when we engage in labor for souls, a power will attend our efforts. The humble Christian will have seasons of devotion which are not spasmodic, fitful, or superstitious, but calm and tranquil, deep, constant, and earnest. The love of God, the practice of holiness, will be pleasant when there is a perfect surrender to God.—*Testimonies for the Church*, vol. 2, 506, 507.

When I discovered your words, I devoured them.
They are my joy and my heart's delight,
for I bear your name,
O LORD God of Heaven's Armies.
—Jeremiah 15:16, NLT

Companionship With Christ a Precious Experience

Like an apple tree among the trees of the wood,
So is my beloved among the sons.
I sat down in his shade with great delight,
And his fruit was sweet to my taste.
He brought me to the banqueting house,
And his banner over me was love.
—Song of Solomon 2:3, 4, NKJV

MANY, EVEN IN THEIR SEASONS of devotion, fail of receiving the blessing of real communion with God. They are in too great haste. With hurried steps they press through the circle of Christ's loving presence, pausing perhaps a moment within the sacred precincts, but not waiting for counsel. They have no time to remain with the divine Teacher. With their burdens they return to their work.

These workers can never attain the highest success until they learn the secret of strength. They must give themselves time to think, to pray, to wait upon God for a renewal of physical, mental, and spiritual power. They need the uplifting influence of His Spirit. Receiving this, they will be quickened by fresh life. The wearied frame and tired brain will be refreshed, the burdened heart will be lightened.

Not a pause for a moment in His presence, but personal contact with Christ, to sit down in companionship with Him—this is our need. Happy . . . the precious experience pictured in these words from the Song of Songs:

"As the apple tree among the trees of the wood,
So is my Beloved among the sons.
I sat down under His shadow with great delight,
And His fruit was sweet to my taste.
He brought me to the banqueting house,
And His banner over me was love." Song of Solomon 2:3, 4.
—*Education*, 260, 261.

DECEMBER 1

An Eternity of Bliss

God Can Always Turn Sorrow Into Joy

For His anger is but a moment,
His favor is for life;
Weeping may endure for a night,
But joy comes in the morning.

—Psalm 30:5, NKJV

IT IS EVER GOD'S PURPOSE to bring light out of darkness, joy out of sorrow, and rest out of weariness for the waiting, longing soul.—*Testimonies for the Church*, vol. 5, 215.

In the time of the end the people of God will sigh and cry for the abominations done in the land. With tears they will warn the wicked of their danger in trampling upon the divine law, and with unutterable sorrow they will humble themselves before the Lord in penitence. The wicked will mock their sorrow and ridicule their solemn appeals. But the anguish and humiliation of God's people is unmistakable evidence that they are regaining the strength and nobility of character lost in consequence of sin. . . .

. . . They have resisted the wiles of the deceiver; they have not been turned from their loyalty by the dragon's roar. Now they are eternally secure from the tempter's devices. . . .

. . . Christ is revealed as the Redeemer and Deliverer of His people. Now indeed are the remnant "men wondered at," as the tears and humiliation of their pilgrimage give place to joy and honor in the presence of God and the Lamb.—*Prophets and Kings*, 590–592.

Hear, O LORD, and have mercy on me;
LORD, be my helper!
You have turned for me my mourning into dancing;
You have put off my sackcloth and clothed me with gladness,
To the end that my glory may sing praise to You and not be silent.
O LORD my God, I will give thanks to You forever.

—Psalm 30:10–12, NKJV

Work Faithfully to Reap Joyfully

Those who plant in tears
will harvest with shouts of joy.

—Psalm 126:5, NLT

As faithful husbandmen in God's great field, we must sow with tears and be patient and hopeful. We must meet troubles and sorrows. Temptations and wearisome toil will afflict the soul, but we must patiently wait in faith to reap with joy. In the final victory God will have no use for those persons who are nowhere to be found in time of peril and danger, when the strength, courage, and influence of all are required to make a charge upon the enemy. Those who stand like faithful soldiers to battle against wrong, and to vindicate the right, warring against principalities and powers, against the rulers of the darkness of this world, against spiritual wickedness in high places, will each receive the commendation from the Master: "Well done, *good* and *faithful* servant: . . . enter thou into the joy of thy Lord" (Matt. 25:21).—*Testimonies for the Church*, vol. 3, 327.

A farmer who plants only a few seeds will get a small crop.
But the one who plants generously will get a generous crop.
You must each decide in your heart how much to give.
And don't give reluctantly or in response to pressure.
"For God loves a person who gives cheerfully."
And God will generously provide all you need.
Then you will always have everything you need
and plenty left over to share with others.

—2 Corinthians 9:6–8, NLT

The Glorious Reward of the Faithful Worker

He who continually goes forth weeping,
Bearing seed for sowing,
Shall doubtless come again with rejoicing,
Bringing his sheaves with him.

—Psalm 126:6, NKJV

A HARVEST OF JOY will be reaped by those who sow the holy seeds of truth. —*Testimonies to Ministers and Gospel Workers*, 174.

Glorious will be the reward bestowed when the faithful workers gather about the throne of God and of the Lamb. When John in his mortal state beheld the glory of God, he fell as one dead; he was not able to endure the sight. But when the children of God shall have put on immortality, they will "see Him as He is." 1 John 3:2. They will stand before the throne, accepted in the Beloved. All their sins have been blotted out, all their transgressions borne away. Now they can look upon the undimmed glory of the throne of God. They have been partakers with Christ in His sufferings, they have been workers together with Him in the plan of redemption, and they are partakers with Him in the joy of seeing souls saved in the kingdom of God, there to praise God through all eternity.—*Testimonies for the Church*, vol. 9, 285.

Behold what manner of love the Father has bestowed on us,
that we should be called children of God! Therefore the world does not know us,
because it did not know Him. Beloved, now we are children of God;
and it has not yet been revealed what we shall be, but we know that when he is revealed,
we shall be like Him, for we shall see Him and He is.
And everyone who has this hope in Him purifies himself, just as He is pure.

—1 John 3:1–3, NKJV

The Reward for Fulfilling the Mission

"He who reaps receives wages, and gathers fruit for eternal life, that both he who sows and he who reaps may rejoice together."
—John 4:36, NKJV

GOD DESIGNS that all shall be workers. The toiling beast of burden answers the purpose of its creation better than does the indolent man. God is a constant worker. The angels are workers; they are ministers of God to the children of men. Those who look forward to a heaven of inactivity will be disappointed; for the economy of heaven provides no place for the gratification of indolence. But to the weary and heavy-laden rest is promised. It is the faithful servant who will be welcomed from his labors to the joy of his Lord. He will lay off his armor with rejoicing, and will forget the noise of battle in the glorious rest prepared for those who conquer through the cross of Christ.—*Messages to Young People*, p. 216.

The weight of the wrath of God will fall upon those who have misspent their time and served mammon instead of their Creator. If you live for God and heaven, pointing out the way of life to others, you will go onward and upward to higher and holier joys. You will be rewarded with the "Well done, thou good and faithful servant: . . . enter thou into the joy of thy Lord."—*Testimonies for the Church*, vol. 4, 54.

I planted, Apollos watered, but God gave the increase.
So then neither he who plants is anything, nor he who waters,
but God who gives the increase. Now he who plants and he who waters are one,
and each one will receive his own reward according to his own labor.
For we are God's fellow workers; you are God's field, you are God's building.
—1 Corinthians 3:6–9, NKJV

Hope That Gladdens the Heart

"When that happens, be happy! Yes, leap for joy!
For a great reward awaits you in heaven.
And remember, their ancestors treated
the ancient prophets that same way."

—Luke 6:23, NLT

WE ARE STILL AMIDST the shadows and turmoil of earthly activities. Let us consider most earnestly the blessed hereafter. Let our faith pierce through every cloud of darkness and behold Him who died for the sins of the world. He has opened the gates of paradise to all who receive and believe on Him. To them He gives power to become the sons and daughters of God. Let the afflictions which pain us so grievously become instructive lessons, teaching us to press forward toward the mark of the prize of our high calling in Christ. Let us be encouraged by the thought that the Lord is soon to come. Let this hope gladden our hearts.—*Testimonies for the Church*, vol. 9, 286.

Let your imagination take hold upon things unseen. Let your thoughts be carried away to the evidences of the great love of God for you. In contemplating the object of which you are in pursuit, you will lose the sense of pain brought by the light afflictions that are but for a moment.—*Testimonies for the Church*, vol. 8, 125.

The Christian is not left to walk in uncertain paths; he is not left to vain regrets and disappointments. If we do not have the pleasures of this life we may still be joyful in looking to the life beyond.—*Steps to Christ*, 124.

The LORD is my shepherd;
I shall not want.
He makes me to lie down in green pastures;
He leads me beside the still waters.
He restores my soul;
He leads me in the paths of righteousness
For His name's sake.
Yea, though I walk through the valley of the shadow of death,
I will fear no evil;
For You are with me;
Your rod and Your staff, they comfort me.

—Psalm 23:1–4, NKJV

Choosing the Heavenly Over the Earthly

For you had compassion on me in my chains,
and joyfully accepted the plundering of your goods,
knowing that you have a better
and an enduring possession for yourselves in heaven.
—Hebrews 10:34, NKJV

THEN LET YOUR PROPERTY go beforehand to heaven. Lay up your treasures beside the throne of God. Make sure your title to the unsearchable riches of Christ.—*Christ's Object Lessons*, 375.

Christ calls upon every one to consider. Make an honest reckoning. Put into one scale Jesus, which means eternal treasure, life, truth, heaven, and the joy of Christ in souls redeemed; put into the other every attraction the world can offer. Into one scale put the loss of your own soul, and the souls of those whom you might have been instrumental in saving; into the other, for yourself and for them, a life that measures with the life of God. Weigh for time and for eternity. While you are thus engaged, Christ speaks: "What shall it profit a man, if he shall gain the whole world, and lose his own soul?" Mark 8:36.

God desires us to choose the heavenly in place of the earthly. He opens before us the possibilities of a heavenly investment. He would give encouragement to our loftiest aims, security to our choicest treasure. He declares, "I will make a man more precious than fine gold; even a man than the golden wedge of Ophir." Isaiah 13:12. When the riches that moth devours and rust corrupts shall be swept away, Christ's followers can rejoice in their heavenly treasure, the riches that are imperishable.—*Christ's Object Lessons*, 374.

"But lay up for yourseleves treasures in heaven,
where neither moth nor rust destroys
and where thieves do not break in and steal."
—Matthew 6:20, NKJV

The Crown for the Fruition of Our Work

After all, what gives us hope and joy,
and what will be our proud reward
and crown as we stand before our Lord Jesus when he returns?
It is you! Yes, you are our pride and joy.
—1 Thessalonians 2:19, 20, NLT

THERE IS A FUTURE JOY to which Paul looked forward as the recompense of his labors—the same joy for the sake of which Christ endured the cross and despised the shame—the joy of seeing the fruition of his work. "What is our hope, or joy, or crown of rejoicing?" he wrote to the Thessalonian converts. "Are not even ye in the presence of our Lord Jesus Christ at His coming? For ye are our glory and joy." 1 Thessalonians 2:19, 20.

Who can measure the results to the world of Paul's lifework? Of all those beneficent influences that alleviate suffering, that comfort sorrow, that restrain evil, that uplift life from the selfish and the sensual, and glorify it with the hope of immortality, how much is due to the labors of Paul and his fellow workers, as with the gospel of the Son of God they made their unnoticed journey from Asia to the shores of Europe?

What is it worth to any life to have been God's instrument in setting in motion such influences of blessing? What will it be worth in eternity to witness the results of such a lifework?—*Education*, 70.

I have fought the good fight, I have finished the race, and I have remained faithful.
And now the prize awaits me—the crown of righteousness, which the Lord,
the righteous Judge, will give me on the day of his return.
And the prize is not just for me but for all who eagerly look forward to his appearing.
—2 Timothy 4:7, 8, NLT

Sharing With Christ the Joy in Redeemed Souls

"His lord said to him, 'Well done, good and faithful servant; you were faithful over a few things, I will make you ruler over many things. Enter into the joy of your lord.' "

—Matthew 25:21, NKJV

WITH UNUTTERABLE LOVE, Jesus welcomes His faithful ones to the joy of their Lord. The Saviour's joy is in seeing, in the kingdom of glory, the souls that have been saved by His agony and humiliation. And the redeemed will be sharers in His joy, as they behold, among the blessed, those who have been won to Christ through their prayers, their labors, and their loving sacrifice. As they gather about the great white throne, gladness unspeakable will fill their hearts, when they behold those whom they have won for Christ, and see that one has gained others, and these still others, all brought into the haven of rest, there to lay their crowns at Jesus' feet and praise Him through the endless cycles of eternity.—*The Great Controversy*, 647.

The days of pain and weeping are forever ended. The King of glory has wiped the tears from all faces; every cause of grief has been removed. Amid the waving of palm branches they pour forth a song of praise, clear, sweet, and harmonious; every voice takes up the strain, until the anthem swells through the vaults of heaven: "Salvation to our God which sitteth upon the throne, and unto the Lamb." And all the inhabitants of heaven respond in the ascription: "Amen: Blessing, and glory, and wisdom, and thanksgiving, and honor, and power, and might, be unto our God for ever and ever." Revelation 7:10, 12.—Ibid., p. 650.

Enter into His gates with thanksgiving,
And into His courts with praise.
Be thankful to Him, and bless His name.

—Psalm 100:4, NKJV

Mission Accomplished

"But none of these things move me;
nor do I count my life dear to myself,
so that I may finish my race with joy,
and the ministry which I received
from the Lord Jesus, to testify to the gospel
of the grace of God."

—Acts 20:24, NKJV

HAS GOD CALLED YOU to be a representative of Christ upon earth, in His stead beseeching sinners to be reconciled to God? This is a solemn, exalted work. . . . You are not released from responsibilities when out of meeting, but should still maintain your consecration to the work of saving souls. You are to be a living epistle, known and read of all men. Ease is not to be consulted. Pleasure is not to be thought of. The salvation of souls is the all-important theme. It is to this work that the minister of the gospel of Christ is called.—*Testimonies for the Church*, vol. 2, 705.

As their reward, the faithful undershepherds will hear from the Chief Shepherd: "Well done, good and faithful servant." He will then place the crown of glory upon their heads and bid them enter into the joy of their Lord. What is that joy? It is beholding with Christ the redeemed saints, reviewing with Him their travail for souls, their self-denial and self-sacrifice, their giving up of ease, of worldly gain, and every earthly inducement, and choosing the reproach, the suffering, the self-abasement, the wearing labor, and the anguish of spirit as men would oppose the counsel of God against their own souls; it is calling to remembrance the chastening of their souls before God, their weeping between the porch and the altar, and their becoming a spectacle unto the world, to angels, and to men. All this is then ended, and the fruits of their labors are seen; souls are saved through their efforts in Christ. The ministers who have been co-workers with Christ enter into the joy of their Lord and are satisfied.—*Testimonies for the Church*, vol. 2, 709.

Knowing We Have Not Worked in Vain

It is by your holding fast to the word of life
that I can boast on the day of Christ
that I did not run in vain or labor in vain.
—Philippians 2:16, NRSV

ALL WHO HAVE BORNE WITH JESUS the cross of sacrifice will be sharers with Him of His glory. It was the joy of Christ in His humiliation and pain that His disciples should be glorified with Him. They are the fruit of His self-sacrifice. The outworking in them of His own character and spirit is His reward, and will be His joy throughout eternity. This joy they share with Him as the fruit of their labor and sacrifice is seen in other hearts and lives. They are workers together with Christ, and the Father will honor them as He honors His Son.—*The Desire of Ages*, 624.

The redeemed will meet and recognize those whose attention they have directed to the uplifted Saviour. What blessed converse they will have with these souls! . . .

What rejoicing there will be as these redeemed ones meet and greet those who have had a burden in their behalf! And those who have lived, not to please themselves, but to be a blessing to the unfortunate who have so few blessings—how their hearts will thrill with satisfaction! They will realize the promise: "Thou shalt be blessed; for they cannot recompense thee: for thou shalt be recompensed at the resurrection of the just."—*Testimonies for the Church*, vol. 6, 311, 312.

They shall be called, "The Holy People,
The Redeemed of the LORD";
and you shall be called, "Sought Out,
A City Not Forsaken."
—Isaiah 62:12, NRSV

Shame to the Wicked

Therefore thus says the Lord God:
"Behold, My servants shall eat,
But you shall be hungry;
Behold, My servants shall drink,
But you shall be thirsty;
Behold, My servants shall rejoice,
But you shall be ashamed."

—Isaiah 65:13, NKJV

WHILE TO THE WICKED the advent of the Lord brings woe and desolation, to the righteous it is fraught with joy and hope.—*The Great Controversy*, 339.

It is at midnight that God manifests His power for the deliverance of His people. The sun appears, shining in its strength. Signs and wonders follow in quick succession. The wicked look with terror and amazement upon the scene, while the righteous behold with solemn joy the tokens of their deliverance. . . .

Soon there appears in the east a small black cloud, about half the size of a man's hand. . . . The people of God know this to be the sign of the Son of man. In solemn silence they gaze upon it as it draws nearer the earth, becoming lighter and more glorious, until it is a great white cloud, its base a glory like consuming fire, and above it the rainbow of the covenant. Jesus rides forth as a mighty conqueror. . . . No human pen can portray the scene; no mortal mind is adequate to conceive its splendor.—*The Great Controversy*, 636, 640.

Those who really love the Saviour cannot but hail with gladness the announcement founded upon the word of God that He in whom their hopes of eternal life are centered is coming again, not to be insulted, despised, and rejected, as at His first advent, but in power and glory, to redeem His people. It is those who do not love the Saviour that desire Him to remain away.—*The Great Controversy*, 339.

"Therefore you also be ready,
for the Son of Man is coming at an hour you do not expect."

—Matthew 24:44, NKJV

DECEMBER 12

An Eternity of Bliss

Faultless Before the Father's Throne

Now to Him who is able to keep you from stumbling,
And to present you faultless
Before the presence of His glory with exceeding joy,
To God our Savior,
Who alone is wise,
Be glory and majesty,
Dominion and power,
Both now and forever.
Amen.

—Jude 24, 25, NKJV

AMID THE REELING OF THE EARTH, the flash of lightning, and the roar of thunder, the voice of the Son of God calls forth the sleeping saints. He looks upon the graves of the righteous, then, raising His hands to heaven, He cries: "Awake, awake, awake, ye that sleep in the dust, and arise!" Throughout the length and breadth of the earth the dead shall hear that voice, and they that hear shall live. And the whole earth shall ring with the tread of the exceeding great army of every nation, kindred, tongue, and people. From the prison house of death they come, clothed with immortal glory, crying: "O death, where is thy sting? O grave, where is thy victory?" 1 Corinthians 15:55. And the living righteous and the risen saints unite their voices in a long, glad shout of victory.—*The Great Controversy*, 644.

There will be a relinking of the family chain. When we look upon our dead, we may think of the morning when the trump of God shall sound, when "the dead shall be raised incorruptible, and we shall be changed." 1 Corinthians 15:52. A little longer, and we shall see the King in His beauty. A little longer, and He will wipe all tears from our eyes. A little longer, and He will present us "faultless before the presence of His glory with exceeding joy." Jude 1:24.—*The Desire of Ages*, 632.

It will happen in a moment, in the blink of an eye, when the last trumpet is blown. . . . And we who are living will also be transformed.

—1 Corinthians 15:52, NLT

Greater Than Sorrow and Shame

Looking unto Jesus, the author and finisher of our faith,
who for the joy that was set before Him endured the cross,
despising the shame, and has sat down
at the right hand of the throne of God.

—Hebrews 12:2, NKJV

IT WAS FOR THE JOY that was set before Him—that He might bring many sons unto glory—that He endured the cross and despised the shame. And inconceivably great as was the sorrow and the shame, yet greater is the joy and the glory. He looks upon the redeemed, renewed in His own image, every heart bearing the perfect impress of the divine, every face reflecting the likeness of their King. He beholds in them the result of the travail of His soul, and He is satisfied. Then, in a voice that reaches the assembled multitudes of the righteous and the wicked, He declares: "Behold the purchase of My blood! For these I suffered, for these I died, that they might dwell in My presence throughout eternal ages." And the song of praise ascends from the white-robed ones about the throne: "Worthy is the Lamb that was slain to receive power, and riches, and wisdom, and strength, and honor, and glory, and blessing." Revelation 5:12.—*The Great Controversy*, 671.

"Blessing and honor and glory and power
Be to Him who sits on the throne,
And to the Lamb, forever and ever!"

—Revelation 5:13, NKJV

We Shall See God's Face

"When he prays to God,
he will be accepted.
And God will receive him with joy
and restore him to good standing."

—Job 33:26, NLT

SINCE SIN BROUGHT separation between man and his Maker, no man has seen God at any time, except as He is manifested through Christ. . . .

"Lord, show us the Father," said Philip, "and it sufficeth us. Jesus saith unto him, Have I been so long time with you, and yet hast thou not known Me, Philip? he that hath seen Me hath seen the Father." . . .

The disciples did not yet understand Christ's words concerning His relation to God. Much of His teaching was still dark to them. Christ desired them to have a clearer, more distinct knowledge of God. . . .

Our knowledge of God is partial and imperfect. When the conflict is ended, and the Man Christ Jesus acknowledges before the Father His faithful workers, who in a world of sin have borne true witness for Him, they will understand clearly what now are mysteries to them.

Christ took with Him to the heavenly courts His glorified humanity. To those who receive Him He gives power to become the sons of God, that at last God may receive them as His, to dwell with Him throughout eternity. If during this life they are loyal to God, they will at last "see His face; and His name shall be in their foreheads." Revelation 22:4. And what is the happiness of heaven but to see God? What greater joy could come to the sinner saved by the grace of Christ than to look upon the face of God and know Him as Father?—*The Ministry of Healing*, 419–421.

We Shall Meet and See the Lord Jesus

It will be said on that day,
"See, this is our God; we have waited for him, so that he might save us.
This is the Lord *for whom we have waited;*
let us be glad and rejoice in his salvation."

—Isaiah 25:9, NRSV

JESUS IS COMING, but not as at His first advent, a babe in Bethlehem; not as He rode into Jerusalem, when the disciples praised God with a loud voice and cried, "Hosanna"; but in the glory of the Father and with all the retinue of holy angels to escort Him on His way to earth. All heaven will be emptied of the angels, while the waiting saints will be looking for Him and gazing into heaven, as were the men of Galilee when He ascended from the Mount of Olivet. Then only those who are holy, those who have followed fully the meek Pattern, will with rapturous joy exclaim as they behold Him, "Lo, this is our God; we have waited for Him, and He will save us." And they will be changed "in a moment, in the twinkling of an eye, at the last trump"—that trump which wakes the sleeping saints, and calls them forth from their dusty beds, clothed with glorious immortality, and shouting, "Victory! Victory over death and the grave!" The changed saints are then caught up together with the angels to meet the Lord in the air, never more to be separated from the object of their love.—*Early Writings*, 110.

For the Lord Himself will descend from heaven with a shout,
with the voice of an archangel, and with the trumpet of God.
And the dead in Christ will rise first. Then we who are alive and remain shall
be caught up together with them in the clouds to meet the Lord in the air.
And thus we shall always be with the Lord.

—1 Thessalonians 4:16, 17, NKJV

We Shall Rejoice at His Appearance

Hear the word of the Lord,
You who tremble at His word:
"Your brethren who hated you,
Who cast you out for My name's sake, said,
'Let the Lord be glorified,
That we may see your joy,'
But they shall be ashamed."

—Isaiah 66:5, NKJV

CHRIST IS COMING with power and great glory. He is coming with His own glory and with the glory of the Father. He is coming with all the holy angels with Him. While all the world is plunged in darkness, there will be light in every dwelling of the saints. They will catch the first light of His second appearing. The unsullied light will shine from His splendor, and Christ the Redeemer will be admired by all who have served Him. While the wicked flee from His presence, Christ's followers will rejoice. The patriarch Job, looking down to the time of Christ's second advent, said, "Whom I shall see for myself, and mine eyes shall behold, and not a stranger." Job 19:27, margin. To His faithful followers Christ has been a daily companion and familiar friend. They have lived in close contact, in constant communion with God. Upon them the glory of the Lord has risen. In them the light of the knowledge of the glory of God in the face of Jesus Christ has been reflected. Now they rejoice in the undimmed rays of the brightness and glory of the King in His majesty. They are prepared for the communion of heaven; for they have heaven in their hearts.—*Christ's Object Lessons*, 420.

Beloved, now we are children of God;
and it has not yet been revealed what we shall be,
but we know that when He is revealed,
we shall be like Him, for we shall see Him as He is.

—1 John 3:2, NKJV

The Joy of Being in His Presence

"You have made known to me the ways of life;
You will make me full of joy in Your presence."

—Acts 2:28, NKJV

LET THOSE MEN AND WOMEN . . . FOR AN INSTANT witness the high, the holy state of perfection that ever abides there,—every soul filled with love; every countenance beaming with joy; enchanting music in melodious strains rising in honor of God and the Lamb; . . . realize that there is higher and greater joy yet to experience, for the more they receive of the enjoyment of God, the more is their capacity increased to rise higher in eternal enjoyment, and thus continue to receive new and greater supplies from the ceaseless sources of glory and bliss inexpressible.—*Testimonies for the Church*, vol. 2, 266.

Heaven is a good place. I long to be there and behold my lovely Jesus.—*Early Writings*, 39.

For now we see in a mirror, dimly, but then face to face.
Now I know in part, but then I shall know just as I also am known.

—1 Corinthians 13:12, NKJV

Then the angel showed me a river with the water of life, clear as crystal,
flowing from the throne of God and of the Lamb.
It flowed down the center of the main street.
On each side of the river grew a tree of life,
bearing twelve crops of fruit, with a fresh crop each month.
The leaves were used for medicine to heal the nations.
No longer will there be a curse upon anything.
For the throne of God and of the Lamb will be there, and his servants will worship him.
And they will see his face, and his name will be written on their foreheads.

—Revelation 22:1–4, NLT

DECEMBER 18

An Eternity of Bliss

The Greatest Honor

Honor and majesty surround him;
strength and joy fill his dwelling.

—1 Chronicles 16:27, NLT

THOSE WHO TAKE CHRIST at His word, and surrender their souls to His keeping, their lives to His ordering, will find peace and quietude. Nothing of the world can make them sad when Jesus makes them glad by His presence. . . .

As through Jesus we enter into rest, heaven begins here. We respond to His invitation, Come, learn of Me, and in thus coming we begin the life eternal. Heaven is a ceaseless approaching to God through Christ. The longer we are in the heaven of bliss, the more and still more of glory will be opened to us; and the more we know of God, the more intense will be our happiness. As we walk with Jesus in this life, we may be filled with His love, satisfied with His presence. All that human nature can bear, we may receive here. But what is this compared with the hereafter?—*The Desire of Ages*, 331.

The true Christian's joys and consolation must and will be in heaven. The longing souls of those who have tasted of the powers of the world to come and have feasted on heavenly joys, will not be satisfied with things of earth. . . . Their amusement will be in contemplating their treasure—the Holy City, the earth made new, their eternal home. And while they dwell upon those things which are lofty, pure, and holy, heaven will be brought near, and they will feel the power of the Holy Spirit, and this will tend to wean them more and more from the world and cause their consolation and chief joy to be in the things of heaven, their sweet home.—*Early Writings*, 112.

Endless Delight

"Then you shall take delight in the LORD,
and I will make you ride on the heights of the earth;
I will feed you with the heritage of Jacob your father,
for the mouth of the LORD has spoken."

—Isaiah 58:14, ESV

THE HERITAGE THAT GOD has promised to His people is not in this world. . . .

. . . All that are Christ's are "Abraham's seed, and heirs according to the promise"—heirs to "an inheritance incorruptible, and undefiled, and that fadeth not away"—the earth freed from the curse of sin. Galatians 3:29; 1 Peter 1:4. For "the kingdom and dominion, and the greatness of the kingdom under the whole heaven, shall be given to the people of the saints of the Most High;" and "the meek shall inherit the earth; and shall delight themselves in the abundance of peace." Daniel 7:27; Psalm 37:11.—*Patriarchs and Prophets*, 169.

You must be there. Whatever you lose here, be determined to make sure of eternal life. Never become discouraged. . . . Live for Jesus. . . . Seek earnestly for the crown of life.—*Testimonies for the Church*, vol. 8, 131.

Look to Jesus, keeping your eyes fixed on the glory at the top of the ladder. Through Christ alone can you make sure of heaven, where all is purity, holiness, peace, and blessedness, where there are glories that mortal lips cannot describe. The nearest we can come to a description of the reward that awaits the overcomer is to say that it is a far more exceeding and eternal weight of glory. It will be an eternity of bliss, a blessed eternity, unfolding new glories throughout the ceaseless ages.—*Testimonies for the Church*, vol. 8, 131.

"For as the new heavens and the new earth
that I make
shall remain before me, says the LORD,
so shall your offspring and your name remain."

—Isaiah 66:22, ESV

We Shall Be Like Him

Beloved, now are we children of God;
and it has not yet been revealed what we shall be,
but we know that when He is revealed,
we shall be like Him, for we shall see Him as He is.
—1 John 3:2, NKJV

THOSE WHO LOVE GOD will have an intelligent knowledge of him. The image of God will shine forth from the faces of his servants, and they will be openly acknowledged as sons and daughters of God. When in the world, they did not claim to be their own, and God set to his seal that they were his. Heaven will be for those who desire it with intense desire, who put forth efforts in proportion to the value of the object which they seek. The thoughts of those who will obtain heaven, will be upon heavenly things; but those who are all taken up with the excitement and pleasure of this world, will have no love whatever for God or heaven.—"Perils of, and Provisions for, the Youth," *Review and Herald*, May 13, 1890, 290.

Those who take no pleasure in thinking and talking of God in this life, will not enjoy the life that is to come, where God is ever present, dwelling among his people. But those who love to think of God will be in their element, breathing in the atmosphere of heaven. Those who on earth love the thought of heaven, will be happy in its holy associations and pleasures. The prophet says, " . . . His servants shall serve him; and they shall see his face; and his name shall be in their foreheads."—"Perils of, and Provisions for, the Youth," *Review and Herald*, May 13, 1890, 289, 290.

"Faultless before the presence of His glory with exceeding joy" (Jude 24), Christ presents to the Father the purchase of His blood, declaring: "Here am I, and the children whom Thou hast given Me." "Those that Thou gavest Me I have kept." Oh, the wonders of redeeming love! the rapture of that hour when the infinite Father, looking upon the ransomed, shall behold His image, sin's discord banished, its blight removed, and the human once more in harmony with the divine!—*The Great Controversy*, 646.

"For God so loved the world that He gave His only begotten Son,
that whoever believes in Him should not perish but have everlasting life.
For God did not send His Son into the world to condemn the world,
but that the world through Him might be saved."
—John 3:16, 17, NKJV

A Sinless New Earth

The wilderness and the wasteland shall be glad for them,
And the desert shall rejoice and blossom as the rose; . . .
Then the eyes of the blind shall be opened,
And the ears of the deaf shall be unstopped.
Then the lame shall leap like a deer,
And the tongue of the dumb sing. . . .
And the ransomed of the LORD *shall return,*
And come to Zion with singing,
With everlasting joy on their heads.
They shall obtain joy and gladness,
And sorrow and sighing shall flee away.

—Isaiah 35:1, 5, 6, 10, NKJV

IN THE BIBLE the inheritance of the saved is called "a country." Hebrews 11:14–16. There the heavenly Shepherd leads His flock to fountains of living waters. The tree of life yields its fruit every month, and the leaves of the tree are for the service of the nations. There are ever-flowing streams, clear as crystal, and beside them waving trees cast their shadows upon the paths prepared for the ransomed of the Lord. There the wide-spreading plains swell into hills of beauty, and the mountains of God rear their lofty summits. On those peaceful plains, beside those living streams, God's people, so long pilgrims and wanderers, shall find a home.—*The Great Controversy*, 675.

"Look, God's home is now among his people!
He will live with them, and they will be his people.
God himself will be with them. He will wipe every tear from their eyes,
and there will be no more death or sorrow or crying or pain.
All these things are gone forever."

—Revelation 21:3, 4, NLT

There Will Only Be Joy and Singing

It shall blossom abundantly and rejoice,
Even with joy and singing.
The glory of Lebanon shall be given to it,
The excellence of Carmel and Sharon.
They shall see the glory of the Lord,
The excellency of our God.

—Isaiah 35:2, NKJV

EYE HATH NOT SEEN, nor ear heard, neither have entered into the heart of man, the things which God hath prepared for them that love Him." 1 Corinthians 2:9. Only through His word can a knowledge of these things be gained; and even this affords but a partial revelation.—*Education*, 301.

There, when the veil that darkens our vision shall be removed, and our eyes shall behold that world of beauty of which we now catch glimpses through the microscope; when we look on the glories of the heavens, now scanned afar through the telescope; when, the blight of sin removed, the whole earth shall appear in "the beauty of the Lord our God," what a field will be open to our study! There the student of science may read the records of creation and discern no reminders of the law of evil. He may listen to the music of nature's voices and detect no note of wailing or undertone of sorrow. In all created things he may trace one handwriting—in the vast universe behold "God's name writ large," and not in earth or sea or sky one sign of ill remaining.—*Education*, 303.

For now we see in a mirror, dimly, but then face to face.
Now I know in part, but then I shall know just as I also am known.

—1 Corinthians 13:12, NKJV

The Garden of Eden's Restitution

For the LORD will comfort Zion,
He will comfort all her waste places;
He will make her wilderness like Eden,
And her desert like the garden of the LORD;
Joy and gladness will be found in it,
Thanksgiving and the voice of melody.

—Isaiah 51:3, NKJV

THE GARDEN OF EDEN remained upon the earth long after man had become an outcast from its pleasant paths. The fallen race were long permitted to gaze upon the home of innocence, their entrance barred only by the watching angels. At the cherubim-guarded gate of Paradise the divine glory was revealed. Hither came Adam and his sons to worship God. Here they renewed their vows of obedience to that law the transgression of which had banished them from Eden. When the tide of iniquity overspread the world, and the wickedness of men determined their destruction by a flood of waters, the hand that had planted Eden withdrew it from the earth. But in the final restitution, when there shall be "a new heaven and a new earth" (Revelation 21:1), it is to be restored more gloriously adorned than at the beginning.

Then they that have kept God's commandments shall breathe in immortal vigor beneath the tree of life; and through unending ages the inhabitants of sinless worlds shall behold, in that garden of delight, a sample of the perfect work of God's creation, untouched by the curse of sin—a sample of what the whole earth would have become, had man but fulfilled the Creator's glorious plan.—*Patriarchs and Prophets*, 62.

Now I saw a new heaven and a new earth, for the first heaven and the first earth
had passed away. Also there was no more sea. Then I, John, saw the holy city,
New Jerusalem, coming down out of heaven from God,
prepared as a bride adorned for her husband.
And I heard a loud voic from heaven saying, "Behold, the tabernacle of God
is with men, and he will dwell with them, and they shall be His people.
God Himself will be with them and be their God."

—Revelation 21:1–3, NKJV

The River of Water of Life

There is a river whose streams shall make glad the city of God,
The holy place of the tabernacle of the Most High.
—Psalm 46:4, NKJV

THE PROPHET BEHOLDS THE "RIVER OF WATER OF LIFE, clear as crystal, proceeding out of the throne of God and of the Lamb." "And on this side of the river and on that was the tree of life." "And there shall be no more death, neither sorrow, nor crying, neither shall there be any more pain: for the former things are passed away." Revelation 22:1; 22:2, R.V.; 21:4. . . .

. . . "They shall hunger no more, neither thirst any more; neither shall the sun light on them, nor any heat. For the Lamb which is in the midst of the throne shall feed them, and shall lead them unto living fountains of waters" [Revelation 7:16, 17]. —*Education*, 302, 303.

Oh, for language to express the glory of the bright world to come! I thirst for the living streams that make glad the city of our God.—*Early Writings*, 39.

Let all that is beautiful in our earthly home remind us of the crystal river and green fields, the waving trees and living fountains, the shining city and the white-robed singers, of our heavenly home—that world of beauty which no artist can picture, no mortal tongue describe.—*Counsels to Parents, Teachers, and Students*, 55.

"Look! I am creating new heavens and a new earth,
and no one will even think about the old ones anymore.
Be glad; rejoice forever in my creation!
And look! I will create Jerusalem as a place of happiness.
Her people will be a source of joy."
—Isaiah 65:17, 18, NLT

The City of God

"Whereas you have been forsaken and hated,
So that no one went through you,
I will make you an eternal excellence,
A joy of many generations."

—Isaiah 60:15, NKJV

There are homes for the pilgrims of earth. There are robes for the righteous, with crowns of glory and palms of victory. All that has perplexed us in the providences of God will in the world to come be made plain. The things hard to be understood will then find explanation. The mysteries of grace will unfold before us. Where our finite minds discovered only confusion and broken promises, we shall see the most perfect and beautiful harmony. We shall know that infinite love ordered the experiences that seemed most trying. As we realize the tender care of Him who makes all things work together for our good, we shall rejoice with joy unspeakable and full of glory.

Pain cannot exist in the atmosphere of heaven. In the home of the redeemed there will be no tears, no funeral trains, no badges of mourning. "The inhabitant shall not say, I am sick: the people that dwell therein shall be forgiven their iniquity." Isaiah 33:24. One rich tide of happiness will flow and deepen as eternity rolls on. —*Testimonies for the Church*, vol. 9, 286.

"Also the sons of those who afflicted you
Shall come bowing to you,
And all those who despised you shall fall prostrate at the soles of your feet;
And they shall call you The City of the Lord,
Zion of the Holy One of Israel."

—Isaiah 60:14, NKJV

No Sorrow or Sadness

"I will rejoice in Jerusalem,
And joy in My people;
The voice of weeping shall no longer be heard in her,
Nor the voice of crying."

—Isaiah 65:19, NKJV

WE ARE HOMEWARD BOUND. He who loved us so much as to die for us hath builded for us a city. The New Jerusalem is our place of rest. There will be no sadness in the city of God. No wail of sorrow, no dirge of crushed hopes and buried affections, will evermore be heard. Soon the garments of heaviness will be changed for the wedding garment. Soon we shall witness the coronation of our King. Those whose lives have been hidden with Christ, those who on this earth have fought the good fight of faith, will shine forth with the Redeemer's glory in the kingdom of God.—*Testimonies for the Church*, vol. 9, 287.

The will of God is to be done on earth, as it is done in heaven. Then the nations will own no other law than the law of heaven. All will be a happy, united family, clothed with the garments of praise and thanksgiving—the robe of Christ's righteousness. All nature, in its surpassing loveliness, will offer to God a constant tribute of praise and adoration. The world will be bathed in the light of heaven. The years will move on in gladness. The light of the moon will be as the light of the sun, and the light of the sun will be sevenfold greater than it is now. Over the scene the morning stars will sing together, and the sons of God will shout for joy, while God and Christ will unite in proclaiming: "There shall be no more sin, neither shall there be any more death." —*Testimonies for the Church*, vol. 8, 42.

"He will wipe every tear from their eyes,
and there will be no more death or sorrow or crying or pain.
All these things are gone forever."

—Revelation 21:4, NLT

We Shall Enjoy the Work of Our Hands

"In those days people will live in the houses they build
and eat the fruit of their own vineyards.
Unlike the past, invaders will not take their houses
and confiscate their vineyards."

—Isaiah 65:21, 22, NLT

IN THE EARTH MADE NEW, the redeemed will engage in the occupations and pleasures that brought happiness to Adam and Eve in the beginning. The Eden life will be lived, the life in garden and field. "They shall build houses, and inhabit them; and they shall plant vineyards, and eat the fruit of them. . . . For as the days of a tree are the days of My people, and Mine elect shall long enjoy the work of their hands." Isaiah 65:21, 22. . . .

The prophets to whom these great scenes were revealed longed to understand their full import. They "inquired and searched diligently: . . . searching what, or what manner of time the Spirit of Christ which was in them did signify. . . . Unto whom it was revealed, that not unto themselves, but unto us they did minister the things, which are now reported unto you." 1 Peter 1:10–12.

To us who are standing on the very verge of their fulfillment, of what deep moment, what living interest, are these delineations of the things to come—events for which, since our first parents turned their steps from Eden, God's children have watched and waited, longed and prayed!—*Prophets and Kings*, 730, 731.

"They will not work in vain,
and their children will not be doomed to misfortune.
For they are people blessed by the LORD,
and their children, too, will be blessed."

—Isaiah 65:23, NLT

Eternal Delight in Our Father's Kingdom

"So don't be afraid, little flock.
For it gives your Father great happiness
to give you the Kingdom."

—Luke 12:32, NLT

IN COMPARISON WITH THE MILLIONS of the world, God's people will be, as they have ever been, a little flock; but if they stand for the truth as revealed in His word, God will be their refuge. They stand under the broad shield of Omnipotence. God is always a majority. When the sound of the last trump shall penetrate the prison house of the dead, and the righteous shall come forth with triumph, exclaiming, "O death, where is thy sting? O grave, where is thy victory?" (1 Corinthians 15:55)—standing then with God, with Christ, with the angels, and with the loyal and true of all ages, the children of God will be far in the majority. . . .

In this world their minds were consecrated to God; they served Him with the intellect and with the heart; and now He can place His name "in their foreheads." "And they shall reign for ever and ever." Revelation 22:5. They do not go in and out as those who beg a place. They are of that number to whom Christ says, "Come, ye blessed of My Father, inherit the kingdom prepared for you from the foundation of the world." He welcomes them as His children, saying, "Enter thou into the joy of thy Lord." Matthew 25:34, 21.—*The Acts of the Apostles*, 590.

"The master was full of praise. 'Well done, my good and faithful servant.
You have been faithful in handling this small amount,
so now I will give you many more responsibilities. Let's celebrate together!' "

—Matthew 25:21, NLT

We Shall Have Unending Joy

And the ransomed of the Lord shall return,
and come to Zion with singing;
everlasting joy shall be upon their heads;
they shall obtain joy and gladness,
and sorrow and sighing shall flee away.

—Isaiah 35:10, NRSV

THE PROPHET CAUGHT the sound of music there, and song, such music and song as, save in the visions of God, no mortal ear has heard or mind conceived. "The ransomed of the Lord shall return, and come to Zion with songs and everlasting joy upon their heads: they shall obtain joy and gladness, and sorrow and sighing shall flee away." "Joy and gladness shall be found therein, thanksgiving, and the voice of melody." "As well the singers as the players on instruments shall be there." "They shall lift up their voice, they shall sing for the majesty of the Lord." Isaiah 35:10; 51:3; Psalm 87:7; Isaiah 24:14.—*Prophets and Kings*, 730.

There the redeemed shall know, even as also they are known. The loves and sympathies which God Himself has planted in the soul shall there find truest and sweetest exercise. The pure communion with holy beings, the harmonious social life with the blessed angels and with the faithful ones of all ages who have washed their robes and made them white in the blood of the Lamb, the sacred ties that bind together "the whole family in heaven and earth" (Ephesians 3:15)—these help to constitute the happiness of the redeemed.—*The Great Controversy*, 677.

They raise their voices, they shout for joy;
from the west they acclaim the Lord's majesty.
Therefore in the east give glory to the Lord;
exalt the name of the Lord, the God of Israel,
in the islands of the sea.
From the ends of the earth we hear singing: "Glory to the Righteous One."

—Isaiah 24:14–16, NIV

A New and Perfect Creation

"But be glad and rejoice forever
in what I will create,
for I will create Jerusalem to be a delight
and its people a joy."

—Isaiah 65:18, NIV

THERE, IMMORTAL MINDS will contemplate with never-failing delight the wonders of creative power, the mysteries of redeeming love. There will be no cruel, deceiving foe to tempt to forgetfulness of God. Every faculty will be developed, every capacity increased. The acquirement of knowledge will not weary the mind or exhaust the energies. There the grandest enterprises may be carried forward, the loftiest aspirations reached, the highest ambitions realized; and still there will arise new heights to surmount, new wonders to admire, new truths to comprehend, fresh objects to call forth the powers of mind and soul and body.

All the treasures of the universe will be open to the study of God's redeemed. Unfettered by mortality, they wing their tireless flight to worlds afar—worlds that thrilled with sorrow at the spectacle of human woe and rang with songs of gladness at the tidings of a ransomed soul. With unutterable delight the children of earth enter into the joy and the wisdom of unfallen beings. They share the treasures of knowledge and understanding gained through ages upon ages in contemplation of God's handiwork. With undimmed vision they gaze upon the glory of creation—suns and stars and systems, all in their appointed order circling the throne of Deity. Upon all things, from the least to the greatest, the Creator's name is written, and in all are the riches of His power displayed.—*The Great Controversy*, 677.

"See, I will create
new heavens and a new earth.
The former things will not be remembered,
nor will they come to mind."

—Isaiah 65:17, NIV

Happiness and Eternal Fulfillment

You will show me the way of life,
granting me the joy of your presence
and the pleasures of living with you forever.

—Psalm 16:11, NLT

THE YEARS OF ETERNITY, as they roll, will bring richer and still more glorious revelations of God and of Christ. As knowledge is progressive, so will love, reverence, and happiness increase. The more men learn of God, the greater will be their admiration of His character. As Jesus opens before them the riches of redemption and the amazing achievements in the great controversy with Satan, the hearts of the ransomed thrill with more fervent devotion, and with more rapturous joy they sweep the harps of gold; and ten thousand times ten thousand and thousands of thousands of voices unite to swell the mighty chorus of praise. . . .

The great controversy is ended. Sin and sinners are no more. The entire universe is clean. One pulse of harmony and gladness beats through the vast creation. From Him who created all, flow life and light and gladness, throughout the realms of illimitable space. From the minutest atom to the greatest world, all things, animate and inanimate, in their unshadowed beauty and perfect joy, declare that God is love.—*The Great Controversy*, 678.

"Look, I am coming soon, bringing my reward with me
to repay all people according to their deeds.
I am the Alpha and the Omega, the First and the Last,
the Beginning and the End."

—Revelation 22:12, 13, NLT

Read the Bible in One Year

JANUARY

- ❑ 1. Genesis 1; 2
- ❑ 2. Genesis 3–5
- ❑ 3. Genesis 6–9
- ❑ 4. Genesis 10; 11
- ❑ 5. Genesis 12–15
- ❑ 6. Genesis 16–19
- ❑ 7. Genesis 20–22
- ❑ 8. Genesis 23–26
- ❑ 9. Genesis 27–29
- ❑ 10. Genesis 30–32
- ❑ 11. Genesis 33–36
- ❑ 12. Genesis 37–39
- ❑ 13. Genesis 40–42
- ❑ 14. Genesis 43–46
- ❑ 15. Genesis 47–50
- ❑ 16. Job 1–4
- ❑ 17. Job 5–7
- ❑ 18. Job 8–10
- ❑ 19. Job 11–13
- ❑ 20. Job 14–17
- ❑ 21. Job 18–20
- ❑ 22. Job 21–24
- ❑ 23. Job 25–27
- ❑ 24. Job 28–31
- ❑ 25. Job 32–34
- ❑ 26. Job 35–37
- ❑ 27. Job 38–42
- ❑ 28. Exodus 1–4
- ❑ 29. Exodus 5–7
- ❑ 30. Exodus 8–10
- ❑ 31. Exodus 11–13

FEBRUARY

- ❑ 1. Exodus 14–17
- ❑ 2. Exodus 18–20
- ❑ 3. Exodus 21–24
- ❑ 4. Exodus 25–27
- ❑ 5. Exodus 28–31
- ❑ 6. Exodus 32–34
- ❑ 7. Exodus 35–37
- ❑ 8. Exodus 38–40
- ❑ 9. Leviticus 1–4
- ❑ 10. Leviticus 5–7
- ❑ 11. Leviticus 8–10
- ❑ 12. Leviticus 11–13
- ❑ 13. Leviticus 14–16
- ❑ 14. Leviticus 17–19
- ❑ 15. Leviticus 20–23
- ❑ 16. Leviticus 24–27
- ❑ 17. Numbers 1–3
- ❑ 18. Numbers 4–6
- ❑ 19. Numbers 7–10
- ❑ 20. Numbers 11–14
- ❑ 21. Numbers 15–17
- ❑ 22. Numbers 18–20
- ❑ 23. Numbers 21–24
- ❑ 24. Numbers 25–27
- ❑ 25. Numbers 28–30
- ❑ 26. Numbers 31–33
- ❑ 27. Numbers 34–36
- ❑ 28. Deuteronomy 1–5

MARCH

- ❑ 1. Deuteronomy 6; 7
- ❑ 2. Deuteronomy 8; 9
- ❑ 3. Deuteronomy 10–12
- ❑ 4. Deuteronomy 13–16
- ❑ 5. Deuteronomy 17–19
- ❑ 6. Deuteronomy 20–22
- ❑ 7. Deuteronomy 23–25
- ❑ 8. Deuteronomy 26–28
- ❑ 9. Deuteronomy 29–31
- ❑ 10. Deuteronomy 32–34
- ❑ 11. Joshua 1–3
- ❑ 12. Joshua 4–6
- ❑ 13. Joshua 7–9
- ❑ 14. Joshua 10–12
- ❑ 15. Joshua 13–15
- ❑ 16. Joshua 16–18
- ❑ 17. Joshua 19–21
- ❑ 18. Joshua 22–24
- ❑ 19. Judges 1–4
- ❑ 20. Judges 5–8
- ❑ 21. Judges 9–12
- ❑ 22. Judges 13–15
- ❑ 23. Judges 16–18
- ❑ 24. Judges 19–21
- ❑ 25. Ruth 1–4
- ❑ 26. 1 Samuel 1–3
- ❑ 27. 1 Samuel 4–7
- ❑ 28. 1 Samuel 8–10
- ❑ 29. 1 Samuel 11–13
- ❑ 30. 1 Samuel 14–16
- ❑ 31. 1 Samuel 17–20

APRIL

- ❑ 1. 1 Samuel 21–24
- ❑ 2. 1 Samuel 25–28
- ❑ 3. 1 Samuel 29–31
- ❑ 4. 2 Samuel 1–4
- ❑ 5. 2 Samuel 5–8
- ❑ 6. 2 Samuel 9–12
- ❑ 7. 2 Samuel 13–15
- ❑ 8. 2 Samuel 16–18
- ❑ 9. 2 Samuel 19–21
- ❑ 10. 2 Samuel 22–24
- ❑ 11. Psalm 1–3
- ❑ 12. Psalm 4–6
- ❑ 13. Psalm 7–9
- ❑ 14. Psalm 10–12
- ❑ 15. Psalm 13–15
- ❑ 16. Psalm 16–18
- ❑ 17. Psalm 19–21
- ❑ 18. Psalm 22–24
- ❑ 19. Psalm 25–27
- ❑ 20. Psalm 28–30
- ❑ 21. Psalm 31–33
- ❑ 22. Psalm 34–36
- ❑ 23. Psalm 37–39
- ❑ 24. Psalm 40–42
- ❑ 25. Psalm 43–45
- ❑ 26. Psalm 46–48
- ❑ 27. Psalm 49–51
- ❑ 28. Psalm 52–54
- ❑ 29. Psalm 55–57
- ❑ 30. Psalm 58–60

MAY

- ❑ 1. Psalm 61–63
- ❑ 2. Psalm 64–66
- ❑ 3. Psalm 67–69
- ❑ 4. Psalm 70–72
- ❑ 5. Psalm 73–75
- ❑ 6. Psalm 76–78
- ❑ 7. Psalm 79–81
- ❑ 8. Psalm 82–84
- ❑ 9. Psalm 85–87
- ❑ 10. Psalm 88–90
- ❑ 11. Psalm 91–93
- ❑ 12. Psalm 94–96
- ❑ 13. Psalm 97–99
- ❑ 14. Psalm 100–102
- ❑ 15. Psalm 103–105
- ❑ 16. Psalm 106–108
- ❑ 17. Psalm 109–111
- ❑ 18. Psalm 112–114
- ❑ 19. Psalm 115–118
- ❑ 20. Psalm 119
- ❑ 21. Psalm 120–123
- ❑ 22. Psalm 124–126
- ❑ 23. Psalm 127–129
- ❑ 24. Psalm 130–132
- ❑ 25. Psalm 133–135
- ❑ 26. Psalm 136–138
- ❑ 27. Psalm 139–141
- ❑ 28. Psalm 142–144
- ❑ 29. Psalm 145–147
- ❑ 30. Psalm 148–150
- ❑ 31. 1 Kings 1–4

JUNE

- ❑ 1. Proverbs 1–3
- ❑ 2. Proverbs 4–7
- ❑ 3. Proverbs 8–11
- ❑ 4. Proverbs 12–14
- ❑ 5. Proverbs 15–18
- ❑ 6. Proverbs 19–21
- ❑ 7. Proverbs 22–24
- ❑ 8. Proverbs 25–28
- ❑ 9. Proverbs 29–31
- ❑ 10. Ecclesiastes 1–3
- ❑ 11. Ecclesiastes 4–6
- ❑ 12. Ecclesiastes 7–9
- ❑ 13. Ecclesiastes 10–12
- ❑ 14. Song of Solomon 1–4
- ❑ 15. Song of Solomon 5–8
- ❑ 16. 1 Kings 5–7
- ❑ 17. 1 Kings 8–10
- ❑ 18. 1 Kings 11–13
- ❑ 19. 1 Kings 14–16
- ❑ 20. 1 Kings 17–19
- ❑ 21. 1 Kings 20–22
- ❑ 22. 2 Kings 1–3
- ❑ 23. 2 Kings 4–6
- ❑ 24. 2 Kings 7–10
- ❑ 25. 2 Kings 11–14:20
- ❑ 26. Joel 1–3
- ❑ 27. 2 Kings 14:21–25
Jonah 1–4
- ❑ 28. 2 Kings 14:26–29
Amos 1–3
- ❑ 29. Amos 4–6
- ❑ 30. Amos 7–9

JULY

- ❑ 1. 2 Kings 15–17
- ❑ 2. Hosea 1–4
- ❑ 3. Hosea 5–7
- ❑ 4. Hosea 8–10
- ❑ 5. Hosea 11–14
- ❑ 6. 2 Kings 18; 19
- ❑ 7. Isaiah 1–3
- ❑ 8. Isaiah 4–6
- ❑ 9. Isaiah 7–9
- ❑ 10. Isaiah 10–12
- ❑ 11. Isaiah 13–15
- ❑ 12. Isaiah 16–18
- ❑ 13. Isaiah 19–21
- ❑ 14. Isaiah 22–24
- ❑ 15. Isaiah 25–27
- ❑ 16. Isaiah 28–30
- ❑ 17. Isaiah 31–33
- ❑ 18. Isaiah 34–36
- ❑ 19. Isaiah 37–39
- ❑ 20. Isaiah 40–42
- ❑ 21. Isaiah 43–45
- ❑ 22. Isaiah 46–48
- ❑ 23. Isaiah 49–51
- ❑ 24. Isaiah 52–54
- ❑ 25. Isaiah 55–57
- ❑ 26. Isaiah 58–60
- ❑ 27. Isaiah 61–63
- ❑ 28. Isaiah 64–66
- ❑ 29. Micah 1–4
- ❑ 30. Micah 5–7
- ❑ 31. Nahum 1–3

AUGUST

- ❑ 1. 2 Kings 20; 21
- ❑ 2. Zephaniah 1–3
- ❑ 3. Habakkuk 1–3
- ❑ 4. 2 Kings 22–25
- ❑ 5. Obadiah and Jeremiah 1; 2
- ❑ 6. Jeremiah 3–5
- ❑ 7. Jeremiah 6–8
- ❑ 8. Jeremiah 9–12
- ❑ 9. Jeremiah 13–16
- ❑ 10. Jeremiah 17–20
- ❑ 11. Jeremiah 21–23
- ❑ 12. Jeremiah 24–26
- ❑ 13. Jeremiah 27–29
- ❑ 14. Jeremiah 30–32
- ❑ 15. Jeremiah 33–36
- ❑ 16. Jeremiah 37–39
- ❑ 17. Jeremiah 40–42
- ❑ 18. Jeremiah 43–46
- ❑ 19. Jeremiah 47–49
- ❑ 20. Jeremiah 50–52
- ❑ 21. Lamentations
- ❑ 22. 1 Chronicles 1–3
- ❑ 23. 1 Chronicles 4–6
- ❑ 24. 1 Chronicles 7–9
- ❑ 25. 1 Chronicles 10–13
- ❑ 26. 1 Chronicles 14–16
- ❑ 27. 1 Chronicles 17–19
- ❑ 28. 1 Chronicles 20–23
- ❑ 29. 1 Chronicles 24–26
- ❑ 30. 1 Chronicles 27–29
- ❑ 31. 2 Chronicles 1–3

SEPTEMBER

- ❑ 1. 2 Chronicles 4–6
- ❑ 2. 2 Chronicles 7–9
- ❑ 3. 2 Chronicles 10–13
- ❑ 4. 2 Chronicles 14–16
- ❑ 5. 2 Chronicles 17–19
- ❑ 6. 2 Chronicles 20–22
- ❑ 7. 2 Chronicles 23–25
- ❑ 8. 2 Chronicles 26–29
- ❑ 9. 2 Chronicles 30–32
- ❑ 10. 2 Chronicles 33–36
- ❑ 11. Ezekiel 1–3
- ❑ 12. Ezekiel 4–7
- ❑ 13. Ezekiel 8–11
- ❑ 14. Ezekiel 12–14
- ❑ 15. Ezekiel 15–18
- ❑ 16. Ezekiel 19–21
- ❑ 17. Ezekiel 22–24
- ❑ 18. Ezekiel 25–27
- ❑ 19. Ezekiel 28–30
- ❑ 20. Ezekiel 31–33
- ❑ 21. Ezekiel 34–36
- ❑ 22. Ezekiel 37–39
- ❑ 23. Ezekiel 40–42
- ❑ 24. Ezekiel 43–45
- ❑ 25. Ezekiel 46–48
- ❑ 26. Daniel 1–3
- ❑ 27. Daniel 4–6
- ❑ 28. Daniel 7–9
- ❑ 29. Daniel 10–12
- ❑ 30. Esther 1–3

OCTOBER

- ❑ 1. Esther 4–7
- ❑ 2. Esther 8–10
- ❑ 3. Ezra 1–4
- ❑ 4. Haggai 1; 2
  Zechariah 1; 2
- ❑ 5. Zechariah 3–6
- ❑ 6. Zechariah 7–10
- ❑ 7. Zechariah 11–14
- ❑ 8. Ezra 5–7
- ❑ 9. Ezra 8–10
- ❑ 10. Nehemiah 1–3
- ❑ 11. Nehemiah 4–6
- ❑ 12. Nehemiah 7–9
- ❑ 13. Nehemiah 10–13
- ❑ 14. Malachi 1–4
- ❑ 15. Matthew 1–4
- ❑ 16. Matthew 5–7
- ❑ 17. Matthew 8–11
- ❑ 18. Matthew 12–15
- ❑ 19. Matthew 16–19
- ❑ 20. Matthew 20–22
- ❑ 21. Matthew 23–25
- ❑ 22. Matthew 26–28
- ❑ 23. Mark 1–3
- ❑ 24. Mark 4–6
- ❑ 25. Mark 7–10
- ❑ 26. Mark 11–13
- ❑ 27. Mark 14–16
- ❑ 28. Luke 1–3
- ❑ 29. Luke 4–6
- ❑ 30. Luke 7–9
- ❑ 31. Luke 10–13

NOVEMBER

- ❑ 1. Luke 14–17
- ❑ 2. Luke 18–21
- ❑ 3. Luke 22–24
- ❑ 4. John 1–3
- ❑ 5. John 4–6
- ❑ 6. John 7–10
- ❑ 7. John 11–13
- ❑ 8. John 14–17
- ❑ 9. John 18–21
- ❑ 10. Acts 1; 2
- ❑ 11. Acts 3–5
- ❑ 12. Acts 6–9
- ❑ 13. Acts 10–12
- ❑ 14. Acts 13; 14
- ❑ 15. James 1; 2
- ❑ 16. James 3–5
- ❑ 17. Galatians 1–3
- ❑ 18. Galatian 4–6
- ❑ 19. Acts 15–18:11
- ❑ 20. 1 Thessalonians 1–5
- ❑ 21. 2 Thessalonians 1–3
  Acts 18:12–19:20
- ❑ 22. 1 Corinthians 1–4
- ❑ 23. 1 Corinthians 5–8
- ❑ 24. 1 Corinthians 9–12
- ❑ 25. 1 Corinthians 13–16
- ❑ 26. Acts 19:21–20:1
  2 Corinthians 1–3
- ❑ 27. 2 Corinthians 4–6
- ❑ 28. 2 Corinthians 7–9
- ❑ 29. 2 Corinthians 10–13
- ❑ 30. Acts 20:2
  Romans 1–4

DECEMBER

- ❑ 1. Romans 5–8
- ❑ 2. Romans 9–11
- ❑ 3. Romans 12–16
- ❑ 4. Acts 20:3–22:30
- ❑ 5. Acts 23–25
- ❑ 6. Acts 26–28
- ❑ 7. Ephesians 1–3
- ❑ 8. Ephesians 4–6
- ❑ 9. Philippians 1–4
- ❑ 10. Colossians 1–4
- ❑ 11. Hebrews 1–4
- ❑ 12. Hebrews 5–7
- ❑ 13. Hebrews 8–10
- ❑ 14. Hebrews 11–13
- ❑ 15. Philemon
  1 Peter 1; 2
- ❑ 16. 1 Peter 3–5
- ❑ 17. 2 Peter 1–3
- ❑ 18. 1 Timothy 1–3
- ❑ 19. 1 Timothy 4–6
- ❑ 20. Titus 1–3
- ❑ 21. 2 Timothy 1–4
- ❑ 22. 1 John 1; 2
- ❑ 23. 1 John 3–5
- ❑ 24. 2 John
  3 John and Jude
- ❑ 25. Revelation 1–3
- ❑ 26. Revelation 4–6
- ❑ 27. Revelation 7–9
- ❑ 28. Revelation 10–12
- ❑ 29. Revelation 13–15
- ❑ 30. Revelation 16–18
- ❑ 31. Revelation 19–22